MW00769373

IT CAN BE DONE!

IT CAN BE DONE!

MY MEMOIR OF FAMILY, FAITH, FLYING, AND BUSINESS

DAVID CHARLES GASMIRE

TAMPA, FLORIDA

IT CAN BE DONE!
My memoir of family, faith, flying, and business

Published by Gatekeeper Press
7853 Gunn Hwy, Suite 209
Tampa, FL 33626
www.GatekeeperPress.com

Library of Congress Control Number: 2023932675

ISBN (hardcover): 9781662937828

ISBN (paperback): 9781662937835

ACKNOWLEDGMENTS

New Year's Day, 2021. 5:23 a.m. Well, here goes.

It would be impossible to mention every person who has been a part of my life and had an impact on who I was, who I was becoming, and how I was going to get there. Writing about the events of my life would be incomplete without all the wonderful relationships God has blessed me with along the way. Every time I think I may be done with my book, I think of something else to add. The journey, in that regard, becomes endless, and as much as I would like to write about everything that I have experienced—well, almost everything—it would take, as of today, sixty-seven years to write. So, I know I have left out some events that are relative to my story that I will think of later, but oh well, this is what I got.

My lifelong thanks and love to my wife, Sandee, for being my copilot all these many years. And to Natalie and Charlie for growing to be so accomplished in the important character aspects of life. They have the self-respecting character that every parent prays their children will find and live under. They think of others in a way that, quite frankly, more of our society needs today. I am so proud of them both that I simply do not know how to express those feelings here.

And thank you and love to Corey Page Gasmire, who took the step into the Gasmire family when she married Charlie in November 2017 and who had our two beautiful grandchildren thirteen months apart, Caleb Thomas and Collins Page. Such beautiful babies; I feel like I am looking at God when I fall into each of their eyes. These two grandchildren are now part of our life path. I have learned that as you do the memoir look-back, although life keeps moving forward, there are heartfelt ways to enjoy where your journey has already taken you.

My love and thanks to my brother and sister, Jay Gasmire and Sue Ellen Werley, for being the mosaic of my life from the beginning. We have so many stories, and some of them are relived here in good old black and white, in plain sight. We have always been very close, and I deeply love them both. And love shout-outs to Denise and Samantha Gasmire, Troy Werley, Jaden and Elizabeth (engaged as of this writing), and Tessa Werley.

Thank you to so many great friends who have touched our family in so many ways. Thank you for being my friends!

FOREWORD

I have been thinking about writing my autobiography for a while now. My story is not unlike millions of others, but since every life is a splendid adaptation of one's own God-given soul, it is interesting, as are others, in its own unique way. Sure, I would like to change things that have happened in my life, and I suspect there are elements in your life that you wish qualified for a redo. But every experience you go through becomes the tapestry of life called "you." You have a personal story, as do I, and I have chosen to embark on the joys and sorrows of reliving much of it here in good old black and white. Writing your memoir is not for the faint of heart, but it just might help someone else also spinning through the galaxy.

This is my personal story, much of which I find quite amusing if you look at it through the correct lens of not taking yourself too seriously. I try to do that in my stories here. My early intentions, as I contemplated this body of work, were to simply memorialize my family history and recount memorable events that my family might enjoy reading. However, as I got deeper into describing my journey, I realized there was more to tell, with the intent of imparting an element of jocularity along with life's lessons.

It is my goal that you can relate to many of the events in my life and be able to relate to the highs and lows. I have found nostalgia is a complex emotion. On one hand, it can feed the heart with useful introspection and at the same time, create a roadblock to acceptance and create collateral damage that is hard to repair. At the time of this writing, our two grandchildren, Caleb Thomas Gasmire and Collins

Page Gasmire, are not even two years old. And yet, as I hold them, I wonder if they will have a curiosity about family who preceded them. If, like most people, that interest will ignite when they have less time in front of them than they do in the years behind them. I do hope they find the meaningful unity Sandee and I have. After decades of marriage, we continue to adore each other, to the betterment of a stable family. They, too, will learn that relationships are, at their essence, a challenge worthy and necessary of undertaking, but simply not simple.

This book is to tell my story, and to some extent, a little bit of my wife Sandee's story since we have known each other since 1969 and have been together for more than fifty years. Are there some tall tales? Yes. True? Yes. These incidents and reflections can help cement family legacy and pride in themselves and their love for family. Not in what we have accomplished, but what we have overcome and how we looked at those life experiences. It just might create ambition for their own lives.

From my point of view, and a large reason I have written this book, all experiences in life are the precursors to a significant life of achievement. Your meaningful failures, of all kinds, are just as important as your successes when you simply believe, at your core, that your pursuits can be accomplished, despite all of life's twists and turns, and YOU are the one who can do it. I try to explain, from my point of view at the time, firsthand experiences that shaped the way I saw life, thought about myself, my determination, my past, and finally, my future.

There are so many mistakes and misjudgments and some plain old stupidity that I must admit to in this book. I watched *The Three Stooges* for tactical advice growing up, mostly about how to treat my brother Jay. In life, you get the experience first, then the lesson second. It is a painful way to learn things, but it makes it easier to remember them the next time.

From my first lemonade stand to my first genuine business ventures in high school and college, to start-ups resulting in company transactions, including initial public offerings and equity sales with exit valuations in the hundreds of millions of dollars, to developing even more companies, it all started with my parents and included lots of spankings. Hard ones. Belts. Boards and shoes. Always on the backside, never in the face, and I always deserved the painful reminder of unacceptable behavior. But it was all a necessary part of growing up. Nothing like a good ass-whooping to set you straight. And I certainly got my share.

I have been told by friends that some of my real-life stories are worthy of others reading about them, and I hope to make those experiences useful and relevant here. My story is more about events, the background of how they occurred, and the lessons learned from them, than it is a historical family tree of everyone involved from three generations ago, although I make some family historical references for the legacy benefit of my family. Many of the Gasmires still live today in West Virginia and Pennsylvania, as well as Ohio. We have been in Texas since 1969 and believe we may be the first Texan Gasmires. The move to Texas turned us into a bunch of Gasmire cowboys and cowgirls, for sure!

Today we live at our ranch with our dogs and horses and a nice piece of property to enjoy in the Texas Hill Country. A very big part of my story is how we landed in Texas after a few of our early years in Toledo, long enough for me and my younger brother Jay to be born in 1955 and 1957 respectively, followed by St. Charles in west Chicago, Illinois, for a couple of years, followed by ten years in Glendale, Missouri, a suburb of St. Louis, where our sister, Sue Ellen, was born in 1963.

During my research and writing of this book I have had the chance to talk to many people about writing an autobiography. I found that some people are interested in their own pasts and curious about their beginnings, and others are not reflective or choose not to look back with any active interest. I also noticed that those two positions are largely determined by where they grew up. If they never moved away from their birth hometown and never had distance as a barrier to their memories, they feel there is no need to go back in time because time never changed for them. They are still where they have always been, and curiosity does not take them on a journey to connect to the past. The past is in the present because the geography has not changed.

However, if your past experiences and memories are from a distant land, it is natural to want to revisit those places. Such is the case with me. I am fiercely nostalgic and find personal joy, comfort, and challenge in looking back. I need to so I can decide on what the future needs to look like. To make a great future, it is helpful to assess the past. By exploring those places of lore, I can get a view of the whole picture. The purpose of this book is to keep my story, for me and our grandchildren to follow, in living color, with some relevance that connects family. If I do not write these stories down, then one day, the stories will not exist.

My book is also intended to shed some light on meaningful events that shaped my faith in Jesus Christ through the years. I also want to take you through my business journey, from small to large, from my first job sweeping floors in a barbershop to working in a world of venture capital, private equity, and many things entrepreneurial. I am not a historian, an intellectual, or a visionary with years in academia, loaded with letters after my name. I am a normal guy who has had to figure things out along my life's journey. What I can do is find ways to make things happen, which I believe are within reach, and in some cases, out of reach, at least for the moment. If I just persevere and believe in myself, my faith, family, and friends, I can get it done! And you can too!

Your challenges are the change makers of your life. You have strength you have never used before, and you won't get stronger by only doing things that are comfortable. I try to convey here that you would not believe how much power is in you by believing. In fact, it has been said and quoted by a lot of people more published than me, that it is impossible to beat someone who just never gives up. And that can be you. You just have to believe in yourself through the trying times and keep on showing up even when you don't feel like it.

One of the joys of my life at this "later stage" is reflecting on how my early years shaped my interest in everything I am still interested in today. I remember vividly the first experiences that led me to my love for music, flying, running, boating, hunting, golf, theater, sports, entrepreneurship, and others. These interests and early experiences took place between seven and twelve years of age and have been instrumental in understanding how I still dream and plan today. How I was raised, along with my brother Jay and my sister Sue Ellen, created a lot of "want to" in me, surrounded by enormous amounts of "have to," for a variety of reasons.

Once I was on my way to college and out of the house at seventeen years old, things got real, and they got tough. I was devoured. My earliest recollections of things real are centered on the few short years we lived in St. Louis. We were brought up in a relational family with aunts and uncles and cousins, most of whom lived in distant Indiana, Michigan, and Ohio, and remarkably close friends of our parents and our close school chums, some of whom I am still in close contact with today. We were taught growing up that relationships are everything in the sense that people are fun; they can teach us things; they can create competition and ambition, and, at times, get your ass kicked.

At fourteen years old, my brother threw a knife at me after Dad left us on an island on Lake Texoma so that we could work out our differences. He was tired of giving fatherly advice. He needed the threat of death to try its hand at controlling Jay and me. Dad came back to the island by boat the next day and picked us up. We would have to postpone our "disagreement" for another time.

MOST THINGS IN LIFE ARE TAUGHT THROUGH OR BECAUSE OF RELATIONSHIPS

The people that I can singlehandedly identify as having a critical role in my life, both good, bad, and controversial, are people not of grandeur or wealth, not of world significance or social popularity. These are people who planted seeds in my faith and initial interest in all the activities I still do today. I will tell you about some of my life's influencers and how their simple acts of lending encouragement or teaching simple skills enabled me to learn some of life's lessons without even knowing they were doing so.

Is it possible to have a hero that you really did not like, but what they taught you becomes so valuable in your life, either as an example of what to do or what to avoid, that they still deserve to get some credit for intersecting your life and giving you something that you might not have received otherwise? I know one of those, and you will hear about him in my book. And as I look at my mentors, I see that some are independent operators, taking more of a solo approach to their ambitions and ways of thinking about things. They are less collaborators and more focused on the personal achievement and getting things done their way. Some of my mentors are initiative-taking collaborators, working the team to the goal line of accomplishment.

Sports are a good metaphor for describing leadership and mentorship. There are team sports, and there are individual sports and athletes of each that require the right mettle to succeed in that environment. In my early years in sports, I did both, as most kids do. Try your best, then move on. But the stuff you love, you move on … with. Even participating in those various sporting games in adolescence may seem like just social fun and physical development, but those experiences in an early developing mind can water and feed the young and maturing soul to crave the pieces that build the story of their life. Even when they do not know how to, but they want to.

One of my life's greatest actionable lessons is that a want-to spirit and ambition are more important than just a can-do personality, particularly when that can-do has no want-to. You either want it or you do not. It can be done, if you want it. Give me a teammate with more want-to than can-do, and we can win. You can teach "can-do," but you can't teach "want-to." That is what happened with me.

I also hope that by reading my book you will find events and moments here to which you can also relate. I do not claim to have run into problems that no other has had to overcome; however, each person's situation is different because of the context in which it occurs. I try to give enough background so you can see the way I thought about key events before, during, and after those growth struggles. Some failures that led to victories later really paid off, not only financially but in personal and family growth. I tell young people who have run into personal or business failures that seemed insurmountable that they cannot grow and haven't even lived until those things happen to them.

If you work hard, with ambition and a thirst for progress and success, you will not be without stumbles, such as being fired, being broke, losing the love of your life, or being sued in business. Life is a mixed bag of joy and sorrow, pros and cons, yins and yangs, but your determination and faith will become the cornerstones of your story. They will help how you think about things, and they will be helpful to others who are looking for someone who can relate to their life's struggles. They will have a direct impact on the person you choose to become.

The type of person you become is directly a product of who you choose to be. You have a choice, and your life experiences will put you to the test. God has a plan for your life, but He is not giving you a gravy train. He will allow difficulties to emerge just when you want and need them the least. That is how our character and faith are built and developed! I hope you see this in yourself as you read my journey through things good and bad.

As Sandee and I approach our seventies in just a few short years, we are blessed to have hung in there with and for each other for decades. We hope to have another thirty years, but God has that plan too. For now, we are living life and enjoying our family and the grandchildren who are here, with hopefully more coming one day. And finally, as I recall some of the trying moments of my life and the successes, it has been a rebirth for me to think how God has blessed my life and saved me from myself. I hope my reflections here are somehow encouraging to you.

I have been fortunate to have lived this long, and I want to share it. So much to tell you about, so let us begin. As John Wayne said in Sandee's favorite movie *McLintock*, when he told his estranged wife, Maureen O'Hara, "Let's just get to the rat killin'," if you can think it and dream it, It Can Be Done. Let us do this together.

1

The early Gasmire years, life in the Midwest, correction by corporal punishment, life in St. Louis, first guitar, first band, the first realized value of a buck, hunting/fishing, the mysterious deaths at the Ann Arbor VA, Michael Joseph Owens

THE EARLY YEARS AS A GASMIRE

In looking back to my early years in Toledo, St. Charles, and mostly, St. Louis, I can say that the interests and activities that my parents introduced to me from when I was six or seven years old until about twelve to thirteen years old cemented my paths of interest, passion, and commitment for the rest of my life. It was during those years that I was given the opportunity to explore many new things. Sure, we dug in the backyard, made mud pies, built forts, and rode our bikes around the neighborhood and harassed all our neighbors "Dennis the Menace" style, but Dad and Mom's interests produced some exciting and never-to-forget life experiences.

At an early age, my dad introduced me to and I became hooked on flying and outdoors sports, including hunting and fishing, golf, target shooting, acting, music, boating, long-distance running, and learning to think creatively to create new things of any kind. There was usually some way to combine some of these together, which Dad usually produced, and I caught on very quickly.

Everything I do today has a direct connection to our few short years in St. Louis, which were ultimately carried to Dallas, then continued for the next fifty years.

But everything preceding the events in St. Louis began where I was born in Toledo, Ohio, on November 17, 1955. Although I was born in Ohio, I have been in Texas for so long now that I do not remember being called a Yankee or even a Midwesterner. But that is where it all began for me, my younger brother, Jay William, and our even younger sister, Sue Ellen.

My earliest memories of life with my parents Richard C. (Dick) and Ellen (Ellie) Gasmire surrounded my dad's career at Owens-Illinois (O-I). The company's world headquarters were in Toledo, Ohio, although I have only very vague memories of living there. My mom and Dad were married in their early twenties and just crazy about each other. They each had an outgoing personality. Dad was very driven to have a successful career, and Mom supported their collective dreams as they began to raise me, my brother, and my sister, fairly early in their marriage.

I don't remember much about Toledo since I was a toddler, but I do know that during the brief time we lived there, I was attacked by a neighbor's boxer dog who ripped my face up when I strayed into its yard without my mom noticing. I do not remember the attack because I was only two years old, but I still have the scar next to my mouth and right eye where stitches were placed, the old-fashioned way, with big needles, using thick string with wide stitch placement.

Mom was such a loving person and took very good care of us kids. She is the reason that I learned about encouragement very early in my life. She was positive, enthusiastic, and loved to laugh, even when we did stuff that she had to deal with that involved serious injury at home. I do not remember how I got into my mom's kitchen knives and sliced my left forefinger, almost severing it. That also required the ugly stitches. Later in life, when I had to hitchhike in college to get around to my various jobs, Mom reminded me that I still had ten fingers. It was the beginning of a lifetime of inflicted wounds and injuries that were more inconveniences than big health problems, but they were not fun experiences, and Mom took care of us when they occurred. The real damages happened while living in St. Louis and many other interesting medical events in Texas.

On the bright side, I do vaguely remember in the late 1950s, going to kindergarten and first grade in St. Charles, Illinois. My mother dressed me up in a Raggedy Andy costume for a school play, and it is my first recollection of being on a stage in front of a bunch of strangers. The legendary characters of Raggedy Ann and Raggedy Andy must have been the cute spot for young mothers. She made my costume and dressed me up in baggy blue coveralls with a plaid shirt, socks over my hands to look like a rag doll, a red, stringy wig, and a funny hat. She also put makeup on my face, including drawing a triangle for my nose. I looked like a rag doll, all right. Look up the character sometime and you will see what I went through.

I have a strange sense that I did like doing that because it got me out of getting the spankings at home that I deserved. I was about four years old and already under strict rule! Spankings were not only socially acceptable but a staple in every American household, delivered by the world's "greatest generation." Nothing like five or six firm licks to the backside to remind you not to steal quarters from Daddy's piggy bank, although I never got caught for that, even though I should have been.

My parents were born in the Midwest. My dad was born October 31, 1929, in Louisville, Ohio, and my mom was born in Wakarusa, Indiana, on August 17, 1932. Dad passed away in May 2017, and Mom left us in September 2012. Both of their passings were sad events, and I will cover each event later in this book.

LIFE IN THE MIDWEST

During the first fifty years of the twentieth century, the industrial Midwest and Northeast spawned manufacturing industries, which they built to palliate an insatiable need for products. The American machine was in full bloom. While the last half of the nineteenth century built the railroads and steamships, the first fifty years in the twentieth century exploded with manufacturing advances and life-changing energy supplies, such as useable electricity, cars, airplanes, home heating and cooling, and appliance conveniences of every kind for the home. After radio and television were invented, the popular culture of things of comfort and great social use was developed at an amazingly fast clip. From 1950 to 2000, continued advancements were taking place geographically outside of the Midwest.

MICHAEL JOSEPH OWENS (1859–1923)

The Gasmire families working in the mid- to late-1800s and early 1900s had hardworking manufacturing jobs, which were difficult but life-sustaining. Our relatives earned everything they needed to live day to day, without knowing that Owens's influence would be passed forward to multiple generations. Although my great grandfather, John Frederick Gasmire, who was married to Sophia Gasmire, was a dentist/physician by training primarily in West Virginia and Pennsylvania, he was also involved with a manufacturing glass bottle plant in West Virginia.

Michael Owens had a profound impact on the life of us Gasmires, whose relatives were under the tutelage of Michael Owens. The culture he created as a young man, as he forged a way to build a glass-bottling empire, made him the Steve Jobs of his day.

Michael Owens believed that anything could be done. So much so that he built a culture around the personal commitment that anything worth considering, big and small, could be done.

We have an incredibly old picture of a very young Michael Owens, who was a teenage apprentice working for a glass manufacturer in Newark, Ohio. The plant Owens worked in with John F. Gasmire was constructed of wood and eventually burned down. Not a total surprise since they were using large supplies of natural gas and high silica-content sandstone—the two items necessary for glass manufacturing. Glass bottle production would never be the same, and it developed into plastic blow molding in subsequent years.

Owens invented an automatic glass bottle manufacturing machine that revolutionized the glass bottle industry. Think about how life changed with bottles of any kind. Does anyone really care about glass bottles? Why does anyone care about anything? It is the calling and determination inside a person. Within a brief period of time, Owens became a plant manager for Libbey in Findley, Ohio. Owens wanted to build a machine that would automate the glass-blowing process rather than relying on blowing glass by hand, which was terribly slow and tedious. In August 1904, Owens successfully patented a machine that could automatically manufacture glass bottles. It could produce four bottles per second. During his life, Michael Owens secured forty-five patents.

CHANGING LIVES WITH A SINGLE MISSION, BELIEVING IT COULD BE DONE

Owens was born in 1859, and my granddad Charlie was born in December 1887. Dad told me that my great grandfather, John F. Gasmire, worked with Michael Owens while also maintaining his dental practice, but I am not sure how accurate that account really is. However, I do know there was a relationship between John F. Gasmire, the glass plant, and Michael Owens, and the picture proves it. Think about that the next time you have a plastic bottle in your hand. Turn it over and look at the labeling blown into the plastic. If you see an O-I stamped into the plastic or a reference to Owen, that is where it all started.

The company was renamed Owens-Illinois, Inc in 1965. Owens died in Toledo in 1923, and his lore in our family took on great meaning as Dad and his brother, Wilbur (Al) Schaich, set out in their careers at O-I in the late 1940s and 1950s, Dad in engineering and manufacturing, and Al in new product patent development as a patent attorney. For more than twenty years, Dad raised us in the arms and shadows of O-I.

I discovered during my research for this book a quote that Michael Owens was known for, which drove the culture in the early days at O-I: [1]"It can be done." Based upon a life upbringing with my dad, Richard C. Gasmire, he grabbed on to that positive thinking and proved it correct. He passed it down to me, and I am very grateful for that subtle but powerful way of thinking.

My grandfather, Charles Gasmire (no middle name), was one of ten children. His brothers were Elwood, Manford, Albert (who was never married and died at forty years old), and John. His sisters were Ada, MaVerda, Mary, Louise, Rella, and Hallie. When I was a child, I remember knowing Louise and Rella and MaVerda (pronounced May-Verda). Louise was a hoot, and Rella was the perfect likeness of her brother Charlie, my grandfather. Louise and Rella, along with Charlie, were the musical talents in the family, and those interests and talents continued for a couple more generations. They played the violin, guitar, and mandolin, which is now proudly displayed in our entryway at the ranch.

Charlie's father, John F. Gasmire, was killed in an auto crash at the age of seventy-seven in June 1931. The crash occurred when they were hit by a truck on Steubenville Pike in Pittsburgh. His wife Sophia, son Manford, and another son were injured. I never found out which one of Charlie's other brothers was in the car that claimed their father's life.

---

1 New York Times, 1923

I have a savings account book from Diamond National Bank in Pittsburgh, where Charlie and his mother shared the account from May 2, 1921, until June 29, 1932, when the account was closed with a closing balance of $2,074.21 one year after John's death.

After John's death, Sophia lived another eight and a half years and died on January 25, 1941, leaving behind seven of her nine children, including my grandfather, Charlie. What is very interesting is Sophia's family lineage. Both of her parents were born in Germany with the names of Wilhelm Bauer (1823–1890) and Fredericka Specht (1831–1919). Many of the Gasmires from these two generations are buried in Union Dale Cemetery in Pittsburgh, PA. Sophia and John were both born in Wheeling, West Virginia, and are buried at Union Dale Cemetery.

Charlie Gasmire, my grandfather, worked as a salesman for the Metropolitan Insurance Company, calling on customers to sell new policies and renewal policies and collect all premiums due. He carried a handgun on the collection runs but never had to use it, at least as far as I know. My grandfather came out of WWI with an honorable discharge as a private in 2nd Company, 1st Battalion 155th Depot Brigade in 1919 after just over seven months of active duty from June 1918 to February 1919. He was born in 1887 and served in the Great War when he was twenty-one years old. He did not get married until he was forty years old. He told Dad that he waited "as long as he could" because when you're married, if you go to dinner and a picture show, you will have to buy two dinners and two tickets, not just one. He would hold up two fingers for emphasis when he explained it. We all just agreed with a chuckle and shook our heads.

Although Charlie only had an eighth-grade education, he exhibited a punctilious focus on his finances. After he passed away on March 22, 1984, we found the journal that he used to keep track of his expenditures. After his wife, my grandma Alma, passed away on July

31, 1974, Charlie lived by himself and kept track of everything. He scribbled his spending transactions in pencil on little attached pieces of a notepad the size of a pack of cigarettes. He listed expenses as small as one penny, with the date spent. Most were in the fifty-cent range, but a few expenditures made it as high as $1.75. There were multiple entries where he bought Red Man chewing tobacco. That was his vice, chewing tobacco. And along with his journal entries were the actual pennies, nickels, and some dimes that he was hanging on to. There were no quarters, as I recall.

These are the signs of a man who kept track of everything. When you don't have much to start with, tracking and cataloging life's expenses can be the difference between making it versus going to the land of the paupers. It's a good business lesson: the little things are the big things. Tend to the smaller drivers of what makes a business work, and the big things have a better chance of taking care of themselves.

Charlie continued working for the Metropolitan Insurance Company until he became the second husband to Alma Amanda Moorhead, who was born in Pittsburgh in Allegheny County on August 17, 1892. Charlie and Alma were married on January 19, 1928, four years after her first husband, William Lewis Schaich, died of scarlet fever when Al was just nine years old. We are ever so grateful for Alma's first marriage, as they had two children, both my uncles Wilbur (Al) and Robert, who we called Uncle Bob. Uncle Al and my father had a special relationship and were separated in age by a whopping fourteen years.

William's father was a construction worker and built William and Alma their own home next door to his own home, just west of Pittsburgh. When William died in their home from the fever, Alma and her two boys, Al and Bob, moved into the other house that William's father had built. Years later, Bill Schaich, Al's second oldest child and first of four sons, attempted to find the original homes and learned that developers had torn down our family homes along with others to clear land for Riverfront Stadium, home of the Pittsburgh Pirates and Pittsburgh Steelers. Too bad to have lost those legacy buildings.

After William died, Alma remained on her own in Pittsburgh, burdened with caring for her two young sons, Al and Bob, until marrying Charlie in 1928. Think of how hard that must have been. It takes a commanding work ethic and dedication to get things done to survive, and in today's world, it is easy to overlook or even pity the work of our ancestors. But if they hadn't had the mettle to survive, to endure the daily grind, I'm not sure I would have the same story that I have today. And probably the same for you and your family matriarchs and patriarchs. Sooner or later, work has to be done, and these were the pioneers that gave me a fighting chance to grind it out. I hope our ancestors in years to come learn all the dominos that have had to fall for generations to give them the chances and opportunities they will have one day. A look back should be a look forward.

Perhaps Alma saw Charlie as a charming bachelor. He had a good job and had no children, so he was the perfect suitor to help raise her two young boys. He was five years older than Alma. He was forty, and she was thirty-five when they married. It was his first and only marriage. Soon after they were married, Charlie left the life of a traveling insurance salesman behind and took a job working as a high school custodian. Dad would tell us stories of how he began helping Granddad at the high school to make ends meet. Dad also worked in a grocery store as a kid and helped Granddad when he needed the extra hand.

I am incredibly grateful that Granddad was able to spend more time with Dad, even though it changed their financial dynamics. Dad learned things from Granddad and Grandma that were passed down to me, and now, to our kids. Those things included hunting, fishing, and traveling. Alma was a real angler. She could fry them in the pan too, and she was not afraid to work. I really do not think she was afraid of anything. She did not even blink when the nightcrawler worms that Granddad and I had dug up by the mailbox and put in the refrigerator to keep them fresh got out of their box and climbed all over the food inside. It freaked me out because I thought I was going to get clobbered. Granddad took the hit for that one instead. He just put in another chew and moved on about it.

Grandma, for all her toughness, was really the encouraging influence for Dad to get more than a high school education. She was not a glamorous woman. She was a working homebody who wanted Dad to go to college. If Charlie graduated from the eighth grade, then she wanted Dad to go to college. And he expected the same of us as we came along years later. We grew to learn new skills handed down from Granddad and Grandma. I learned to shoot a shotgun using Granddad's single-shot twelve gauge at around ten years old.

Dad was relentless on the safety aspects of hunting, of carrying around a loaded firearm, and would bust our chops if he caught us being unsafe with the handling and shooting of any firearm. Granddad's twelve-gauge kicked the fire out of my shoulder, but not before it kicked the life out of a squirrel in a mulberry tree in southern Missouri while we hunted on a pig farm that Dad dug up from some relationship he had at O-I.

At Granddad's home in Michigan, he had a little fourteen-foot fishing boat with oars and a small gas-powered motor requiring yanks and pulls to get started. I remember Granddad dragging the motor out of the basement below the house in Brighton, Michigan, to attach it to the boat floating in his backyard on Lake Woodlawn, about an hour northwest of Detroit. He would lift it off its stand that was sitting on an uneven dirt floor.

I can still remember the smell of that basement. It smelled musty, with a fragrance of wood, dust, oil, chemicals, and whatever Grandma was cooking upstairs. He had toolboxes galore, and even more tackle boxes. Fishing tackle of every kind hung from the ceiling or was stuffed neatly into converted tobacco boxes clearly marked with what lure they needed to store—lures that looked like they had either caught a boatload of fish or were in bad need of repair and new paint. All the lures were made of wood. The real deal. The stuff old fishing movies are made of: handmade and effective. I never saw Granddad buy a plastic lure, although I am sure he did; he just wrote it down in his spending journal and never let it get out of his basement.

There was a hand water pump from a well they had at one time; there were hand tools to carve, drill, and cut wood; and there were lubricants for all. It was not a large room, but it was a fun place to explore with Granddad when he would get us ready to go fishing. He would carry the motor in one hand, and the other hand and arm he would extend out from his body to cantilever the load. I know where Dad got that move as he demonstrated it to me years later when we lived in St. Louis. I have a picture of Dad bringing in firewood from the backyard through the kitchen door. With wood in one arm and negotiating the door with the other, he was trying to crack a smile for the photo I took of him with the new Swinger Polaroid camera he and Mom gave me for my birthday that November.

He carried the wood through the kitchen while my mom's cooking filled the air with either chicken or squirrel in the frying pan. Either way, we ate it all and loved it, save for spitting out shot on the plate if it was squirrel or rabbit. We ate a lot of both, due to Dad, Granddad, and Grandma too. I remember one afternoon when we were visiting Granddad and Grandma at their lake home, which was purchased by Uncle Al, Dad's half brother and mentor, and loaned back to Granddad and Grandma to live in for the rest of their lives. I do not recall visiting them in any other home but that one on the lake.

Granddad and I had been out digging up fishing worms by his mailbox in front of where they lived on Oak Knoll Rd. when he spotted something down the road. He said, "Davey, let's have a look," and we walked toward it to see what it was. Well, it was not what I expected. It was a huge snapping turtle! In the middle of the road. He said, "My, my, would you look at that, Davey! Let's take him to Grandma so she can make some turtle soup!"

He picked that turtle up by the tail and carried him cantilevered far out to his right so as not to lose a kneecap from a vicious, nasty, and pissed-off snapping turtle from Michigan. I watched him "process" it, and the next day or two, we had turtle soup on the veranda overlooking the lake. In later years, whenever I passed by that turtle-pick-up-spot, I just had to chuckle with a warm feeling of gratitude that I learned how to hunt and fish.

THE MYSTERIOUS DEATHS AT THE ANN ARBOR VA HOSPITAL

In 1975, after Alma had passed away in 1974, Granddad and Dad became witnesses to the mysterious deaths at the Ann Arbor VA hospital. It was a national story, and a book was written about the murders. A group of nurses systematically attempted to murder as many as a hundred elderly patients over a period of years. The FBI investigated eight deaths, although there were more. The book written about the scandal included excerpts and summaries of the Gasmire involvement. It read:

> In addition to Neely, a family member of Charles Gasmire, another of the victims, identified Perez as a suspect. On July 29th, Richard Gasmire, the son of Charles, had entered his father's room and saw a nurse near the head of his father's bed doing something with the IV apparatus. She had her back to him and did not see him enter. He stood there for about two minutes. His father was sleeping when suddenly he sat up in bed and then collapsed. Charles Gasmire was going into a Pavulon induced respiratory failure.
> Richard Gasmire identified the nurse as Leonora Perez. To confirm his identification, the FBI set up a line-up of 18 women wearing

nurses' uniforms, 15 of which were Asian. Gasmire immediately identified Perez as the nurse he had seen in his father's room. Richard Gasmire did testify to what he had seen at the trial.[2]

I remember it at the time because I had already graduated from high school in Dallas and had just moved out of the house for college. It was important in our family, and more importantly, they almost killed Granddad. If my dad had not been there when he was, then Granddad would surely have died. Dad sounded the alarm, and the floor staff went to work on Granddad as a full code and saved his life.

In the full book written about all the events in detail, Granddad was on the witness stand and was hard of hearing. When the lawyer asked him questions, Granddad would cup his ear and say, "Eh?" but not before hitting the open microphone soundly with his hand and sending booming vibrations throughout the courtroom.

Always remember that you should always have a good sound system, and Granddad proved it again. He lived until 1984 and died at his lake home of cardiac arrest. We speculate that he was watching his favorite TV show—wrestling—and probably got himself so worked up (he believed it was real) he just might have keeled over from his easy rocking chair and landed on the floor in his living room. A neighbor found him there. So sad that he died alone. He was ninety-six.

THE GASMIRES INVADE ST. LOUIS; MIDWEST VALUES, SPORTS, AND SHOWS

Our family structure was very traditional Midwest values. Demanding work by the husbands and fathers, and even harder work at home by the wives and mothers. Our home was no exception. Mom took care of us at home and in our outside activities, such as getting us signed

2 The mysterious deaths at Ann Arbor by Robert K Wilcox, January 1, 1977

up for school events, sporting teams, and birthday parties. However, in the 1950s and 1960s, kids were not overloaded with multiple social priorities at the same time. We played one sport each season. I played baseball, football, and hockey. Fell in love with the St. Louis Cardinals, both baseball and football, and St. Louis Blues hockey. But all this normalcy was surrounded by Dad's career at O-I. Everything was O-I.

I still have Dad's favorite stapler with the O-I logo on it from the sixties. We would take family road trips and drive eight hours in a car full of smoke with the windows rolled up from St. Louis up to see Uncle Al and Aunt Lilian in Toledo, Ohio, during summers and winters. Uncle Bob and Aunt Jean moved to Tennessee, and we did not see them very often after they moved. But we had a close and developing relationship with Al. He and Dad were very close. Al mentored my dad, I believe.

When Al planned on marrying the first love of his life, Lilian Halfaker, he had to plan carefully. Anticipating Alma's less-than-encouraging reaction to Al's intent of marrying, he waited until one week after he had turned twenty-one so that she could not tell him he couldn't marry Lilian. It was not an issue Alma had with Lilian, but rather with losing a hardworking son to a married life that would take him further from home. It must have run in the times back then.

When my dad told Charlie he was going to marry my mother, Ellie Holdeman, Charlie told him not to say anything to Alma until a day or two before the wedding, or there would be trouble. Alma was of Irish descent and just had a robust way of reacting to such things. But she put the mission of education in each of her boys, Bob, Al, and my father, Richard (Dick).

When Al was in college at the University of Ohio, he got a low-paying janitor job cleaning a fraternity house and joined the ROTC, where he could make some extra money. The Reserve Officer Training Corps was a path many men took and still do today, along with many women.

He graduated from college in 1940, which was a perfect time to get drafted by the army for WWII. The army shipped him to Massachusetts to work for the weapons depot there. He was assigned the work of developing patents for the new weapons that were being discovered during manufacturing and development. He became a patent attorney and landed at O-I sometime after the war.

After he and Lillian were married, they traveled with Al's jobs, which required them to move every two years. Once their first of five children was born (Nancy), Lillian put her foot down to stop the incessant moving of their home so frequently. They settled in Maumee, Ohio, and lived there for more than fifteen years. All five of their children—our cousins Serin, Bill, Terry, Tom, and Bob—graduated from Maumee High School. I remember visiting their home.

From then on, Al built an incredible legal career at O-I and shepherded Dad into the company after Dad graduated from Tri-State College in Angola, Indiana. Founded in 1884, it is now named Trine University. Trine is a private school with a tri-state presence in Indiana, Michigan, and Ohio, with five thousand students. Al worked as a patent attorney most of his professional life and was instrumental in encouraging Dad to become an engineer. Dad confided in me during a personal talk one time about how, when he was in high school, he believed he wanted to be a preacher. I was really surprised because other than him wanting to attend church each Sunday, we had no idea of his desires in his early years. He wanted to go to seminary and get into ministry. That did not develop further professionally, although throughout his life he was always involved with church activities and politics and found ways to perform with the choir and various acting opportunities. He loved acting, and he combined that passion and ministry, and it worked out great.

Many a story can be told about shows we saw Dad perform in, and it put a morsel of interest in my mind about acting or the arts in some capacity. He seemed happy working on those shows and the rehearsals that he would drag us to watch. I remember getting the neighborhood kids together in St. Louis and putting on plays for the neighbors, charging them ten cents. I put Jay in charge of the money, and for some reason, we never saw any. I think he forgot to charge them when they were seated.

We had an outdoor area on our back patio, which had an enormous oak tree smack dab in the center of it. That served as the theater stage during the summer, and we flooded it with water to make the ice rink in the winter. Dad and Mom would take us to Forest Park and the Muny Opera at the St. Louis Zoo each summer to watch professional shows that left an impression on me. The evening heat in the summer was oppressive, so the outdoor theater had enormous fans on top of stanchions coming out of the ground throughout the seating, but we still dressed up to go to "the Muny."[3]

I developed a personal fascination with the Muny as a result of Mom and Dad taking us there. It was on a grand scale to me at the age of eight or nine years old. Everyone was so dressed up in the heat, waiting for the sun to go down and the show lights to come up. In July 1964, our family went to see a production of *Tom Sawyer*, starring Danny Lockin as Tom Sawyer. That same year, the Muny produced other shows, such as entertainment legends *My Fair Lady, Showboat,* and *The Sound of Music*. It was the real deal, with real superstars performing over the years.

---

3 The Municipal Opera Association of St. Louis, Missouri, is the largest municipally owned outdoor theater in the US, seating as many as eleven thousand for a single show. Located in Forest Park just west of downtown St. Louis and near the St. Louis Zoo, it always had an electric atmosphere of enthusiasm for the arts, as I recall. The theater was built in 1917, with six performances during its first season, and typically included shows with local talent, usually more of a stage play than musicals. In more recent years, leading up to its hundred-year anniversary in 2017, the performances have been mostly musical. Since it is outdoors, it is only open three months per year, from June until August.

After going to see Dad rehearse and perform in our small community theater, followed by seeing the big stage production at the Muny, I really took notice of that kind of pomp and circumstance and I got very interested in acting. I even remember taking the show program home for the names of the actors so I could flip through the white pages of the phone book to see if I could find their phone numbers so I could call them. I did not realize they did not actually live in St. Louis. For all I knew, they lived just up the street. They seemed mystical to me. They were real, but not really. They played make-believe in a way any kid would love. It stuck with me, and I pursued some acting roles in St. Louis as a kid and landed a couple and got dumped by a few.

I remember one role my mom made me try out for, so it would get me out of the house for a few hours each day. (She later told me that I drove her crazy.) It was over in Brentwood, as I recall, at a small troupe theater that I do not remember the name of. But I tried out for a part and was assigned the role of the shah of Persia. I was nine or ten years old. Really? The shah of Persia? I did not even know what a shah was! Not sure that I know today, other than I cannot say, "I never met a shah I didn't like." Who meets shahs? How do you play a shah at ten years old?

Well, it led to my mom taking me to a much larger theater tryout, where I had to read lines to the director while on the stage in front of him and his assistant critics. I was scared stiff. I got to the tryout about ten minutes before my reading after school and dinner at home. I do not know how my mom did all that she did. I read the lines to myself a couple of times and tried to understand the character whose lines they were, and I never got a handle on it by the time they called my name to read. I got up on the big stage with the lights beaming down on me, and I bombed. I was told I would not be asked back. Well, at least I was a shah. It's good to get dumped early in life and occasionally throughout life. Not all participants get trophies.

Mom also found, and I do not know how, a way to get a few of my friends and me on a local children's television program[4] modeled after Captain Kangaroo, in more of a showboat stage layout design.

We lived right on the Mississippi River, and riverboats were a large part of our town's history. Mom took us out of school early one day and took us down to the television station. Our job as the show's "kids" was just to sit or stand and be kids. No lines, no acting, no nothing. But the lights were bright, and the cameras looked intimidating, and it was live TV. It was a fun experience, thanks again to Mom!

It was those early experiences of getting up in front of a crowd and learning how to speak publicly with confidence that equipped me for the demands of my advanced business life throughout the years. My mother was of great encouragement to me in learning the self-confidence of public speaking. It also helped me when I became a disc jockey in college, fronting a band, acting and singing in shows, and presenting during road shows for fundraising and public offerings.

My dad's career at O-I led him to work on and file a few dozen US patents that are still in place, although technology has rendered the unused patents rather useless today. Still, Dad had an engineering mind, along with his acting talents and interest in church work. It is remarkably interesting that Dad, who was great at math and science, was equally gifted in fine arts. His engineering abilities came into great and frequent use at home and on vacations. If something broke, like an attic fan, a boiler or heater, or even the car, Dad could be found sitting cross-legged on the floor, or grass, or driveway, wherever the problem was, with a toolbox, his shirt off, working hard on figuring the damn thing out.

---

4 It was called *Captain 11's Showboat*. I used to watch this show because it was best known for airing Three Stooges shorts to viewers in the St. Louis area. The show aired from May 1959, before we moved to St. Louis, until August 1968. Local performer Harry Fender played Captain 11, and it was a popular late-afternoon local favorite.

When we would go to the Lake of the Ozarks or the Mississippi River, or even Grandma and Granddad's lake, where they lived on Lake Woodlawn, in Michigan, Dad was always working on the engine. One time we drove to the lake in Michigan for a family summer vacation. We towed the boat behind the O-I company car all the way there. When we got there, we realized that we had left the keys to the boat at home. Before we even launched the boat in the water, Dad was cross-legged on the boat floor, hot wiring the electrical system. He showed me how to do it. On the way home from that trip, as we were towing the boat seventy miles per hour down the highway, an Illinois State Trooper pulled us over. Dad rolled down the window, expecting to get a speeding ticket. Instead, the trooper handed Dad a suitcase we had left at Grandma's. She had called the troopers and had them pick it up and run us down to give it to us. Nothing like road service and good old-fashioned police work in the 1960s.

Our seventeen-foot StarCraft aluminum boat had a 75 hp Johnson outboard on the back. Many times, the motor had the lid off so Dad could work on it, or even just start it. We would drain the oil before each cold winter, and he was meticulous about his tools. I found that out the hard way. He was an amazing mechanic. His skills and interests complemented one another. On one hand, he could think through a very challenging mechanical engineering problem and pull together whatever was available at the time and place that he could fix it, and yet, he could also get in the car and sing at the top of his lungs along with the AM radio playing Frank Sinatra. He loved both, and all ends, from technology and mechanics to a finely harmonized choir. He could punch in and out of some very different situations, from solving big problems in a factory or managing an on-scene disaster to playing pretend airplane with the switches in the car on the way home.

THE OWENS-ILLINOIS FIRE

I remember an awfully bad night for O-I and Dad's plant in St. Louis. We received a call in the middle of the night that one of the warehouses next to the plant had caught on fire and was actively burning. For some reason, I ended up in the car with Dad, and Jay was there too. I vividly recall arriving at the plant on a very wintry night, with fire truck lights flashing and water hoses going every direction in and out of the warehouse. There was so much water put on that fire, due to the combustible nature of the plastic bottles and cardboard boxes where they were stored, that the wooden bricks used to make the floor became loose and floated in the water on the ground everywhere. I'll never forget the look on Dad's face, and Jay and I stayed out of the way and got back in the car. It was freezing outside.

From that fire we then drove a considerable distance to one of the O-I warehouses, where saved product was being moved from the burned-out warehouse. When we got there, Jay and I remained in Dad's company car, huddled up in the front seat, trying to keep warm. I remember the car heat coming in from the center of the floor, and we had our feet tucked up against it. We were seeing Dad's leadership style in action. As I recall, no one was seriously hurt, and Dad was extremely glad for that, as that was his first concern. But the plant suffered damage, and it damaged Dad because he loved that place, the people, and the company.

I remember Dad asking me as we drove away from the warehouse, "Davey, are you going to put up the flaps and the landing gear?"

I said, "Sure, Dad," then I turned the fan on high and slid the heat to normal.

"Takeoff checklist complete. Let's head home." He was like that because he needed it too. I could tell Dad was gripped by what was happening, and yet, he remained balanced by demonstrating fatherly leadership while protecting us from the event itself.

Dad could multi-process more than the average plastics plant manager executive. Jay and I, on occasion, would go to the office with Dad on weekends when he needed to be there. We took over his office by drawing innovative fifth-grader designs of plastic bottles that he could consider for his customers. Little did we know that those decisions were made at the home office for each customer, but Jay and I were trying to see if we could produce something more than just a normal-shaped bottle. We were trying to be business guys just like Dad and trying to get noticed for our efforts.

It was important to Dad to succeed, to get it done with intensity, then enjoy the outcome. Something that added to Dad's intensity was how he thought about solving a problem. If it could be done, he was the one that would figure it out. Usually, he would solve it in one of two ways. First, he would think about what he had available to him right there, in that space and time, to fix it quickly. His creative brain would kick in to ask himself, "How can I use this tin can as a screwdriver?" or "If I use this nickel, can I plug this hole?" His instinct was to get it done quickly so he could move on to whatever was next.

Or, second, he would think, "How can I turn this into an event of gigantic proportions?" It was either quick and now, or later and big. One example of this was when he had a problem with the riding lawn mower. It did not maintain steady RPMs to run the belted mower drive, and as a result, it bogged down a bit. He tried a normal fix with adjustments and a new part or two, but the problem continued. So, he went to plan B, which sometimes was really plan A all along. He organized a neighborhood riding lawn mower parade and party and invited and expected all his friends in the neighborhood to participate. And they did.

The event included judging each riding mower for performance and decoration. He had neighbors bring trumpets, grills and coolers, transistor radios, and whiskey. By creating this deadline for himself, he had to perform. He loved to perform. If he could not fix it, he was going to have a fun time getting everyone else to participate so that he had a bigger reason than just mowing the lawn. He was an expert at that, and I ended up with some of that too. And Mom loved it too because she loved a good party.

Another good example of Dad taking a problem and turning it into a need, which is also a great and necessary skill in business, was when I would bring home a school project. I had a physical science project in sixth grade that required me to make something that explained the human circulatory system. I was stumped, and who really cared anyway? I figured I would just get some butcher paper from Tom Boy, our local grocer/hangout joint run by a guy named Leonard, and get some paint and draw what I saw from a picture. It was not going very well, and I asked Mom and Dad for suggestions or alternatives. The project was due in two days, and I was running out of time. O-I to the rescue.

In the factory, part of the process to make plastic bottles was to extrude plastic into long, spaghetti-like pieces that could be ground into small plastic pellets, which could be mixed with virgin plastic material, melted down, then injected into a machine to make blow mold plastic bottles. If you took the spaghetti phase of that process before chopping it up, it could look like a circulatory system. So, using the quick-fix "with what we have" strategy (strategy A), Dad brought about a hundred feet of this stiff yet somewhat flexible yellow plastic spaghetti material home, and I did the best with what I had. No other kid in the class had a plastic extruded circulatory system model. And I turned it in on time.

After that close call, Dad surprised all three of us kids, although Sue-Sue was about three or four at the time, with about fifty large Clorox bottles complete with caps. We turned that gem of an opportunity into the best neighborhood creek raft by building a wooden frame and attaching all the bottles underneath for flotation. It was awesome. We had a creek in our side yard and when it rained, we stared out the window until the creek was raging with fast-moving water, then dragged, then floated our raft to the head of the creek. That was when we found out that part of the engineering of the raft needed to include a way to retain all the bottles under the frame so they would stay attached.

In a short time, there were bottles all over the neighborhood and a frame that was left to be picked up after things dried out. A very good lesson in how to test your thinking on an idea. A very early and simple introduction to the business concept "what will kill us next?" I've never forgotten to always think about what keeps things afloat and manage to protect it.

GREAT PARENTS AND GREAT TEACHERS WITH INFINITE PATIENCE WITH ME

I think Dad knew he had the skills to be able to focus on many different things, and he could see when I would get out of line with my focus. It would drive him, Mom, and my teachers nuts. An example is when my favorite teacher in elementary and middle school, Mrs. Barbara Handley, asked my parents for a parent-teacher conference to talk about my inability to behave in class. I remember that discussion in third grade. I was told that from then on, I needed to make a tally mark in pencil on the top of my desk every time Mrs. Handley said I had just interrupted the class or misbehaved. I had no problem understanding the need to keep track of things, but that was ridiculous! How many pencils did this school have? We would need all of them! And a good wall pencil sharpener to reload pencils by the case.

I attended Henry Hough Elementary School in Glendale, MO. In 2022, Glendale was recognized as the safest city in Missouri, and to this day, I really believe it. It was a small, very intimate neighborhood of friends and hardworking families. It should have been a backdrop for the perfect American city, full of patriotic, churchgoing folks who loved to shoot shotguns off their front porches on New Year's Eve and gather for caroling from house to home during Christmas.

How Mom and Dad landed in that neighborhood is a very thankful mystery. I loved growing up there. I loved those schooldays and can probably still tell you the names of some of my classmates there. I am still in touch with a few of them. Silly kids' stuff in the neighborhood, walking to and from school, knowing all our neighbors, selling newspapers, either the *St. Louis Post Dispatch* or the *Globe Democrat,* barking, "Git your paypa hee-uh!" to cars driving by for a nickel a copy, then hitting the car with a snowball and getting paid twenty-five cents for an hour of sales.

It was all a great way to grow up. Safe. Local. Convenient. There was no wokeness, which permeates a portion of society in cities of the 2020s. We lived with lots of trees and green grass, with large lots for yard sports. It was a playground of life. I loved it. And our family was happy.

We were not rich. We were a five-member family on one income and an average Glendale home. It was a two-story wood-and-red-brick square footprint that had a sunroom overlooking our creek in our side yard. Above the sunroom was a sundeck that was accessible through the master bedroom door on the second floor. I remember being scared to be up there and did not find a reason to be there if I did not need to be. We learned to load our own shotgun shells in the sunroom while we watched sporting events.

HUMAN ENDURANCE AND HOW IT CAN BE DONE ... BUT WHY BOATING?

I remember watching the Summer Olympics while making some not-so-high-quality shotgun reloads and was in awe of the long-distance running events. When I heard the announcer say that these runners we were watching were running a marathon, I did not make much of a big deal about it until they said a full marathon was 26.2 miles!

How can anyone run that far? In less than three hours? That must be impossible! I thought to myself. I was really impressed and sort of in disbelief that the feat could be done in the first place, much less as a race, but it did feed my interest in running up and down the big hill on our street that went up and right as we walked out from our front door at 257 Parkland Avenue. It was a great hill. In the summer we would ride our bikes up and down it. We would also run up and down it, and in the winter, we would sled and saucer down it. Long-distance running and the benefits of such became a bigger deal in my life than I realized at the time I admired those Olympians.

One of the fun elements of watching sports on television is that for a crazy moment or two, we start thinking, "Hey, I think I might be able to do that." But why does it matter if we can do that or not? It probably would not be of interest if it was easy, and to our honest selves, we are impressed with the feats of others. In my family, we had so many interests that were budding and brewing that sometimes we forgot what to do next. Every normal aspect of everyday middle-class life became a race to see if we could do it, all while we were still working on something from two years ago. Today I think we call it normal, but when I grew up, it was a diagnosis somewhere between ADHD and dementia.

I was in the early stages of thinking about and trying long-distance running, then boating was introduced smack-dab in the middle of getting ready for summer bike riding and running with neighborhood kids. It didn't help that we had a single-car garage that kept Mom's car protected and a workshop immediately behind it where we kept our bicycles, tools, paints, chemicals, and general junk that could not fit in the garage. I climbed on those paint cabinets once, detached one from the wall, and ended up on the floor with paint cans all over me and a very angry mother.

With only one single garage, we had a parking dilemma when Dad talked Mom into buying a boat for the family. After all, he grew up with fishing boats around that were owned by his older brother and parents, who would take frequent fishing trips together whenever they talked themselves into spending the money to do so, primarily in their later years. Dad was influenced by some of the shop workers in his factory, and, ever the leader, included them in his social and adventure exploits. He would take them up on things such as crazy boat rides on the Mississippi River. Pappy Ruets, one of his favorite men at the plant, took me, Dad, and Jay, to the river in a fourteen-foot wood fishing boat and showed us how his little stinker of a boat performed. His attention was on how his Coors longneck bottle rode all alone on the bench seat next to him. With every life-threatening steep turn, he watched the bottle to see if it would be dislodged by centrifugal force or remain upright by the fate of gravity.

It is actually an interesting engineering feat that just happened to scare us to death, but I think about that ride every time I see a Coors longneck beer more than fifty years later.

The decision to buy a boat did not come without some adolescent brain damage for me, Jay, and Sue. Dad told us the salesman was taking us on a demonstration ride in the boat on the Mississippi River. Another boating demo on Huck Finn's river. He wanted to put the little StarCraft through its paces. At the time, we had never been on a river as a whole family and did not think too much about it, except for the ride with Pappy. Until we did.

Our whole family was aboard, and I remember the key elements of the ride very well. It scared the living shit out of me. He had that boat at full speed, making steep turns right and left, crossing that funny thing behind us called a "wake," and throwing us around like rag dolls. Having already been Raggedy Andy once in my life, I did not appreciate a repeat performance at thirty miles per hour. I do not remember where Sue-Sue went to hide, maybe in Mom's lap, but Jay and I climbed under the instrument panel and buried our faces and heads in big orange life jackets. The ugly kind.

The Mississippi River might be a good place for Tom Sawyer and Huck Finn (and do not forget a very hot Becky Thatcher), but the three-to-six-knot constant rage of that dirty water heading to the Gulf of Mexico was too much for me. It had sticks, trees, junk, bodies of who knows what, all floating at a speed that you could ski on without a boat.

I do not recall the post-ride discussion between the salesperson and our family, but the decision was made to make the purchase, and among the five of us, I would say the results were mixed. Dad loved it. Mom went with it. Sue did not know better. Jay thought it might be fun only if we never went back on the Mississippi River, and my vote was a very-chicken-like, "Sure! It will be fun."

A few weeks later, horror of horrors was repeated. Only worse. Dad took us back to the river to teach us how to water ski. I hated it. We all hated it. I did get up on two skis though, and I did everything I could not to fall. You did not know on what or on whom you would land. Then, if you did fall, you were heading to New Orleans, and there was not anything you could do about it. I lived through it but was not happy about it. Then we all watched as Dad talked Mom into trying it. We just knew we were going to lose her and might never find her body. We pictured the headlines: "Doris Day found on the shores of Louisiana," and we were scared for her. But she got up! Then, to our horror, she kicked a ski to only ski on one ski. One ski!

"What happened?! She lost a ski, Dad!" we shouted.

Dad yelled back, "Nah, she kicked it so she could ski on one. It is more fun on one!"

After she wore herself out and dropped back into the slime, we picked Mom up and headed downriver to find her other ski. It had been drifting toward a river barge the size of New Hampshire. I remember pulling up to the ski and the barge to pick it up. I thought we were dead. Not to Dad! Time to go back to the landing, load her up, and go home.

We were so done with the Mississippi River. Every time we drove over the Eads Bridge or the Veterans Bridge, built decades earlier and high above the water, I could not look outside and down to the water. I had nightmares about those bridges for years. What were we thinking? Geez. I get the shakes now, just thinking about what it was like back then. But there we were, a new boating family that has now been boating for fifty years and climbing.

THE LEADERSHIP VALUE OF LEARNING TEAM AND INDIVIDUAL SPORTS

Team sports were something I had an interest in during the early years in St. Louis. I played baseball for the Jansen Giants, who were sponsored by the local grocery store, named Jansen's. I loved the St. Louis Cardinals baseball team, listened to games throughout the summers, and practiced with Jay in the backyard at our home in Glendale. I played outfield. I loved the game. I just was not very good at it … particularly batting with a hardball pitcher. I was afraid of that ball hitting me in the face. After all, I had a boxer dog hit me in the face with teeth when I was two, so I was a little "flinchy" when objects came flying at my head.

While in St. Louis I took stitches to my head a couple of times in non-baseball injuries, and I sure did not want a baseball with one hundred and eight handmade stitches holding it together to have the opportunity to be thrown as a fastball up my nose. No, sir. I backed away from nearly every pitch in practice and in games. Needless to say, I didn't see much playing time. Until my dad saw me play. I think I embarrassed him by chickening out and stepping out of the batter's box before the ball even left the hand of the pitcher. It was a fantastic way to watch a pitch come over the plate. As a spectator.

After one game, my dad decided to help me get over the fear of being hit by a pitch. He figured if he could get me focused on something more frightening than staring down a game ball, then maybe I would hang in there and wait for the pitch and no big deal. His solution was to back me against a tree in the backyard and have my little brother pitch to me. The tree prevented me from backing up, but not from closing my eyes and scrunching my face. The tree also did nothing for Jay's control as a pitcher. He used the same poor form to throw a knife at me years later at Lake Texoma.

I never did get used to staying in the batter's box until one fateful at-bat. Two out, two on, game tied in late innings … The coach sent Davey Gasmire to the plate. What was he thinking? I still swear Dad paid him off. Here came the pitch, eyes closed, swung on, and CRACK—I accidentally hit it. And the ball flew over the right fielder's head. It was like slow motion to me. I rounded first and had to keep going. The crowd and team were cheering as I rounded second. I saw the ball picked up back by the fence and thrown in my direction. I do not think I had ever run that far, much less the 26.2-mile marathon that I saw on TV.

The ball was closing in on me, so at the third base, Dad held up the HOLD sign to me, but I did not know what it meant. Unwittingly, I tripped on the third base bag, hit the dirt face-first, and quickly crawled back to the base just in time to be called SAFE! I was mobbed in the dirt at third base. Two runs scored. The Giants won. Then I retired from baseball. Sometimes you need to know when to go out on top.

If you are in the game, no matter your station, position, or reputation, you can change the outcome of that game if you keep swinging, keep digging, and believe something great will happen. I sure was surprised, but I shouldn't have been; this was why they sent me to the batter's box to begin with. Thanks for putting me in, Coach! Next time you are at the plate, ask yourself, "Why am I here?" Then do it.

Football was a little better for me. I played on the Kirkwood Cardinals, and like most kids, played both sides of the ball. On offense I was a guard, and on defense I was the middle linebacker. I loved the kill-the-man-with-the-ball strategy on defense. We played in all kinds of weather in the winter, and it was a blast getting all muddy and going home to show off the dirt. I played in sixth, seventh, eighth, and tenth grade before I realized there was a pretty girl down the street that I wanted to devote some attention to, so practices were pesky and in the way.

In my last team picture as a sophomore while living in Dallas and attending W.T. White High School, I wore #76. When I took the team picture home, my mom noticed that my jersey number looked larger than all the others. My #76 was the larger back number of the jersey, but I put it on backward without even noticing it. Such a social faux pas when you are a teenager in high school, trying to impress the girl down the street.

I had my earliest memory of capitalism during those early years in Glendale. A favorite activity our family enjoyed was going to Hall's Pharmacy in Glendale after church on Sunday afternoons. At Hall's, we would get thick malts and milkshakes made from a Hamilton Beach blender that became so cold it froze the metal container it was mixed in. It would be served alongside a tall glass so you could enjoy pouring it from the frozen container into the glass for drinking with a big fat straw. Slurp, slurp. It was great. For Jay and me, it was a reason to go to church in the first place. Sue went along with everything in those days; she had some catching up to do on our ages.

On Saturdays, after family chores, or during the week after school, my best elementary and middle school childhood friend, Bill Merten, and I would sometimes go to Hall's Pharmacy to read *Mad Magazine* comic books off the shelf and sit on the barstools drinking a concoction called a Zombie. A Zombie had every flavor the soda fountain had on tap, including chocolate. It was so good, and Mr. Hall did not make us buy the comic books, but he did sell us a lot of Bazooka bubble gum, complete with a comic in each piece, pretend cigarettes, and an occasional magic trick.

Across the street from Hall's was a barbershop run by a barber named Mac McGillis. Mac McGillis' Barbershop was the first establishment that paid me cash to do some work. I would go there after school or on the weekend and sweep his floor of all the hair that had been cut that day. I would get twenty-five cents, then go back across the street to Hall's for a twenty-five cent Zombie, then walk the four or five blocks home in time for dinner. I earned it. I spent it.

Mom and Dad attempted to teach me and Jay, and later, Sue, the fine art of work. Work. Weekends. Work. After school. Work. Each of us got a weekly allowance of fifty cents. An annual raise of 10 percent on our birthdays. Dad said that was higher than raises he gave at the plant, but I still scratched my head. I knew it was not much of a raise. And we only got paid if we successfully completed our assigned chores to the satisfaction of the payer—Dad. Imagine that: pay for a quality job well done. None of this union work and wages stuff for this workforce.

I would say we got paid about 50 percent of the time, which cut deeply into our individual cash flow. We made up for it by taking Dad up on his challenge to pay us for achieving physical fitness goals. A favorite of mine was when Dad offered us a gift at the local sporting goods store in exchange for demonstrating how many push-ups and sit-ups we could do. Dad liked giving us fitness goals. He would provide cash incentives for achieving some of these goals. He was big on push-ups and sit-ups. As John Pinette, the late comedian, once said, "I don't do ups. I only do downs. I sit down. I lay down. I woof it down, but I do not do ups." Funny stuff, that John Pinette.

At that age, I could get twenty-five or thirty counted off, but not before Dad expected more. By the time I could do fifty or so push-ups and fifty or more sit-ups, he made good on his offer and took me to the sporting goods store. A typical prize might be a new baseball, caps for my cap gun, or BBs for the BB gun we would shoot at our target in the basement at home.

The next challenge was running, and that is when I was further introduced to the idea of running more than fifty feet without stopping. I thought that could be done but had trouble grasping 26.2 miles. We would run up the hill on our street, then walk back down. Then the next time, we would run up the hill and to the next block. Over time, we were able to run around the block without stopping. I loved it, and so did Dad.

Those days inspired me to keep running, and long-distance running became a passion of my early adulthood all the way to my forties and still is today. Little did I know that marathons and triathlons would be a way of life for me, resulting in some incredible personal athletic accomplishments. More exercise grew into larger gifts, and that is when we got into model rockets. It wasn't lost on me that the concept of "cause and effect" taught in elementary school might be a concept to get me to college. Run this far, get this much. More push-ups, more parental praise. I was beginning to understand that if I did this, I got that. And I think I was the only one of my friends beginning to dial into achievement of any kind. Wow, was that fun.

Model rockets introduced the element of danger with explosive rocket engines that could take your face off if you did not have some safety procedures. The rocket days also merged nicely with my developing interest in airplanes and flying. If we could do all this other stuff, why couldn't we fly?

MY FIRST AWARENESS OF AVIATION —A LASTING MEMORY WITH MY DAD

As is probably true for most people, the years that I believe gave me the start in nearly all my interests were from seven to thirteen years old. During that time, from 1962 until 1968 or 1969, I experienced many early firsts that fueled my interest to further pursue these hobbies with curiosity to see if they would be life's calling. In 1963, before President Kennedy was shot by Lee Harvey Oswald in Dallas in November, Dad had a business trip to take, flying commercially from St. Louis to Detroit's Willow Run Airport. Willow Run has a long aviation legacy, dating back before WWII, and continues to serve the flying public.

For some reason, Dad wanted to take me with him, then leave me at Grandma and Granddad's at the lake in Brighton while he conducted business in Detroit and Toledo, Ohio. It is my very first memory of airplanes, and I remember it in vivid detail today. Dad got us tickets to fly out of Lambert Airfield. Lambert St. Louis Flying Field, as people first called it, has a tremendous amount of history. The airport board named the field after Albert Bond Lambert, who passed away in 1946. Lambert learned to fly with the Wright Brothers, receiving his pilot's license in 1911. He served in the US Army in WWI, reaching the rank of major. Lambert and the Missouri Aeronautical Society leased one hundred and seventy acres of farmland to serve as an airfield.

Lambert was responsible for bringing the 1923 International Air Races to St. Louis. It was a spectacular vision in those days to race machines of manned flight that, only twenty years earlier, had first been invented. In attendance at those air races was a twenty-one-year-old Charles Lindbergh. After the air races, Lindbergh decided to remain at Lambert as an instructor. Lindbergh made history by being the first to cross the Atlantic Ocean, flying solo nonstop from New York to Paris in 1927.

Our flight to Detroit was a night flight on TWA or Ozark on a noticeably big airplane with four radial engines that spit out white smoke when they started. Dad and I were dressed in our finest clothes, dressed for success for the glamorous flight in an airplane. Never underestimate dressing for success. You can never be overdressed for any event but can easily be underdressed for every event. And pay attention to your shoes. I recall that Mom packed my clothes and made sure I had my little suitcase ready for the week with Grandma and Granddad.

It was exciting, climbing the long rolling metal stairway from the tarmac up to the front door of the giant airplane. It was very cold, and the stewardess met us at the door and took us to our seats on the left side of the airplane. To strap on a seat belt for the very first time in any vehicle, and the firm clicking sound when the clasp buckled, then the light pulls of friction to tighten it around my waist, was like something out of Flash Gordon, a popular child's program at the time. We did not even have seat belts in our car yet. I felt like a space hero; we were going to be leaving the ground, and my dad was right next to me.

I remember the feeling of the shake and rumble and noise of those engines, Cyclone radials, and how the entire tube of people all facing the same direction just stayed one behind the other row after row and bounced simultaneously when we hit bumps. It was new to experience bumps even though we were not on the ground, but I thought they were part of what we should enjoy. My view on that has changed after forty years as a pilot. It did not seem like an exceedingly long flight, as I recall. It was so exciting, and I'm sure Dad was having fun too. I hope so, anyway.

When we landed in Detroit, it was cold and snowing. Dad and I walked up the aisle with our coats and hats, heading to the door, which was right behind the cockpit, where there seemed like a room full of men tending to the airplane. They were all trying to sit or stand, leaned over because of the low ceiling, and greeting passengers as they deplaned. When it was our turn, the flight attendant stopped us. She asked me if it was my first flight and if I enjoyed it. The smile on my face was from ear to ear. Then, as my first experience of aviation love, she pinned a set of wings on my jacket and gave me a double pack of Wrigley's Double-Mint Gum, the chewing gum favorite of the day back then. Then she took me into the cockpit for a moment to meet the pilot—a real pilot! I was staring up at all those switches and knobs and gadgets and hearing radio and equipment noises, and it was all too exciting for me. It was an amazing dream, trying to take it all in. Sleeping that night was difficult. It was almost a reverse Christmas in that I got the gift first, then made the attempt to sleep second.

It was a life-changing experience and memory for me, and Dad loved it too, although he was thinking about work. We still had to rent a car and drive an hour north in the snow to Grandma's. He rented a very stylish Chevy Impala. Black on black. That one flight, in the dark night over the Midwest, into and out of historic airfields, led to another wonderful experience that Dad and I shared together a few short years later, which put the flying bug in my heart forever.

2

Politics and music of the '60s and '70s, first guitar, the Beatles, the Vietnam War, women's lib, social strife and capitalism, Dallas

Dad was developing as a multi-skilled man with a couple of boys, me and Jay, watching every move he made for seven years before Sue was born in St. Louis on March 30, 1963. While Dad's work at O-I really interested him, particularly in St. Louis, where he was the plant manager, making millions of plastic bottles used for household products, from Clorox bottles to dish soap bottles and beer carriers—you name a bottle and they made it—it was wearing my mom out. Life was all about O-I and she felt left out, and I totally understand that now but did not understand it at the time.

In the sixties and early seventies, the women's liberation movement was really getting rolling, and there was much social unrest. It was made worse by opposition to the Vietnam War, which had no successful end in sight. The pop culture of peace, drugs, and rock and roll, was unleashing people's personal preferences and devotion to self-liberation. It was everywhere in music, and I remember it. Many popular artists, including Bob Dylan; Crosby, Stills, Nash & Young; Creedence Clearwater Revival; and dozens of others sang about social issues of freedom and self-expression. The Beatles's John Lennon had drifted from Beatles pop into his own genre of anti-war, peace, and love, into several big hits of the day, including "Imagine" and "Give Peace a Chance."

Although Yoko Ono has always been blamed for breaking up the Beatles, it was not entirely her fault at all. She was actually the inspiration that John was looking for in his quest for new songs, and change was all around. Few people knew this at the time, but when John's post-Beatles music came out, Yoko had handwritten the songs while John was working out the lyrics on the piano. They would then agree to the songs together. They were quite a pair, and they were the sign of the times.

PERMISSION GRANTED TO BREAK THE MOLD AND FEEL GOOD ABOUT IT

There was social rebellion everywhere, with the "younger generation," race relations, labor unions, and foreign countries, and it produced the music that became the sixties. Most of us would sing along with the songs on the radio, with our parents driving us somewhere, not even knowing we were singing about the "eve of destruction." It was great music, masking the darker rebellion it was intended to convey. There was even a space race with the Russians mixed in with everything else. On the television at night, there were images from the war in Vietnam, race riots in Detroit, and the Woodstock music festival in upstate New York. Dr. Martin Luther King, Jr. was gunned down in Memphis in 1967, and race relations were intense as our country tried to adjust to the things that were taking place. It was a real smorgasbord of news events that was squeezed into a thirty-minute broadcast of Walter Cronkite every evening. The TV shows were edgy by the standards of that day and included favorites such as *Rowan and Martin's Laugh-In*, which featured jokes of rebellion and scandal, and lots of pretty girls, including Goldie Hawn, with a laugh track just to tell the audience it was okay.

But I was dialed into the pop songs that were the sixties. To this day, I can hear those songs, and each will remind me of a specific person, a specific place, and the activities we were doing at the time. Those early years and my love of the music at the time gave me the dream of one day being in a band, if it could be done.

THE WOMEN'S LIBERATION MOVEMENT AND HOW IT LANDED IN OUR HOME

There was resistance to all the social turmoil in a lot of ways because it was creating such dramatic changes to the way we were living. A nationally recognized writer was an emerging American feminist journalist and social political activist, and she was getting a lot of attention and publicity. She and others were leading the charge for women to claim liberation, pushing for improvements in everything from higher pay to higher promotions to political positions to burning brassieres and American flags. The sign of the times was that women wanted to be counted fairly as contributing leaders and respected for their own ambition, not just for catering to their husbands' ambitions or conforming to the established social mores. Gloria Steinem wrote many books about liberation, finding a higher plan to live by, and general self-improvement type of prose, but it had a rebellious bent to it. She was a prolific writer. She sold a lot of books, and still does.

Mom did not go to college after high school in Indiana. In St. Louis, she got very active in trying to continue building her life by stepping forward and enrolling for the first time in Merrimac Junior College, and she began taking some courses to begin shaping her own "want-to," all the while keeping her chin up and caring for our family. Her parents did not go to college. Her twin brother did not go on to advanced education after high school. Mom was not raised on that expectation. On the other hand, Dad went to college, as did both of his stepbrothers. On that side of the family were the brainiacs, very educated in institutions, sometimes difficult to talk to socially because they used big words without much emotion. On the dad and mom side of the family, there were vast amounts of expressive behavior and zeal for life at every turn. I thought it was normal, but the step-uncle side of the family thought we were crazy, and over time we hung out with our cousins on that side of the family more and more. We were what they needed, and we enjoyed their company.

I did not think Dad took Mom seriously, and to be gut-wrenchingly honest, he took offense to it. He could not see why she would need more than what he was providing her because that was the male generation reality that he grew up in and was taught. To be fair, Dad liked seeing her doing the things she enjoyed, but she needed to build her own esteem for her own self-worth through her own efforts. I remember thinking it was cool having a mom who was in college. My friends did not have any of their moms in college, but I did. She did not want to settle for what was but wanted to seek out what could be. She was beginning a fresh thinking about herself and had ambition that transcended her role at home.

From a young person's point of view, I know that I was happy for her, and our family view was beginning to include what Mom wanted, and Dad was not ready for that. Not unless it included a good old-fashioned party with booze, beer, and all the trimmings. Mom was always very encouraging to me, and saw some skills developing that she liked and some behavior that she loathed. She thought I should go into advertising and write commercials. I took a stab at it in college because she recommended it. We would sing commercial jingles together on the radio and laugh hysterically at them because the words were rather stupid. One hit song that is forever locked in my mind that reminds me of her every time I hear it is Gilbert O'Sullivan's song "Alone Again, Naturally." I can see Mom holding a finger in the air and singing "Alone Again, Naturally." It is a sad song about losing those you love, and I always get tears in both eyes when it comes on the radio. She was a lovely person, and I miss her.

Society in those days had not necessarily turned on women, in my view, but it also had not given them the social support that was legitimate enough to change, in this case, how my mother was feeling. Our family was close, primarily because of all the interests Mom and Dad shared with us, but Mom was getting very discontented before we left St. Louis for Dallas. Her new friends were fringe players with artistic interests rather than the next suburban homemaker who was in the O-I family.

The call that rocked our humble but happy lifestyle forever came through late one afternoon. I answered the phone downstairs in the kitchen while Mom answered upstairs, and I overheard Dad tell her we were moving to Dallas, Texas. Silence. I about hit the floor. MOVING TO TEXAS? NO! He didn't even wait to get home to tell us, and I guess that is okay, but all of Mom's friends and support would be left behind, and it was a major emotional trainwreck for her. But she kept her beautiful chin up and played the important supportive role of wife and mother.[5] It was during the early spring of 1969, just when the music was getting good, in my view.

Not long after we moved to Dallas, Mom was in close touch with the famous feminine activist Gloria Steinem and connected with her and her movement. At one point, in an interesting development, the

---

5 Mom was the spitting image of Doris Day, and it was not uncommon for passersby to ask for her autograph. I saw her sign a couple of them while we were at a St. Louis Cardinals baseball game outside of Busch Stadium, not far from the yet-to-be completed Gateway Arch on the Mississippi River. It happened again down at the Opera House, Gaslight Square, where all sorts of music was played, particularly Dixieland jazz music. One entertainer that Mom and Dad enjoyed going to see and hear, and took us with them to see, was the Singleton Palmer Dixieland Six band. Singleton Palmer learned to play the trumpet at age eleven, and by the time he was fifteen, he was regularly playing the tuba on the riverboats that cruised the Mississippi River. He was hired by Count Basie in 1947 and toured with the Count Basie Band for three years and then moved back to St. Louis, where he formed his band that Mom and Dad would take us to see. Even while his band was working regularly, Singleton Palmer worked as a janitor for a nearby factory. He died of bone cancer in 1993 at the age of eighty. Prophetic, since after Mom and Dad finally divorced in 1976, she ended up with the last name Singleton-Foley, getting remarried before we even knew she was engaged.

activist was organizing rallies in north Texas and was looking for local support for housing and transportation. By then Dad was a private pilot and owned his own single-engine Piper Cherokee airplane. The touring activist speaker needed the convenience of local air transportation during the rally, so Mom asked Dad if he would fly her, along with Mom, where they needed to go. I remember the conversation, and Dad was supportive and interested in doing so because it was a reason to fly and she was a celebrity, but it never happened. Mom was fully aboard the feminist movement, and it had long-term consequences.

I remember that O-I had about fifteen plants nationally, and Dad was doing a fine job running his plant in the top three in production for several years. While Dad's social life very much included his employees, Mom's social life was with neighbors, her bridge club, and the golf social club. They both were social drinkers, and there was no time like the present for the next party. He told me when I got my first management job years later that I should work to get my employees to become my close friends. Because that is what he did. We hung around O-I people nearly all the time. Mom became friends with the wives of the guys with whom Dad worked, but it was not enough for her. And they both kept drinking.

I think as I was growing older, around eleven years old, and was increasingly more aware of their relationship, I began to feel very threatened by this looming obstacle to continued family bliss.

BE PREPARED

During elementary school, I was a Boy Scout with Troop 302 at Webster Hills Methodist Church. I was working toward being a Life Scout, then an Eagle Scout, but never made it past Star Scout. Each rank consisted of accomplishing certain demonstration of skills learned or community service provided in a measurable way. To achieve each rank, merit badges were earned. After the beginner ranks of Webelos and Second Class came the merit badge ranks, beginning with Star. It took five merit badges to earn the Star Rank. I earned mine in the skills of semaphore (using hand signals with flags to spell out words being observed from a distance); demonstrating swimming and life-saving skills in a pool; hiking (we had several long hikes accompanied by other Scouts and leaders, including a twenty-mile night hike); canoeing, which included having to swamp the canoe and survive in the water by turning our clothes into flotation devices; and my fifth badge was in first aid.

One of our mottos and Scout commitments was to "be prepared" (which is also a useful business edict), and I was not prepared, nor did I know how to prepare, for the descent that was beginning in our family. There had begun a pattern of starting things but not finishing them. From homework to lawn work to fixing my bike, things started to get messy at home, and our family unit was deteriorating, so I hung on to my friends. Discipline and the lack of patience by both Mom and Dad easily led to outbursts aimed at the offender and were becoming more frequent. We had a dinner bell by our back door, and it was fine with Mom for me and Jay and Sue to roam the neighborhood as long as when we heard Mom ring that dinner bell at dark, we better be home before she had to ring it again, or we'd get our butts whipped by Dad when he got home from work. The proverbial "just wait until your father gets home" was true. But it hurt, so it was easy to remember for a short while. So, when that bell rang, we hightailed it home.

While we were still in St. Louis, Dad decided it would be good to also join the local Indian Guides organization at the same time we were in Boy Scouts. Somehow, I got named "Little Thunderbird," and to keep it easy, he was named "Big Thunderbird." Those were cool names, particularly when we would go to see the Air Force Thunderbirds at local air shows. I was a Thunderbird too! It was a lot of fun because we got to go camping and learn even more outdoor skills to go with our survival repertoire from the Boys Scouts.

I attended an Indian Guide camp one year for about a week during the summer. It was to be a development outing and was sort of an issued challenge to compete with the other Indians and show that you should be selected for tribal positions of leadership. There was, and still is, I believe, an active program called "Order of the Arrow." We called it "OA." At OA, the leaders decided by secret vote which boys had the most potential for whatever was next in life and beyond. We were in elementary school, for Pete's sake. If you were selected, you were "tapped out."

Tap Out was a night ceremony along the edge of the lake where all the Indian Guides would stand shoulder to shoulder, staring straight ahead, waiting for the Indian chief, a crazed, war-painted, manic-looking guy. He would run down the line of boys carrying a lit torch in one hand and using his other hand to "tap out" those boys favored for selection into the Order of the Arrow. I remember that guy came running down the line of Indians toward us with bells on his ankles ringing out, ching, ching, ching, with each step, in a rapid run-march cadence with leather straps around his arms and a mean "I'm going to kick your ass" look on his face. He ran down the long line of us, all standing at attention shoulder to shoulder and staring straight ahead. He stopped. He faced an Indian Guide kid, stepped left, stepped right, then, with an open palm, clobbered the chest of the selected inductee. Leaders standing behind him held a hand over his head so that the tap-out warrior would know who to park in his back pockets. The leaders would catch them, drag them off, not being seen again until morning. Pretty creepy.

When he came back by again and stopped in front of me, I could hear him breathing, my heartbeat, and a lot of crickets. He stared straight at me, then punched the guy out on my left, then kept on running. I had missed out on another opportunity! I had bombed again and did not even know it. No trophy again! Not even an honorable or dishonorable mention. But at least I did not get knocked on my keister by an Indian warrior. Sometimes you are the bug, and sometimes you are the windshield. It was so secretive I never could get anyone to tell me where they went or what they did.

Even though Dad had me involved with organizations and activities that promoted excellent-quality decision-making, conduct, and respect for people, I was still a typical restless kid. I was in wrestling when I went to junior high school at Nipher Junior High in Kirkwood. Dad taught me some moves the night before I had a match with a big guy the next morning in the gym. I practiced on him and was ready. It did not work. He kicked my ass. When Dad asked me that evening how the match went, I told him I got clobbered. He just laughed and said, "I told you it might not work."

We did some rather delinquent and really stupid stuff running around our neighborhood as kids. We also did the time-honored tradition of stealing cigarettes or a nip of whiskey from our parents, both Bill's and mine, and trying to smoke them in the creek. Mr. Merten, Bill's dad, was the master of brewing Operations for Anheuser-Busch beer in St. Louis. He smoked and he drank, so we always had home inventory to take to the creek with us. Mr. Merten died years later of cirrhosis of the liver.

I saw a guy on TV one night smoking a Lucky Strike while singing a song, and I thought it looked cool. My parents both smoked. Dad smoked Winstons, and Mom smoked the ever-powerful and dreadful Pall Malls with no filter. So, one day after school, with no one home but me, I went to our basement and lit one up. Then I ate a peanut butter sandwich and went upstairs and barfed it all up. I have not smoked a cigarette since. I also found a way to break some of Dad's keepsakes, including breaking a family heirloom guitar by taking it out of the house, putting it in a side bicycle basket, and riding up to the park with Bill. During the ride there, I hit a bump and out the guitar came, all but demolished in the street. It was at least sixty years old, maybe older. I had a hard time explaining that one. I guess there are some life lessons there, such as you do not know what a dumbass you can be until you realize you are one, and then it is too late.

As my need to create self-supporting commerce increased after the age of thirteen, the shenanigans began to settle down. So, why, you ask, is all of this important? I think it shows how, in my early years, I was all over the place, trying to figure out, well, everything. When you do stupid stuff growing up, it had better change if you are going to be anything more than a social lemming being chased by authorities of every kind. I'm not proud of any of these less-than-intelligent behaviors, but that is where I was at the time. Sure, at the time it might have seemed fun, giving in to peer pressure to do this or that, but we knew it wasn't right to do that stuff, and it was just a matter of time before our awesome parents would intervene to remind us of how awesome they thought they were. But again, before life got serious at the mano a mano level, some of these memories were fun.

Admit it now: reading this, you are thinking of, almost bragging about, the time you did this or that. You snuck out at night and filled a friend's mailbox with whipped cream or put mice into one of your friend's parents' cars. All kinds of stupid stuff. Gather around the beer tap and ask your friends, "Hey, did you do any stupid stuff when you were young?" and you might get, "Of course, and I'm still doing some of that stuff." The bottom line is to draw a distinction between what you are doing and what you are teaching. Make sure it is worth teaching for the betterment of the person and for the good of mankind. A moron is as a moron does.

If your parents are the ones doing stupid stuff, you know it is stupid stuff but cannot say anything about it because you think it really is kind of cool. Just saying. On holidays, particularly New Year's Eve and the Fourth of July, neighbors, and I mean all neighbors, would shoot their shotguns into the air from their front porches, then listen for the shot to rain down on the house down the street, which was also shooting into the air. I always thought that was sketchy, but back in those days, the police did not mind. Not many criminals out when most of the residents were armed and actively shooting. So, they did not bother us. But ignite a pile of leaves in the sewer and find out how many fire trucks and police vehicles blazed a path to your door. You had to be selective about how much and what kind of attention you wanted rolling onto your street.

In some ways, you have to do things as an experiment in the Petri dish of life, knowing that physics and the laws of life will ultimately win.

Those were amazing times, but eventually you must grow up, and as the time neared to move to Texas, I found things I enjoyed doing, with an eye toward learning how to make some spending money along the way.

In St. Louis, if we were not doing outside stuff, we were doing something with music. One very memorable party they threw at our home on Parkland Ave. in Glendale, included Dad hiring a three-piece "combo," as they were called in the sixties, and having them perform for friends in our basement, of all places. My parents both loved music, and the party scene in our home could be crazy, as I remember. We always had a nice Hi-Fi stereo record player that got constant use. During that time, I was in sixth grade and spent time listening on a small transistor radio to bands like The Beatles, The Monkees, Herman's Hermits, the Grass Roots, Tommy James and the Shondells, Mitch Ryder and the Detroit Wheels, and Paul Revere and the Raiders.

I listened to AM radio late at night, putting it under my pillow so Mom wouldn't know I wasn't sleeping. I couldn't believe all those popular bands were playing live at the radio station. I soon learned the truth that these were only recordings being spun by the cool disc jockey Wolfman Jack, and my interest in vinyl took off like a Boeing 707. In school, my best friend since second grade, Bill Merten (we are still friends today), and I would trade writings of the lyrics of some of the popular songs of the day. We just wrote down what we thought they were singing so that when we heard them on the radio, we could sing along. Sometimes we were close, but most of the time, it was hard to understand rock and roll singing, particularly when you were in elementary school.

Dad and Mom got the whole neighborhood over, at least the partiers, and got this combo cranking out the hits. Dad had me and Jay go upstairs, as Sue was not yet born, as I remember, to stay in our rooms. However, we had a laundry chute that allowed us to drop laundry all the way to the basement for Mom's convenience. Pretty high-tech for laundry in the sixties, I must say. But it had an even more important function. It was a great gatherer of sound from the basement and sent it all the way to the open chute door in the hallway on the second floor. Jay and I kept taking turns sticking our heads in the chute to get the full impact of that sound of live music. This turned out to be training for Jay years later when he temporarily lost his hearing at a concert by sticking his head in Ted Nugent's amplifier.

The rock and roll coming through the laundry chute was like a yellow brick road of live music. I had to go down to the basement. Hey, if I could be the shah of Persia, then I could be a Monkee. I got to the bottom step of that basement, probably during a break by the band, and my parents let me stay. I talked to the lead band singer and asked if I could look at all the groovy instruments—an electric guitar, a bass guitar, and a full kit of drums. And they had a keyboard. And when the lead guy asked me if I wanted to try to sing something, I don't know how I said yes, but the keyboard guy started belting out the six-chord descending organ riff beginning "I'm a Believer" by The Monkees. And off I went, singing with my first band. I will never forget it. I have a very satisfying memory of Mom and Dad enjoying me up there, even though I was not supposed to be there in the first place.

Good thing I went to school, because that is where Bill and I figured out most of the words to many popular songs of that day. By about the third grade, I had managed to talk my parents into buying me my first guitar. A used six-string electric guitar made by Teisco, with a one-speaker amp that stood about fifteen inches high. I had no idea how to play it until I found a neighbor two doors up the street who knew how to play. He was probably about twelve, and I was about eight, so I thought he was a pro. His name was Marc Strid. For all I know, he may have changed his name to Stevie Ray Vaughan. He was good, and he taught me one song. Just the chords and the words.

Bill Merten had a drum kit in his basement that his parents let him bang on, and for our age, he was actually pretty good. But I needed to learn the guitar. How can you go on tour at nine years old if you cannot play the guitar? The first song I learned, and that Bill and I played together, was "House of the Rising Sun" by The Animals. At that age, I had no idea it was about a whorehouse, but the words were cool, "They call the rising sun ..."

We had us a two-man band. It made listening to The Beatles that much more fun. We entered a talent show at school but could not get the equipment to work. Another life tip: never underestimate the importance of a great sound system. If it sucks, so do you. A few short years later, we had to break up our band of two for our family move to Dallas. I took the Teisco to Dallas. I always think of that story when I play that song. Sounds rather good if you change the words to "Amazing Grace." Try changing the words to "Amazing Grace" instead the next time you hear "House of the Rising Sun." A couple guitar friends of mine did just that at a blues jam in Corona, California, on a Sunday morning, and it was a hit, so I know it works, or is at least "interesting." It may put a smile on your face.

Music for me during and after living in St. Louis had a lot of memories and meaning. The sixties and first half of the 1970s had great pop and Motown music. The groove of soul with the backbeat of rock and roll made so many of the songs very popular. I can honestly say, most songs that I heard between 1966 and 1975 carry lifetime memories for me of one kind or another. When one comes on the radio, I identify and experience it just as I remember it. That is one joy of music. It can reconnect you to moments as if they happened a second time in a way that recaptures all the senses that you experienced when you first heard it. It is similar to any first in your life. You always remember the firsts. Music has a way of putting you back in place and time and is an automatic language to be shared with friends who might have the same musical interest.

The first album that I bought was "Blues Magoos Electric Comic Book" from a department store in Warson Woods shopping center around 1966. Pretty cheesy sixties rock with songs that lasted only a couple of minutes. I still remember most of the words to every song on that album— "Life is a Cher O'Bowlies" and "Albert Common is Dead" were a couple of my favorites. I never dreamed then that one day I would get to experience the joy of rocking the house down with my own band, with my son next to me belting out the oldies in pretty cool places, including Gilley's in Dallas.

My favorite music year, without question, was 1969. Great life stuff. If you ever plan on being considered a renaissance person, you better have some chops about music, the arts, and you should know who Chuck Berry was. We all connect with music. In business, if you connect with someone with the same musical interests, there is a whole lot of room to pursue deals with the backdrop of that music.

3

My dear mother and her family

Mom's family hailed from Indiana. She and Dad met while driving on the strip in downtown Elkhart, Indiana, running in cars with other teenagers who had cars. Dad told me that he saw a beautiful blonde in one of those cars and had to meet her. She was three years younger than Dad, and he was smitten with her. She was a gorgeous blonde. They were married in 1951, before Dad's military service was complete in the army during the conflict in the Philippines. When they were first married, they lived in Philadelphia, later moving to Toledo as Dad got started with O-I.

Mom's mother, Minnie, and her stepfather, Russ, were wonderfully sweet people. We really loved visiting them on our family road trips to see Dad's family in Michigan and Ohio. Elkhart, Indiana, the home of RVs across the nation, had seen better days economically, but when we visited in the sixties to have fun with our cousins and Mom's twin brother Jay, it was a blast.

Minnie's first husband, Levon, passed away suddenly at the age of twenty-seven after Minnie birthed a stillborn baby, followed by Mom and her twin brother Jay. She subsequently married Russ Whisler, who owned a meat-packing plant. I remember Grandpa Russ taking us to show us how the pigs and cattle were "processed." At that age, I thought it meant checked-in, interviewed, or trained. I did not know they slaughtered them. Quite a "process." But we really enjoyed our trips there, minus the drive.

Grandpa Russ always wore a sweater and a necktie, if not a jacket and a tie. I always admired how solid and together he looked and acted. He had a cool pipe that he could smoke in the house. He had a bear rug on the wall in the basement, which freaked us out when the cousins were told to sleep downstairs. But when we found that Grandpa Russ's bathroom in the basement had a girly poster in it, where you would lift the plastic overlay of her dress to discover nothing but Mother Nature underneath, we could not wait to sleep in the basement. They had a bumper pool table and a record player down there and a wall of cabinets with every kind of game or toy you could dream of. Cool metal cars, board games, army men, and even some girly stuff that Grandma Minnie would use to make girl clothes, dolls, and original toys. I do not remember the television being on very much because we were having too much fun doing other things.

Grandpa Russ would not let us touch his stuff in the garage; it was a big hands-off or you lost your hands. Until he got out the riding lawn mower. We were all over that, trying to climb on his lap, which really annoyed him. He kept telling us we were going to lose our toes in the mower, so we backed off and headed back down to the basement or down the street to the drugstore to buy a record if we could gather enough money. Mom's family was simple, hardworking, and a lot of fun. It was an innocent time, traveling with our family, and I am very grateful for all the memories. It is the good in our families growing up that we want to recreate and experience with our own families as we go into adulthood. We learned a lot about getting along with others, first in our family as a foundation, then in the outside world, in order to survive.

4

My first flight in the left seat, President Kennedy's assassination, my first lesson with cash, learning to smoke cigarettes, camping and hunting, learning to cuss, getting electrocuted, playing guitar, shooting Mickey, our family dog

THE FIRST FLIGHT IN THE LEFT SEAT

Having had the earlier commercial flying experience on an airliner to Detroit with Dad, we always enjoyed and played airplane any time we were in the car. Then, one evening at dinner, he said he had a surprise for me the following week but was going to have to take me out of school early in order to do what he had in mind. It was common for parents to take their kids out of school for family, medical needs, or special events, but it was something to look forward to when you knew it was going to happen in a few short days. On that early afternoon in 1966, when I was not yet ten years old, Mom and Dad picked me up at Henry Hough Elementary School for a ride out into the country. I had no idea where we were going but was hoping it was not waterskiing on the Mississippi. Anything but that.

After a short while, Dad drove us on to a dirt road lined with green trees on each side and telephone and power lines following our journey down the road. We turned behind and around some buildings, then drove into the open and stopped in front of a high-wing tail-dragger airplane. I did not know my airplanes very well back at that time, although I did spend hours drawing pictures of them rather than doing my homework.

To my surprise, there was a kind man there that Mom and Dad said hello to, then introduced me to him. His name was Harold Little. He was a decorated pilot in WWII, with tours in the South Pacific. He was retired and somehow, somewhere, through someone, Dad had arranged for me to take my first flight in the pilot's seat of an airplane, and Harold had agreed to take me.

I want to say the airplane was a Stinson or a Cessna 140, but I am not sure. I do recall that he put me in the left seat, where the captain sits, and he took the right seat. As a flight instructor, he was equally comfortable in either seat, so I think it was extra special of him to let this nine-year-old boy experience that first flight from the left seat. I was in complete candy land with all the switches and dials and buttons and knobs, and Harold let me touch some of them with his help. When we accelerated for takeoff, the world sped up, and in moments we lifted away from the grass runway and climbed into the late afternoon air. I have no idea where we were, but I believe we were west or south of St. Louis. It did not matter. We were flying!

Harold let me hold the yoke and told me I was flying the airplane. I still get a chill and a tear in my eye, thinking how magical that was and how it influenced my love for flying all these years later. After we landed, Dad thanked Harold and we drove home. I remember drawing pictures of airplanes that night and telling Bill and all my friends the next day. I could not have asked for a more wonderful experience. And little did I know that in my future, in large part due to this flight with Harold, I would become an accomplished pilot with thousands of flight hours and personally own more than ten different airplanes over the next fifty-five years. A salute to you, Harold Little.[6] You are loved and will always be appreciated.

WORLD EVENTS FOR A FIFTH GRADER

President John Fitzgerald Kennedy was assassinated on November 22, 1963. I was in fifth grade. I heard about it while relieving myself in the boys' bathroom when a kid in the urinal down the way asked me if I had heard the president had been shot. A strange place to remember hearing about this world event. My family and the world were shocked. Although Dad was always a conservative Republican, he still liked the Kennedys. He would talk politics, but Mom would stay out of the conversation until it amped her up enough with disagreement that she gathered the courage to speak her mind.

We were all glued to the television set, watching the sad but memorable funeral procession and casket lying in state as little John Kennedy saluted his father's coffin. Life was taking a pause as we knew it, for at least a little while. Later in 1968, I was with Dad when he was watching television late at night when Sirhan Sirhan murdered Bobby Kennedy after a campaign speech in the Ambassador Hotel in Los Angeles. I remember him jumping up from the bed and reacting to the event. I had just turned twelve the week before and was getting some orientation on political awareness and reactions to it. Dad was a patriot. He served his country and flew the American flag proudly. He taught us how to say the Pledge of Allegiance; he expected prayer before dinner, and he

---

6 Harold Eugene Little was eighty-two when he died on November 1, 2003. He retired as the manager of the Atlanta Airports District Office Federal Aviation Administration in 1985. He directed all FAA airport activities in the states of Georgia, South Carolina, and North Carolina. He was an F-84 Pilot with the 116th Fighter Squadron, Georgia Air National Guard, Dobbins Air Force Base. He was called to active duty in the air force during the Korean War and was based in Japan and Korea. During WWII, he was a P-38 pilot based in Fogia, Italy, with the 37th Fighter Squadron, 15th Army Air Force, and was awarded five Bronze Stars for combat duty in the European Theater.

did not tolerate wimps who would not stand up to defend our land. I do know that he did not agree with the Vietnam War.

EARLY LESSON ON THE EXCHANGE OF GOODS AND SERVICES

One of the things I learned early on is that there is cash, then there is everything else, which can become cash or be used as payment instead of cash. Seems like a natural human instinct to me. This view developed into the reality that if you want something badly enough, you somehow have to find a way of paying for it. But this is not a hard and fast rule all the time. For example:

Once you are out of cash or inventory, your resources are dried up. So regardless of your spending habits, do not run out of both. Bartering works with your parents, siblings, and friends and is most effective on strangers who only have the asset in the game and not all the friend/family issues that come with any transfer of wealth, no matter how great or how small. For example, in grade school, where all the strategic thinking cells are created, the currency was baseball cards. Currency was firecrackers. Currency was time loaned on your bike with the banana seat and monkey handlebars. Currency was taking a friend hunting or fishing in exchange for a sleepover at someone's house.

The fair exchange of what I needed in exchange for what they needed was endless.

And another important rule is learned here. While a firecracker may appeal to the new person receiving it, you may have no value for it, but keep that to yourself. If you are afraid owning that firecracker is a risk and a liability, it may be best to remove it from inventory. But not before some lip-licking soul must have it, and you can get a Mickey Mantle baseball card for it. Phew, get rid of the quack. But remember, when you go to trade the Mickey Mantle card (don't ever trade a Honus Wagner baseball card. "Hans" played for the Pittsburgh Pirates from 1897 to 1917, and his card is the highest-valued card in existence, worth $6.606 million dollars. There are only fifty remaining in existence) the person you might be trying to trade it to may also have had the same experience, and you might have to work around their expectations for something they have not yet experienced. It all made perfect sense to me.

And this concept applies to every sales transaction of every kind. It works on baseball cards, and it works negotiating to buy or sell a $100-million-dollar business. I will get into this later when we go from being a kid boss to being a boss kid. Not from the point of view of "who, me?" but from the point of view of "yes, you!"

Cigarettes were also in demand with some of our neighbor kids. But not much. In those days, everyone's parents smoked and no kid in the neighborhood wanted them after they tried one and puked for six hours while explaining to their parents that they must have eaten a bad beetle grub down in the creek and it wasn't agreeing with them. But many childhood memories are filled with surprises later in life. Sometime during the early 2000s, a church friend of ours from Hunters Glen Baptist told me that she heard my name on the radio by a Focus on the Family talk show host, Bob Lepine, a nationally syndicated Christian broadcaster. He was talking about his childhood memories while reflecting on losing his mother, who I also knew growing up.

Bob and his family lived just a few houses up the street from us on Parkland in Glendale. He was one of the neighborhood kids who never got in fights, never tried to kill my brother, left my two-year-old sister alone, and was just a good kid. Well, my friend heard Bob talking on the radio about some of our escapades that taught him some life lessons. When my friend told me this, I anticipated he was going to remember a couple of the nice things we did growing up; after all, there weren't many of those. Instead, Bob recounted the wintery night we were camped in my backyard in a tent in about three inches of snow, thinking that we were as tough as Fess Parker on the Daniel Boone show on TV. Although we were freezing our asses off, we did have an exchange that came in handy for Bob's radio show, and he felt obliged to include it in his shows of memories and what he learned growing up.

He told the audience that in order to spend the time in this freezing icebox with only a sleeping bag and a Boy Scout flashlight, I taught him how to cuss. I taught him most of the four-letter cuss words that I heard at my house, sometimes at the dinner table, but always during parental happy hours, which started at 4:00 and ended at 11:00 … a.m. or p.m. We never heard the F-bomb until we were living in Dallas, where that one had to be pulled from the munitions of vocabulary war because the family war was intensifying, but for now, a few choice four-letter words were more than ample to get through grade school and most of junior high.

The cussing using female body parts did not begin until high school, when we finally knew what they were. So, after my friend told me of this quite revealing broadcast from a childhood friend, I called Bob Lepine at his studio in Little Rock. It went like this.

"Bob Lepine speaking," he answered.

"Bob, this is Dave Gasmire," is all that I said.

He began, "How the heck are you, Dave? It has been a long time since Glendale. I have often thought of you from time to time and always had a curiosity about how our neighborhood friends were getting along all these years later!"

I said, "Well, Bob, I have a bone to pick with you. You are using our very private childhood conversations for public consumption, and I got a taste of that from one of your listeners in Texas!"

Bob laughed, and I did too, and I added, "I sure remember those days, and I'm happy and proud to know you have made the big time in broadcasting. And those stories are true, very true, but you left one thing out that I think you should go back on the air to share with your devoted listeners, who obviously look up to you for examples of words to soothe the savage soul and fill the hollow, empty chambers of the human heart."

He asked, "What would you like me to add?"

I said, "For some reason, and I think I know and understand why, you decided to leave out the tiny tidbit that might be useful to your Christian listening audience that you taught me how to cuss!"

He just came apart laughing. He asked me if that was all that I called about, and I jokingly said yes, that I wanted to set the record straight. He said I had not changed much, which I'm not sure is a good thing or not when the last time you saw this friend was in eighth grade. We had a bunch of good laughs, and I expressed sympathy for the loss of his mother, who I always liked.

Before ending the call, we each invited one another to visit our respective homes, and I told him that if he came to our place in Fredericksburg, they wouldn't have to sleep in a tent, but they would be in an old milking barn built in 1888.

He asked, "Where?" and I said, "It may be a barn, but you will love it!"

I hope to see Bob again; he is a great guy and a cherished childhood friend.

MORE CAUSE AND EFFECT, SPORTS, AND A LESSON ON ELECTRICITY

For all the hobbies that Dad was introducing us to without knowing it, some took root for the purposes that Dad had intended. For instance, he loved to play tennis and basketball and other sports that required a lot of running. I was too young to be on a court with Dad without getting run over or trampled, so he would take me "jogging" as a means for both of us to get some exercise, but also to knock some energy out of me. With Dad, all things became competitive to make the event more fun and exciting and with consequences. He was big on teaching us consequences. He would say things like, "Davey, if you put that ball-point pen spring in an electrical wall outlet, it will bite you really bad." I figured I had already been bitten by the dog in Toledo, so what could sticking a pen spring into a wall outlet do to "bite" me? Well, I found out one day when I heard my mom on the phone talking to a neighbor and saying, "I'll send Davey right over with it," at which time I was not interested in running errands around the neighborhood, so I dove behind a big overstuffed living room chair in the corner where there was room to hide.

I heard Mom finishing her conversation on the phone, when lo and behold, lying on the floor next to the chair was a ballpoint pen. I dismantled the pen to get to the spring, stretching it out into one long piece of straight wire about six inches long. Then I noticed the wall outlet. With two hands, I inserted each end of the wire into the two openings of the outlet. There is real juice in there, but it doesn't "bite" you; it "fries" you. Bang-Zap-Pop, and I was screaming for help. The wire exploded and sent burning pieces of shrapnel into both of my hands at an average temperature close to the surface of the sun. Not my best work at adapting on the fly in a stressful situation. But that is how I learned about positive and negative electrical currents.

Seriously, my dad then told me about current, and of course, applied it in a way that wasn't hard to understand after almost burning the house down with us in it. He said, "If you do that again, I am POSITIVE it will have a NEGATIVE impact on your ability to play guitar, drums, or even talk on the phone, so let us try to avoid that one again in the future, huh, Davey?"

The lesson here in business is that it can be applied to thinking through innovative ideas or actions to decide if, metaphorically, it is a light bulb of brilliance lighting up, or perhaps a complete electrical explosion that will take out the company. Choose carefully. The ideas that must accompany a new growth-oriented company need to be not only creative, but there must also be a specific purpose in deploying the resources and energy to pursue them. If you are not sure what will happen with an idea, and you don't know what unintended consequences there will be, better tread lightly before putting that spring of an idea into a wall outlet. Study what you are doing, why you are doing it, and how it should be done. Always consider what will kill you next. On that day, I almost found out one way, but lived to talk about it.

LEARNING TO HUNT AND THE TAKEAWAYS FOR LIFE

Hunting was a family tradition going back a long, long way, and it was taught to us too. I have memories of Dad and Granddad going hunting in Michigan in the deep snow, looking for rabbits. Dad would wear a red-and-black plaid hunting coat that was made of very thick wool, and he had a wool hat with ear flaps to match. He would wear red rubber hunting boots to keep his feet dry. In those days in Michigan, licensed hunters would wear their hunting permits pinned to the back of their coats on the outside so as to be official and seen from a distance. Mom got a plastic cover that the license could slide into so that it would stand up to the weather.

Mom also had a role in how we all looked when we went hunting. Camouflage was something she figured out how to do so that she would not have to buy us new hunting clothes each year because we were growing so quickly. She would take our blue jeans and rub brown and black shoe polish in big blotches to signify trees or obstructions, or who knows what, in order to conceal ourselves from the rabbits or squirrels we were hunting. Then she would spray the now-camouflaged jeans with 3M waterproof spray for wet hunting conditions.

I am not sure the camo idea worked, but I am sure that the waterproof spray did not work. We were wet to the bone after just a few minutes, but Mom sure tried. If she could iron on patches over our knees to cover a hole, she could sure make hunting pants. Mom could make anything, and to be dressed in Mom's camo was an added treat. It taught me how to not rely on new items that are expensive, but adapt available resources and come up with something better.

I was wearing a pair of Mom's famous camouflaged jeans when I accidentally shot our family dog, Mickey. I was the lone kid on a hunting trip with Dad, Granddad, and, I think, one other person, but it was not Jay. We were hunting rabbits in light snow. I was about eleven or twelve and carrying my granddad's single-shot .410 shotgun. Mickey was our favorite pet in the whole world. Dad had taken us to pick a puppy from a litter one night during Christmas. The litter was about six beagle puppies, and I still remember picking Mickey up and holding him for the first time. Puppies smell great. We were crazy over him.

Dad grew up around beagle dogs when he hunted with his father and two brothers growing up, so he thought Mickey would be fine for our family. Mickey would smell the scent of a rabbit from a mile away, and off he would go. It was a real problem living in the suburbs because he could take off, and we could only hope he would find his way home, and for the most part, he always did.

We had taken Mickey to hunt rabbits that afternoon. He would jump out of the car and take off running. Dad would slowly get his gun and gear together and was in no particular hurry to do so. I was worried that Mickey would get lost and told Dad we needed to run after him and follow him. Dad would say, "Nah, he is just out doing his job. He'll be back." After a little bit, you could hear Mickey barking that deep "aa-woo, aa-woo" crazy bark as if to say, "I've got a rabbit, and I'm bringing him to you."

Dad would say, "Just stand in the road right there, Davey, and be ready for when Mickey pushes that rabbit out into the road. Shoot the rabbit, but don't shoot Mickey."

Sure enough, a moment later, that rabbit came out into the road and I shot him. Mickey came in behind him a few seconds later and was all proud of himself. He did great. So, with one in the bag, we headed out into the field to find more rabbits.

I was by myself, probably fifty yards from Dad, and we were working straight ahead through some stacks of fallen trees and tall grass. There were rabbits running everywhere, and Dad was hollering for Mickey to "Git 'em up there, Mick, git 'em up!" Dad and Granddad were shooting like crazy, and I lost sight of Mickey and was scared with all the shooting and little to no experience, with a live shotgun in my hand. Then Dad yelled out, "He's coming your way, Dave! The rabbit is running toward you!"

Then I saw a tuft of white fur, and in my panic, I shot the tuft. It was the tip of Mickey's tail! I was horrified, and I was dang sure I was not going to tell Dad. Not here. Not there. Not anywhere and not at any time. Mickey just kept on hunting, and all I could do was watch him to see if he showed any symptoms of being a shot beagle dog.

Later, on the drive home, Dad and Granddad stopped at a roadside bar for a cold beer. They left me in the car with Mickey in the back seat. That is when I saw blood tainting his white tail tip to a rose pink, with a swelling of his tail a few inches away. I felt terrible for him and should have said something to Dad so we could get Mickey some help. I was so scared of what Dad would do, I did not have the courage to admit what I had done, and it was eating me up inside and did so for years.

Mickey recovered and lived a long life, making it to Dallas, and later, to Houston, where he finally wandered off and never came back

Over fifty years later, and just a couple of months before Dad passed away in May 2017, I was in Florida, near Dad's home there, in his golf cart, sitting there, just the two of us talking. He knew he did not have much time left and took the opportunity to have one final private father/son talk. We had parked near a small lake that had an occasional alligator in it, and we were sitting there in the golf cart, between two trees, watching one of the gators just floating in the water. Dad told me how proud he was of all three of us kids and made his love for us known and undeniable. It had become more of an intention for him to tell us how much he loved us and his friends, the closer he knew the day was coming that would be his last.

In this conversation with me, he knew it would be soon, and we talked alone, both knowing that reality. He asked me to do him a favor. I wondered if it was a simple "pick up something for me" kind of favor or something bigger. I told him, "Sure, Dad, whatever you want."

He said, "I'll be gone soon, and I need you to do something for me, and I'm really counting on you to do it."

I nodded and said, "Sure, Dad, of course."

He said, "I am getting my wish now that I know I am going first. I could not live without Peggy, and I'm being selfish with this right now; I don't want to be here without her. So, I need to know that you will look after her and take care of her for me. She will have some needs. She will need some help, and I am counting on you to do it. Will you do that for me?"

I told him, "Of course we will. You have my promise."

He said, "Okay, thank you."

Then, to lighten it up a bit, and to do myself a favor to get rid of a demon, I said, "Dad, I have something to tell you that has bothered me for years."

He looked over and said, "Like what?"

I paused a few seconds and looked at him on my right and said, "Dad, I don't know how to tell you this, but I shot Mickey."

He said, "What? What do you mean you shot Mickey?"

I said, "Do you remember the time you and Granddad and I went rabbit hunting somewhere near St. Louis, and it was my first time rabbit hunting?"

He said, "I think so."

I said, "I accidentally shot Mickey in the tail that day and didn't have the courage to tell you at the time."

He looked at me, sitting there silently for a few seconds with that thought just hanging there in truth. "You did?" he asked.

I said, "Yes, I did."

He just let it go and said, "Huh, that is a shame. He still lived a long time." Then we moved on to other things and headed back to his house. I am glad he took it as well as he did. But he had other things on his mind.

In the years since wounding our beloved Mickey, I have regretted not standing up to the situation and claiming responsibility for it with my dad. Mickey did just fine, but I felt horrible for hurting him. In business, in life, in fun times, and in turmoil, it is far better to acknowledge what has happened and to be truthful. There is an abundance of help and understanding when trouble arises because it happens to everyone.

In business and in life, trouble will arise, and giving the right measure of reality, with a confident acknowledgment that it will be fixed, is what employees, investors, and regulators are expecting to hear. As much as we want to make no mistakes and claim to be that good, it is not realistic. It is more of a reflection of trust than it is the capabilities of the business and management team. If a mistake is made, you own it. And you can do something about it, but more importantly, learn from it. Put those battle stripes on your sleeve and use the experience the next time you are put in a similar situation.

5

Leaving St. Louis for Dallas, saying goodbye to my best friend, men land on the moon, we buy a house in north Dallas at the last second, a hot chick down the street, high school with no friends, booted from the track team, James Brown, Mark Thompson intro, Stymie Peckerwhite

TEXAS, HERE WE COME

Dad and Mom worked extremely hard, both in terms of keeping things going at home and keeping Dad's paycheck and his career going. A work/life balance was very different back then and mostly was centered around work, achievement, and getting to whatever next step you were trying to get to. It was work sixty hours and a little time on the weekend to hurt yourself with hobbies before going back to work. For us, it was all about O-I, and in 1969, the call came across the telephone line on Yorktown 6 3613 at 257 Parkland Ave in Glendale, Missouri. It was late winter/early spring. Snow was on the ground, and the best music was on the radio. My best friend was two blocks away, and the best malt shop was four blocks away. The best places to run in city drainage pipes began in an open pipe located in our yard, and the best sports teams were in St. Louis. The long-term look of our daily life changed when Dad called home one afternoon. I was also home.

Mom answered the phone upstairs, and I picked up in the kitchen next to the stairs leading to the basement, where so many memories had been and were still being made. I heard my dad tell Mom, "We are moving to Dallas." He just came out and said it.

"TEXAS?" I asked.

"Yes, Dallas, Texas," he crowed on the telephone. Just like that. What a cold call on the telephone to tell your wife and kids to pack the bags and prepare to move. He said, "I'll be home in a little while to tell you more." I thought back to a place for immediate reactive comfort and thought to myself, *Shit. All my friends in my conscious years are here. Everything is here! And now we are leaving?*

I had just noticed hair growing in places it hadn't yet and was beginning to look at girls! I had only had my first beer last summer when Jay and I drank some leftover keg from a party in our backyard! I hung up the phone and rode my bike over to Bill's, hoping he was home so I could tell him we were leaving. The reality was that we were moving because of the great job my father had done at O-I, and now they wanted him in Dallas to fix that plastics bottling plant. Another life and business lesson was unfolding that I didn't yet understand. If you are good at what you do, you will be needed somewhere else one day. Okay, I get that, but Dallas, Texas?

Geez! I was just thirteen years old and had just got the neighborhood economics to work for me! I was making twenty-five cents a week at the barbershop! The malts and milkshakes at Hall's were still only ten cents, and we didn't have to pay for comic books if we just read them at the soda fountain! I had a shoebox full of quacks and some untraded Cardinal baseball cards! I had a favorite record store. Our favorite burger place was Sandy's Burgers, and we boated on the Mississippi River. What could be better than that? What in the world would happen when we moved to Dallas?

I didn't have any connections for continued cash flow; there would be no friends; I would have to go to a new school; I'd have to give up sports; the Beatles were talking about splitting up; and I wouldn't know anyone on our street. I was just about to finish eighth grade at Nipher and move to Kirkwood High School, and all my friends would be going there without me! Bill, Dave, Mark, Rick, and everyone else that lived a fifteen-minute walk or a five-minute banana seat bike ride away through neighbors' yards. I was living the dream, and now it was going to be a nightmare of epic proportions unlike anything I had ever seen before! From there, the next three months were a blur.

Jay and Sue were along for the ride. After all, Jay was ten, and Sue was three; they didn't have the developed infrastructure and empire I had created that was supporting our elementary lifestyles.

The move happened very quickly. From the time we heard "Texas!" to the time we were Texas residents, not yet Texans, was about four months. We had to finish the school year in May and get moved before school started again in September. Yes, school started after Labor Day back then. Dad had done such a fine job running the St. Louis plant to profitability they decided he needed to move to fix the problems at the last-place Dallas plant. That motivated Dad, and he was all excited about getting another plant that he could improve and build upon. I also think he had always been a closet Texan, with all of the outdoor interests and machismo a cowboy needs to have to survive. The plant was paying for the relocation, including the house-hunting trips and all the expenses that went with it.

Right after school let out in May, and right around the time our favorite swim club, Tree Court, was opening, we took a Braniff flight from Lambert Field in St. Louis to Dallas Love Field. I couldn't believe we were giving up a weekend swimming with friends to go look at houses in Dallas. It was a drag. Here's a house, there's another house; this one is big with no backyard; this one is tiny with a big backyard; this one has no neighborhood; this one is on a busy street. This one is this, this one is that ... every house stunk. We hated the trip, and

Dad knew it. Mom went along with it but told Dad on the next trip we needed to build some fun into it. So, they did.

The next trip, a couple of weeks later, we flew one of Braniff's colored planes back to Love Field. This time, we got a hotel in south Dallas near the O-I plant Dad was going to be working at. It was also close to Six Flags, and we took a day journey there. I remember it was fun and very Texan because it was also Fiesta weekend in early May, and all the rides and decorations were a heavily Mexican-style celebration. We made our third trip to Dallas to look some more, and this time we stayed in north Dallas, so we would be closer to Love Field to catch our flight back to St. Louis.

I remember we were only there forty-eight hours, maybe less. We had a good agent, but no cigar on the house front yet until about two hours before our flight home. We were on the way to the airport when the agent said, "If you have just two minutes, I'd like to show you one more house that just came on the market. It is on the way to the airport, and you won't miss your flight."

Mom and Dad agreed, and off we went, hoping not to miss our flight. It was a very hot summer day in late June 1969. Hottest heat I had ever experienced, and I thought to myself, *What are we doing here? No one can survive here. There is no one outside, no yards to play in, and only long, skinny alleys and fences.* I remember thinking, *If it weren't for these free rides on these colorful Braniff airplanes, I'd have to run away and find a workaround to this problem.*

When we pulled up to 4132 Willow Ridge in north Dallas, it was a very new house in a new neighborhood. Nothing really striking to look at, as it looked like all the other builder ranch-style one-story designs making up that newer neighborhood. We ran through it like a herd of feral hogs, and along the way, we decided who would get which rooms. The one designated by and for me was on the far end of the house, away from the other bedrooms. I liked that idea a lot. And it had a ground-level trampoline in the side yard with the ground dug out beneath it so you could bounce, but if you fell off, you were already near the ground.

With only an hour left before our flight from Love Field, which was only ten minutes away in those days, and the days on the calendar ticking by, my parents told the agent they would take it. We had looked at the house for less than fifteen minutes. Now I had something to look forward to. My own bedroom, isolated from the rest of the family and in my complete control as I learned the pros and cons of living in that room.

It was now time to say goodbye to our friends in St. Louis and take one more Braniff airplane ride to Dallas. It was a green airplane, and that was a good sign because it was my favorite color. High hopes and a broken heart leaving St. Louis, and I cried, staring out the window as the jet left the runway for the last time from Lambert Airfield.

HELLO, TEXAS!

It was early July by the time our furniture mover made it to Dallas to move in on Willow Ridge. It was exciting getting my own room for the first time. I also had my own bathroom. Our dog Mickey made the trip, and his room was the laundry room just outside my door. (I think he actually came with the moving truck, and the driver took care of him all the way as he rode in his cab, but he probably didn't know that Mickey got car sick. Especially if you shot him in the tail first.) You went through that room to get to my teenage love shack.

And let's not forget the trampoline. A true safety design that only served as a great place to make out with my girlfriend and almost killed a neighbor friend when he tried a flip and landed on the frame with his face. He should have hit the dirt; it would have been softer.

After we moved in and unpacked boxes, we tried to figure out how the family intercom system would work. The master system was in the kitchen, and each room had a speaker and a way to talk to others through it. It lasted about a month before we lost interest in this "new" technology that didn't jive with real life in a house with four people. Now we text with our phones to the person in the same room. I liked it better back then.

The big news that summer was Apollo 11 and the first lunar landing by astronauts Neil Armstrong and Buzz Aldrin, with Mike Collins circling the moon in the command module. The world's eyes were glued to the TV on July 20, 1969. We hadn't started school yet, so my eyes were glued to our Motorola color TV that sat on a rack that had wheels so you could scoot it around the room like a drink cart. The adventure of space, airplanes, and the lunar landing, along with all the great music of 1969, had a huge impact on my ability to adjust to a new home. I had my own room. I had my Teisco guitar and amp. I had a record player that only played forty-fives and a stack of vinyl. I also had my own bathroom, a black light with psychedelic posters of the day, including the ever-famous picture of Ringo Starr of the Beatles in chromed-out blue shadows holding a pigeon on his finger, the multicolored Adam and Eve poster showing them standing on tall spires of rock overlooking the Grand Canyon, and the most glamorous photo of Farrah Fawcett with that long flowing hair flipped back while in a one-piece bathing suit, showing off for all her fans. Every American boy in high school remembered that one!

My favorite song that I played in my room in July of that year was the hit by a band called Spirit, "I Got a Line on You." I played it constantly because it was up-tempo and had that classic sixties rock drive to it that I still love today. Things were about to work out great, but I didn't know it at the time, and how could I have known? After all, I felt so racked by the move and the disarray of things that, since my earliest memory, had been stable and predictable and safe. I had no idea that God had planted us in Dallas for His purpose, which also included a great future, but it sure didn't feel like it at first. If Dad hadn't been promoted at O-I and supported by my mother, we wouldn't have moved to Dallas, which turned out to be the best thing that ever happened to me in my life.

Change can be good, so embrace it and trust that things will be great.

By about the middle of August, we began to get ready to go to school. Jay had already hooked up with his next dependent family, the Reals. Jay got into that family as only Jay could and still does. He and Mike became very close friends and still are today. There are so many Real stories in those first few weeks because we didn't have any friends yet. Jay was always at the Real house, only one block away, and I was in my room, figuring out what was next for me.

SEEKING A STATION IN LIFE, HEADING INTO HIGH SCHOOL

We always had something in the garage that Dad was working on. A boat, its motor, an engine of this sort or that, and anything else that needed Dad the handyman. He would usually ask—no, tell—me to help him, and I'm glad he did because I developed a curiosity about how things worked. Not so I could further my engineering mind, which hadn't been born yet, but to get the damn thing to work so I could use it. This was a life- changing need and curiosity for me, as I wanted to occupy my early days on Willow Ridge fixing the Honda 50 motorcycle Dad had brought to Dallas from St. Louis. He had bought it a few years earlier on a hunting trip to Colorado with his St. Louis mates and never really rode it much. But all his friends had one in St. Louis, so he bought it. He told us to never ride it. The typical "do as I say and not as I do."

I'd say that the results on that approach were mixed at best, but it did give me something to work on. When I finally got it running, I needed one more part, and that was a master link for the drive chain. I had to adapt a broken one it had, and sometimes it worked for twenty minutes or only two minutes, but I got it running. When Dad wasn't home, I fired that baby up, strapped on his helmet just in case I got caught, headed down the alley toward Snow White Avenue and turned right, then right again onto Willow Ridge, where I wanted it to roar up the street toward our house at the other end.

The Honda 50 with shin guards doesn't really roar; it produces more of a meow, or maybe even more of a purr. It made enough noise because when I flew by 4040 Willow Ridge, there was a pretty blonde girl in the front yard, staring at me like "what the hell is he doing?" I saw her and almost hit a tree and two parked cars. I made it to the end of the street and turned around to get another look and impress her this time with how cool I was.

I did those runs three or four times before she went inside, obviously not impressed and rather uninterested in this new neighbor kid up the street. I was so excited to see her again and find out her name and if she lived there and where she went to school. St. Louis was in the rearview mirror, but it was still in sight. I missed my friends there, but I now had a new friend to meet, just seven houses down the street.

SCHOOL

My remaining year of junior high school was spent attending Thomas C. Marsh Junior High. It was ninth grade, and my mom drove me there for my first day. She had taken us kids to the store to buy new school clothes, and I was at least looking forward to wearing some new cool duds to a school I never had attended and where I knew absolutely no one other than the new friend I had met on the motorcycle just a couple of weeks earlier.

It was pouring down rain on my first day at Marsh. Jay was attending Thomas Gooch Elementary, as was Sue Ellen. Gooch was closer to home than Marsh, but they were all within walking distance. I ended up having two classes with the new girl down the street. We shared physical science (hey, hey) and algebra. It was the first time in my life that I ever looked forward to algebra class. Not the algebra, just the class. I was terrible at algebra. She was there and sitting close enough for me to see all the A's she was getting on her tests. This was an important opportunity for me, being able to see her tests. Now I could pass the class and get to know her. A double play! Since they called roll at the beginning of our classes, I listened intently for the name to be called and for her to raise her hand and say "here."

"Sandy Orr?" the teacher called.

Her cute little hand went up. I think she was wearing a blue dress, as she was always dressed up, and she answered "Here." And I thought, *Sandy Orr. She is stunning me right here, right now. She is cute, pretty, smart, dresses very nice, and she lives just down the street from me.* One thing I could do was make sure that chivalry lived, so I asked if I could carry her books as we walked home together, and she let me! The first thing I learned about her was her name was Sandra, but she went by Sandee, with two E's. Very cool, I thought.

A few weeks later, I got her telephone number and began calling her in the evenings. Her stepfather, Si Winkler, had a rule in his house. No talking on the phone after 9:00 p.m. And he meant it. I could write a book about my relationship with Si Winkler. It would be called *The Book of Si*. It would be two short pages and contain just two topics: Page 1: Golf and Page 2: Archie Bunker. He was all Archie, and he loved to play golf. He was a founding member at Brookhaven Country Club, where my parents also became members. I never played golf with Si. He never asked me. So, I married his stepdaughter, but I did ask him!

The only time he asked me to play golf with him was if I were to stop our wedding five minutes before he was going to walk Sandee down the aisle. He told me that if I agreed to it, and we left right then, we would go straight to the airport, and he would buy us two tickets to Hawaii to play golf for a week. I asked if they would be first-class tickets. He said no. The only time he asked me to play golf was when he knew I would say no. I said no and married his stepdaughter instead.

A few weeks after the start of school, they announced that the football team tryouts were to take place. I had played football in Glendale and had all my friends with me, and it was easy to step forward and try out because I knew what and who I was up against. In Dallas, at Marsh Junior High School, where I knew no one but a pretty blonde down the street, it was simply too intimidating. I went to the tryout. Sat in the locker room and watched all the guys dressing out and slapping each other on the back, and I was scared to insert myself into all of that because of the fear of the unknown. They all had played together the prior year. I had played middle linebacker the prior year in Glendale, but I didn't know these guys.

I went and talked to the coach to see if I could get a little help there, and I didn't get any answers. I still didn't know a single guy there, so I tucked tail and walked home. It bothered me that I didn't have the guts to get in there and give them a whack, but it didn't feel right, which is code for I was scared shitless. (There were a couple of guys on that team; one in particular scared the bejesus out of me, and I had to deal with him later in school; it gave me angry dreams until our fortieth high school reunion.) Later in the school year, when I finally knew a few people, I tried out for the track team as a pole vaulter.

A pole vaulter? I always enjoyed trying new things, and I figured I couldn't beat anyone running or throwing stuff, but I could find my way over a fence, so I just had to learn how to get over it faster and without touching it.

To make the squad, you had to clear an eight-foot bar. So, I began practicing during gym at the end of the school day when we had athletics. The coach showed us some techniques that would be useful to make it over the bar. The first one was not to eat ice cream or any desserts and to lose about 20 percent of our body weight, which would have put us on the Ethiopian cross-country team. Coach said, "The less you carry down that runway, the less you need to haul over the top of it."

A flying analogy; now I got it! I didn't need to lose weight—I just needed a faster takeoff speed. According to my calculations, doing more squats and twenty-yard sprints would get me enough velocity to make it over eight feet. We had three days to demonstrate the minimum flight over the bar. I missed the first two days at about six feet, but at least I got into the air. On day three on my last set of attempts, I ran so hard that when I stuck the pole into the box, the pole wouldn't bend, and I just ran under the crossbar solo. That's when I realized pole vaulting wasn't my lifelong passion. As of 2021, the indoor and outdoor world record height for pole vaulting was set by Mondo Duplantis from Sweden. At the age of twenty, he cleared twenty feet, two inches. His record is safe with me.

When the football season started, I had finally met some acquaintances, so it was more social to go to games. I found out that Sandy Orr had changed her name to Sandee Orr when I read the names of the girls on the list of Marsh Matador Cuadrillas. She was on that list, but her name was spelled with two E's at the end. I liked it a lot. Sandee Orr. I was hoping she would be my first girlfriend.

I would go to the football games and, instead of looking for the bus with the football players on it, I would look for the drill team. I found her every time. As the school year moved on, I began making a few friends, which helped boost my confidence. I was beginning to feel that I wasn't walking on the moon alone, hoping someone would come rescue me. Things were getting better socially as we moved to the senior high school, W.T. White, about a mile from my house in north Dallas.

I began seeing Sandee as much as I could. Before school, during school and after school, before dinner, at dinner, after dinner … until 9:00 p.m., when Si would take the phone from her and hang it up on me. See page two in *The Book of Si*. To underscore page two from *The Book of Si*—Sandee and I agreed to do something one evening, before either of us were driving, so I just walked down the street and knocked on her front door. By then I had managed to pull a few more chin hairs to make them longer, and I had a goatee with a fuzzy mustache and all.

After the second knock on the door, the porch light came on and the doorknob began to turn. I had never met her parents, but I had heard about Si. As the door opened, I stood taller, with my shoulders back and a smile on my face. You only get one chance at making a great first impression. The lasting smile and countenance could last a lifetime—with children. A good performance here could serve several more generations. My chance at a first impression was nigh, but when Si opened the door, he took one look at me and, halfway through saying, "Hi, Mr. Winkler, is Sandee ready to go with me—" he slammed the door on my face. Not a word.

See page two in *The Book of Si*. Si didn't like or appreciate facial hair, and neither did Archie Bunker. That's one of the reasons he hated his son-in-law, Meathead. I had the facial hair, and he wasn't letting me in the house. I think Sandee's mother, Nora Ruth Winkler—everyone called her Ruth—saved the day for Sandee and reopened the door, but I was not going in that house. Nora Ruth Winkler. I didn't know about this Winkler last name stuff because I liked Sandee Orr, and I didn't understand her family situation yet.

Sometime before Christmas that year, Sandee was babysitting for the neighbors that lived across from me and my family, Connie and Russ Ambler. The Amblers were scheduled to go out with my mom and dad. The Amblers hired Sandee to babysit their kids while they all went out. They paid her fifty cents per hour. But when my dad and mom went to their house to pick them up and Dad walked through the door and saw Sandee, ever my dad, he grabbed her hand and asked her if she wanted to get married! She was fifteen. She said, "No, I'm only in ninth grade."

That didn't stop Dad; he simply upped the bet. He was like a god. "I have a son across the street that would just love to marry you!"

I think she probably had that look she still gives me today to say "really?" She told me that story a while later, and it warmed my heart. You never know, Sandee darling. And to think, when we first moved to Dallas, I thought my life was starting over. The big hill on my street in Glendale was replaced with a larger hill that was requiring personal strength and determination to crest. I was beginning to learn that climbing hills is necessary and worthy of every effort to successfully prepare for the next one. And more importantly, relationships were coming into full view, bringing wonderful color to life. I was experiencing for the first time the early development of a love relationship. A personal relationship with someone that wanted to spend time with me, not just to hang out, but to get to know and rely upon each other. I needed this opportunity to become myself, a self that someone else wanted, as I explored the vast and spinning world of someone dear to my heart.

I was beginning to live eyes wide open with interest, curiosity, and ambition.

High school was a rat race. We had all the same social dilemmas facing socially awkward kids today, but we didn't have the technology to make it worse. We had music everyone listened to at the same time. We had three channels on TV and no internet. Nothing to get in the way of relationship building and busting.

My parents began to take notice that I was spending all my time with Sandee. If I wasn't at home, I was down the street at Sandee's, hiding from Si, but enjoying Sandee and Mrs. Winkler's company. I was there so much Ruth began to treat me as family, and she knew that I adored and protected Sandee. I started calling her "Ma." As a way to get out of the house together, we had to find places to go on foot. Sandee's family had two dogs, Panda and CB. Panda was an Alaskan Malamute (perfect for Texas summers?), and CB was a crossbreed, something, I think, between a bulldog and a chihuahua. He hated me. He growled if I looked at him funny. The only thing I had on him was size. By about a hundred and fifty pounds.

It was the first full winter when Sandee and I were together all the time because we liked being together. I brought our family dog Mickey with me down to Sandee's to see if she wanted to take CB for a nice walk in the cold evening air. It was cold, maybe in the thirties. Sandee told her parents we would be back after a walk around the block.

The street behind ours was called Mendenhall, and we were walking, holding hands in one hand and holding dog leashes in the other. We were walking snuggled against each other. She had a dark-colored coat on and wasn't wearing a hat, but her blonde hair was draped in front of her. We were in the dark area between home lights that offered some light of the road, and we both stopped and closed our eyes and kissed each other for the first time. I wanted to marry her right then and there. We had to remind ourselves to keep walking, but then we would stop again to get the kissing right, and we did.

When we finally made it back to her house, her mom asked, "What took you so long?" Duh. It was cold for several days, so we took many dog walks, whether they wanted to go or not. Finally, my mom asked Sandee, "What is it with Dave's interest in walking Mickey every night?" I think she said, "Well, maybe they both need exercise?" I do not think my mom ever connected the dots on that one.

For a birthday present when I turned fifteen, out of the blue, my mom and dad, aka "Santa," gave me a record album by James Brown called "I'm Black and I'm Proud." If that was not weird enough—I mean, I liked James Brown, but how about some Stones?—they also included two tickets to a James Brown concert at Memorial Auditorium in downtown Dallas in just a few weeks. I called Sandee and asked her to go with me and told her my mom and dad could drive. I was excited to ask her.

She said, "Who's James Brown?"

I said, "You know, 'hey, I feel good, ara ara ara ara ugn.'"

She said, "I don't recognize it."

I told her she would enjoy the show and that I really wanted her to come with me, so we went. Mom took us there, and Dad picked us up, as I recall. The show was great! Lots of horns, and I think we were the only white people there, but by then we were kissing each other and sitting high in the bleacher cheap seats. We just hugged and kissed while James was singing "It's A Man's World," "Momma Come Here Quick and Bring Me That Lickin' Stick," and "I'm A Sex Machine."

The black ladies sitting behind us screamed at us, "Honey, you gonna miss the show, and y'all gonna git chapped lips!" I told them we didn't care, that we could hear just fine. We got picked up, and it was our first of many concerts in our life together.

While we were falling in teenage love together, we also fell in love with our favorite Mexican food restaurant. We never ate Mexican food in the Midwest, so it was new to me, as was Texas iced tea. What I was missing all those years! We heard of a Mexican place on Northwest Highway by Love Field called Tupinamba's. We had our parents drop us off there, once again, before we could drive. And we sat on an elevated platform at a table that we liked.

We went so often that we got to know the owner very well and still go to their location, after many location changes, at Walnut Hill and Central Expressway in Dallas. Eddie Dominguez, who is still the owner, says hi to us every time and remembers the early days of our relationship. His adult children run it for him now, but he is there when we are there from time to time. When he's not there, I ask his staff if he is at home counting his money. They usually say something like, "No, he is in Napa Valley, spending it."

We had our wedding rehearsal dinner there in 1981, and since 1970 we have been going to Tupinamba's. They should put a picture of us with Eddie on their wall.

Sandee had some high school friends that she had known since she was in grade school. Laura Sherman was a dear classmate then and is a beloved friend today. When Sandee and Laura were together, they got into trouble. They played hooky from school. They kidnapped me in the middle of the night through the bedroom window in the Dave wing of our house, and they liked to TP houses—lots of toilet paper; not twenty rolls per house, two hundred rolls. They were legends.

One night when Laura was staying overnight with Sandee, they told me they were going to come to my house in the middle of the night and wake me up. Laura told me to tie a string to my wrist and hang it through the slightly open window where they could find it in the bushes and tug on it to wake me up. About 2:00 a.m., I felt my arm twitching and a bunch of muffled laughs coming through my window. It was them. Them. OMG, it was them. They had shown up. Now how was I going to get outside?

Well, I was a Boy Scout, and Boy Scouts are always prepared. So, when they had told me to expect them, I had lubed every sliding track door in the house so I could, shall we say, escape the premises like a ninja. I made it outside to join them. Sandee wanted me to kiss her, and Laura kept saying, "Go on, give her a kiss." When I did, I just about slid off Sandee's face and they laughed into the night sky. They had put on so much lipstick, our lips never made contact; they slid off, heading to Bolivia if I hadn't gotten ahold of them.

I walked them back down to Sandee's house, gave her a sliding kiss, then headed back home, hoping my parents had not gotten up and locked the door on me.

When Sandee and I weren't together, it was because I was working various part-time high school jobs, or she was making the big bucks babysitting or at church on Wednesday nights or at youth group or studying. She studied a lot. And I'm glad she did. It is how I got through high school. We had a couple more classes together in tenth grade, but no more classes together after that. So, I would come to her class during class to disturb it to get her attention. I would do passive things—nothing stupid that might get me in trouble, but I would try to be creative. I found a surgical glove that you could inflate and tie off and put between your legs to look like cow udders. I thought that would be lighthearted and a quiet way of telling Sandee hello during class. I just hunched over outside her class door and very slowly bent over like a four-legged animal with the udders hanging low and made the perfect sound of a tired milk cow going back out to pasture after a good squeeze down. I went back and forth until, I think the third time, I was stopped, escorted to the principal's office, and given just two licks. It was all I needed. I got the point. But more importantly, I got Sandee's attention.

I finally got the nerve to tell her that I loved her at a high school basketball game of all places. We were high up in the bleachers at Loos Fieldhouse, where we played our Longhorn home games. During a game and while we were sitting with friends, Sandee was sitting on my right, and she was talking with friends on her right side. I had my arm around her, watching the game, and just pulled her over and whispered in her ear, "I love you!"

She just looked at me and said, "I love you too," smiled, then went back to her conversation. It was like, "Of course you do, and I do too." So, I let it go at that.

When Sandee gave me her high school picture, she wrote on the back of it: "I'll love you forever, Sandee." But she didn't write my name on it! Were these pictures mass-produced for wide distribution? I still give her a hard time for it.

I enjoyed high school. I was in Thespians, which is a speech and drama organization, and I got into a goofy stage where I really enjoyed pantomime. I entered one-act plays and competed. I had a nice role in our senior play, did some children's theater, and played football as a sophomore. One of Sandee's other friends was Mona Canoles. Mona was the twirler at Marsh, and her boyfriend at the time was Mark Brian Thompson.

Mark has been my best friend since those days at Marsh over fifty years ago. Our friendship is very deep and well deserved for both of us. He and Mona were a dating couple in high school. Mark was a jock. He played football as a wide receiver, was a point guard on the basketball team, and was an overall well-liked athlete. He had a job at Sears selling small electrical appliances. I had a job down the street selling shoes at Kinney's Shoes. Sandee had a job down the street selling clothes at Montgomery Ward's, and Mona was working at Calico Corners or someplace like that. But when we were not working, the four of us were usually going out together.

Life is not complete without a bestie. Not just a casual relationship built at Starbucks last week, but rather a relationship forged in fire, with the ups and downs of life. Everyone should seek, value, and nurture a best-friend relationship. Without one, we are incomplete, and life is monochrome. A best friend comes to your emotional rescue when needed. As a best friend, you look out for their best interests, smile when they laugh, and cry when they hurt. Even better, how about many best friends? Running with a herd of best buddies is one of life's greatest joys.

You may know dozens or even hundreds of people, but best friends can only be counted on one hand.

I hope someone, including Mark, includes me as they count their best friend inventory on one hand.

Mark and I got into all kinds of scuffs and scrapes, and the girls adored us. Mark gave me his tenth-grade school picture just after Mona had broken up with him, and on the back of it, he wrote: "To Dave. I hate girls." He didn't hate girls; he hated being broken up with, but who doesn't? It happened to me in a big and life-changing way that I will describe later. But that is what happens in high school. It is a melee of relationship change and turmoil wrapped around the antics of teenagers. What could go wrong?

I owe a lot to Mark in my life. We have just been as good as friends can be. He helps me. I help him. Mark has been through every up and down in my life, and I love him like a blood brother. I still give him a hard time whenever possible, and he does the same to me. And we laugh. That is what best friends do. He will be one of the six that carry me to the grave. I may make him do it alone, just to bust his chops. I love him and really enjoy him in my life. I can tell him things I can't tell anyone else, and he does the same with me. We have come a long way from punching holes in our walls at home, as he did when he got pissed at Mona in high school once. I will always remember that. I was there. I saw it. And I understood it.

Mark and I were inseparable most of the time. When I slept at his house, I slept in his room on the orange shag carpet. His parents were always on his ass, and as I told him, he deserved some of it, but not all of it. That is just what parents do. His parents, Helen and Harvey Thompson, were very interesting people, and I enjoyed knowing them. They were a fiery couple. Harvey was in the oil field in the Middle East, and they adopted Mark and his sister Janice from Germany back in 1955. He was born on July 8, and I always remember his birthday. It is the day before my start date at my first job out of college and my slow climb out of the depths of economic disaster, so it is easy to remember. We hunted together, fished and camped, and did just about everything else best friends do. We also had a few scrapes along the way that were memorable. I debated about detailing them here, but if you ever want to hear the stories, get two beers because it might take more than that for us to tell them to you.

One thing Mark did to help me along was get me started waiting tables. He worked in some of the best restaurants, from Lubbock when he was at Tech, to Dallas, where he worked at Oz, which is where

I waited my first table. He became my direct boss out at Chandler's Landing Yacht Club, and I really got the waiter thing down under his supervision. Waiting tables carried me through college at various places that all had a positive impact on my ability to exist.

Mark and I got fired at the same time at the 94th Aero Squadron Restaurant at Love Field. I blamed him; he blamed me. It was a blast.

STANDING MY GROUND

Even though high school was socially fun, it had a few bad elements. Let's pretend his name, for the sake of this story, is Stymie Peckerwhite. Stymie haunted me for years because he was so nasty to people, and I had my share of encounters with him. One scrape that just about took me out because I couldn't do much about it was at a football team retreat intended to bring the players together at an overnight lake event at Lake Dallas, now called Lake Lewisville. Stymie was out of control, and by morning I had found refuge by climbing up a pole to get on top of a picnic villa so he wouldn't find me and couldn't get to me if he did.

The team had bedded down for the night in sleeping bags, and Stymie Peckerwhite wouldn't leave anyone alone. He was too big and mean for anyone to handle without the coaches around. I saw him peeing on people while they tried to sleep; he would beat people up and kick them, as he was the pre-bullying poster boy. When the sun came up and he saw me on top of the villa, trying to get down, he mocked me and threatened to come up to get me and kick my ass. I stayed up there and told him I'd kick his face and fingers while he tried getting up there. I started crowing like a rooster and calling him chicken and telling him what a jerk he was. And he was.

So, while I was crowing and giving it right back at him, he found a gallon jar of mustard and started hurling it up at me, and I got slimed more than a couple of times. I just egged him on. "Is that all you got?" I kept yelling at him. Then, around daybreak, with me still perched high on the pavilion, enjoying a nice sunrise, the coaches came to see how the night went.

"Did you guys come together as a team?" one coach asked.

"Yes, Coach," was someone's reply.

Then, at 6:00 a.m., he ordered us back to town to get ready for weekend practice. I finally got down off that picnic pavilion after Stymie was gone, and I can't help but think of that event every time I see one. I was scared to death. For the next forty years, I had dreams about it. I wanted to kick his ass so bad I would wake up in the night and tell Sandee about it.

Peckerwhite was a big dude. He was about six three and was big, strong, fast, and recruited by a major D1 college to be a free safety or cornerback. His job was to hit people. They recruited the right guy for that part of it. He was injured and didn't go on to the pros, but he had the talent. I talked about kicking Stymie's ass all the time. To my family, to my friends, and mostly to Mark, Mona, and Sandee.

Fast-forward forty years. God had a plan, and I got to experience it. At our forty-year high school reunion in Dallas we had a golf tournament before the big dinner dance that evening at Prestonwood Country Club. Sandee and I had flown the airplane to Dallas, and we got there late for me to join up with the starting group I was in with Mark and some other guys. Sandee went shopping and dropped me off at the club first.

Paula Salter, everyone's W.T. White sweetheart and prom queen (and someone I took on an impromptu motorcycle ride, borrowing a friend's "motor"), drove me in the drink cart out to my golf group. On the way there, I called Mark on my cell phone and told him I would be there in a few minutes and if he had seen Stymie Peckerwhite out on the golf course, to tell him to wait for me so I would have a chance to kick his ass.

Mark said, “Yeah, he’s here. Right in front of us. But you better bring about five of your friends, ’cause you’re going to need them.”

When Paula dropped me off, I was glad to see several longtime friends, including Mike Leonard, a buddy that I had a lot of fun with and I hoped would be part of the five guys I needed to kick Peckerwhite’s ass. By the time the round of golf was over, everyone had gotten showered up in the men’s locker room without the customary towel fights. I did fire off a couple at Mark to try to reenact the past, but it never got going with the larger group. Just a bunch of fat old farts getting ready for dinner. But where was Stymie? I couldn’t find him. Perhaps I’d kick his ass on the dance floor or during the reunion picture, or when he was on the way to his car. But I’d find him.

When I did, we were both in line to get a drink at the bar. He was standing right in front of me, talking with someone. I told Sandee to go somewhere else because I needed to talk to Mr. Peckerwhite. When the body language was right and he was turned my way, I said, “Hi, Stymie, Dave Gasmire. It’s good to see you.”

He acted like he almost remembered me, but it wasn’t a homecoming greeting. He said, “Yeah, good to see you too.” Then he turned away to talk with someone else, and I stopped him from turning by touching his elbow like it was no big deal. He looked at me, and I said, “Stymie, I have something that has been bothering me for over forty years that you did to me in high school, and I want it trued up right here. I’m not dealing with this anymore.”

He said, “What’s the problem?”

I told him, “You did so much shit to me in high school. Do you remember the football retreat when you covered me in mustard and peed on people and put me in headlocks and all the rest? Do you remember that? I’m here to get that fixed, ’cause I put up with your shit for too long.” And I just looked at him.

He had an easy, pleasant look on his face and simply said, “I don’t remember that, but if you say I did all that, then I owe you an apology. I’m sorry. Can I buy you a drink?”

And I said, "Yes, you sure can. I'll get the next one." To him, it never happened, but for me it was finally over. God's grace is strong, but I had to be patient. I didn't want to have revenge any longer.

I should have been paying more attention to my own intentions and less to revenge. It is a life zapper. We should all hunt those down in our imaginations and our souls and deal with them as Jesus instructs us to do. I've only had two of these in my life, totally within my control, but I waited much too long to deal with it. The second one came years later.

6

Becoming a Texan, factory work not for the meek, figuring out my economic future, high school jobs, a drunk babysitter, joining the factory union.

While all the pieces had fallen into place for a social reentry in Dallas after leaving St. Louis and with Sandee as my official girlfriend and me her official boyfriend, I set out to get part-time and summer jobs. At various times during those years, I had a job at a local trap and skeet range and was a "pull boy," pulling and scoring traps and skeet. It was a fun job, but I was in the sun all day on the weekends, and sometimes into the night under the lights. I was driving my mom's 1967 Pontiac Lemans convertible and put an eight-track stereo in it with some cool speakers. I really tore her car up doing it, but she allowed me to install it until I got my own car, which didn't happen until college when I pulled together enough money to buy a '67 Mustang convertible.

In high school I also had a job at Dairy Queen running the burger line. I was trying to make the production faster, but that burger broiler belt didn't move very fast, and I couldn't speed it up. I lasted in that job a few weeks and am not sure I remember how I left. The job game changer came when my dad asked if I wanted to work at the O-I plant in south Dallas. My job was working for the plant maintenance and housekeeping janitor, a very nice guy with a drinking problem. His name was Raymond Jenkins. I was under the janitor.

We found out what a drinking problem Raymond had when Dad decided he would be a good babysitter for the three of us at our house while he and Mom went to a party for a weekend somewhere. Dad told me that if Raymond had a beer, he couldn't stop. Raymond brought his own beer to our house, drank a case, passed out, then sobered up enough to get paid when Dad got home. It was disgusting and showed terrible parental judgment. Dad's working guys were also his friends, so he saw everyone in a supporting role. I told him that it was a big mistake and that we looked after Raymond; he didn't look after us.

The perfect place to learn things is from the bottom up. Like Dave Harris, the blues musician in Vancouver we befriended recently, sings, "It's Crowded at The Bottom." That's where I started, and very glad that I did. I began just working Saturdays during school but moved to full rotating shift work during the summer. I rode to work with Dad, and we parked ever proudly in the first parking spot in the parking lot with a sign reading "Plant Manager." Each day when we arrived, the plant manager got out of the car there and so did the guy reporting to the janitor. We had both ends covered.

When I started working shift work, I had to drive myself nearly all of the time. I had been approached by the union president and the shop foreman, encouraging me to join the union. It was the glass blower's union and had a large presence in the US. I had no idea what that was or what it meant. The shop union would have liked nothing more than to have the plant manager's kid join the union to leverage against the management leadership.

I asked Bill White, the president, what it meant to join the union. He told me it meant free hot dogs once a month, some coupons for this and that, and invitations to parties and get-togethers. I asked how much it would cost. He told me $12 per month or about $3 per week. I asked him if there were any other benefits to being a member of this fine union clambake. He clinched it for me when he said I would be paid the minimum wage per hour of $2.32 and a half cents per hour. Where did I sign?

On the way home, riding with Dad in the car that night, he asked me what I was talking to Bill White about when he saw the two of us together in the plant. I told him that Mr. White had asked me to join the union. Dad asked me, "What did you tell him?" And I almost wrecked us on the road when Dad heard me say, "I told him I would join and signed the forms today so I could get the union wage and the free hot dogs."

Dad nearly ran off the road. He told me that I was to resign from the union the next day and that I had to tell Mr. White that myself. He then told me all the reasons he didn't want me to be in the union. He told me that the union was the employee organization that aggregates its power to negotiate a contract to the advantage of the union. He went on to describe the strife that can be in play without a balanced relationship with the individuals in the union. He had great relationships with his factory workers, and he relied on his supportive culture, supporting their needs and treating them like friends. He would invite them to our home, provide retreats to reward them, and was an attentive listener to their job issues. To him, the union was unnecessary if he had a personal relationship with the people, and if I, as his son, was in the union, it created a pawn to be used against Dad and his management.

I didn't see it any further than a free hot dog and fifty cents more per hour compared to my friends. To this day, it makes great sense to me, and is a healthy strategy to avoid putting a wedge between management and union, who were really good friends. The next day I went to Mr. White and told him I had to drop out of the club, I mean, the union. He told me I was already a member. I told him that I hadn't paid the dues yet and I was going to ask Mr. Harrington, the payroll accountant, to not withhold the dues from my paycheck that week.

It got ugly, but I got out of it. They almost had me. I told them I didn't want to be in the way between my dad and the union, and I think that got me out. The truth, plain and simple. The great pay and the hot dogs seemed like a good combination to a sixteen-year-old boss's kid.

But as with most things, there is always more to the story and certain repercussions that loom for the inexperienced and unknowing. But it's a great way to learn lessons that will never be forgotten.

I was given every job no one in the plant would do, and I was glad to get them, but it was a test of my mettle. The show *Dirty Jobs* would have loved to follow me for a day. At some point, I was promoted to junior flunky and reported to one of my dad's top managers. His name was Russ Randle, and he was a friend to my dad. Randle was a tyrant to me, but then again, I was outnumbered everywhere at O-I. I did what I was told but tried to have some fun along the way.

I was told that I needed to have everything spic and span for the corporate bosses who were coming down from Toledo, Ohio. A couple of days before the corporate tour, I told Mr. Randle that he didn't have to worry about the FTC, that I had already taken care of it. The machines in the factory all had acronyms, and he assumed I was referring to one of those. The next day, before I left at the end of the day, I found Mr. Randle and told him the FTC was in better shape than the day before and he thanked me for the update.

The day came for the corporate suits to do their thing. Every manager in the plant was wearing a tie, and I was just waiting for one of their ties to get caught in a machine and rip one of their faces off. The day went off without a hitch. After everyone was gone, Mr. Randle found me and asked how all the maintenance and cleaning I was responsible for was getting done. Specifically, he wanted to know how the FTC was doing since he didn't have any idea what it was. He acted like it was a machine I was running that he didn't know about.

I told him the FTC was just as great that day as it had been yesterday. He finally asked me to remind him what the FTC was, and I told him it was the front trash can. Sometimes you have to create some significance for yourself and get noticed for knowing more than they know. Years later, when I would see Randle, I would say, "Want me to go check the FTC, Mr. Randle?" and he'd say, "I saw it this morning, and everything looked fine." He had a grin on his face because he knew that I was now included in his team.

TURNING WORK ASSIGNMENTS INTO OPPORTUNITIES

I worked at the plant a lot whenever I could because it paid so well. One of the jobs I was assigned was to drive a station wagon full of booze and beer up to Lake Texoma, where the O-I Dallas management team was planning a weekend retreat. I thought, *Really? Why would ... never mind; sounds like a paid road trip to me!* So, on the way up to the Texas/Oklahoma border where Lake Texoma has been since the 1940s, I stopped and picked up Sandee and took her with me. She usually slept in until noon during the summer, but I got her to answer the phone and be ready for me to pick her up. I was sixteen, and she was probably seventeen.

We made it all the way there and stocked the rooms at the Tanglewood Resort. We didn't hit any of their inventory of food and beverages, but we did hit a drive-through on the way back. Sandee sat right next to me in the middle of the front seat, and we enjoyed that we were together, and I was getting paid for doing so. It is a great memory of back in the days of just having fun and getting paid for it. I was really enjoying feeling like a hotshot, responsible for a very important leadership meeting. What I did mattered to me, and it would have an impact beyond just mopping a compressor room floor.

Take advantage of every opportunity to show something can get done, and you are the one to do it.

I was given responsibility that I was accountable for, and I wanted to show off for Sandee. She was my girlfriend, and I wanted her proud of me. Sometimes we work hard for the admiration of others, and that is a powerful driver, so harness that want-to and deploy it where necessary. It was a very early recognition of wanting to be counted on, that I could be trusted, and I would deliver what was expected. This road trip was a first lesson in paid freedom with responsibility. And in this case, I was making money to take Sandee out for dinner and a movie. It was a proverbial win-win-win.

Although Dad was working hard, trying to turn the plant's performance around, which is why we moved to Dallas in the first place, he still made time to develop his new friends, who were people he worked with. His production manager, Bob Ratzman, became one of his lifelong best friends. Bob and his wife Joy (perfect name for one of the most precious people on Earth) became so much "family" to us that we have always stayed in touch and done so many things with them.

When Joy died of ALS over Thanksgiving in the early 2000s, it was one of the saddest losses I can remember. She was a saint, and everyone agrees to this day that Bob didn't deserve her. I think he agrees with that! But while Dad worked with Bob and others, he continued his interest in boating by bringing our boat from St. Louis, the little eighteen-foot StarCraft with the 75 hp Johnson outboard motor, and we took it to Lake Texoma for the first time as a family, just like we used to go to the Lake of the Ozarks in Missouri.

We always were lake people and loved boating, and Dad made sure we found a boating existence in Texas. He also continued with crazy fun adventures just like always, and that made living in Texas not such a new experience and made it fun. He had a bullhorn added to his company car, a late-model Ford Crown Victoria, I believe. The horn was activated with a pull cord that went under the dash, through the firewall, and to the horn mounted on the side of the engine compartment out of sight. We would drive past a herd of cows on the way to Texoma and he would pull that cord, blow the bullhorn, and the cows would come a running! Yee haw!! That never got old. I still may put one in my ranch truck today, if I can find one. Dad and Mom were like that, crazy fun. Whenever there was an idea to be tried, we tried it.

While Dad was in his office at the plant, he began noticing the small private airplanes flying nearby while landing at the local airport in south Dallas called Redbird Airport. He always enjoyed airplanes, and we had those experiences in St. Louis that really set up what was about to happen with Dad's curiosity. One day, he went over to the airport to find out about taking flying lessons. He had found the flight school there, Airhaven Aviation, and met an instructor named Homer French. Homer French—now there is a name for you. Dad began taking flying lessons with Homer (a name that later became more of an adjective than a proper name), flying a Cherokee 140. When he told us he was taking flying lessons, I couldn't believe it. It was so exciting. I remember when he came home one day after having soloed without killing himself. He was alive and excited about getting his private license.

I remember when he successfully completed his solo cross-country flights, passed his written exam, and was preparing for his FAA check ride. When he passed it and had his license, we all celebrated, and I think Homer took us to his favorite bar—he loved bars—called Club Schmitz. It was a legend of a place. A Dallas icon for countless barflies and Dallas-burger-style-fanatics.

So many things were celebrated at Club Schmitz. You name it, we celebrated it at Schmitz. They sold T-shirts that read, "I got Schmitz-faced at Schmitz." Before it closed on the last day of May 2014, I took our son Charlie there to experience one of the last nights it was open, and we sat and enjoyed our last Schmitz burger and fries, drank a pitcher of beer, and I told him those stories of yesteryear. I thought it would be fun to remember all those good times so long ago and share those stories with Charlie. I am very nostalgic, and memorable places have always been a return to destination for me, and that is partly why I am writing this book: the look-back is a look forward.

MY TURN TO CONTINUE OUR FLYING HERITAGE

After Dad got his pilot license and became close friends with Homer, they started doing everything together, along with his wife, Chris, and Bob and Joy Ratzman. Now that was a six-some looking for a place to happen. Homer talked Dad into, or maybe Dad talked Homer into, buying a Cherokee 180 from a watermelon patch on a farm in Ennis, Texas. Dad got a "deal" on it, and he and Homer flew it out of that watermelon patch the short distance to Airhaven at Redbird Airport. I remember that so well.

When they landed and parked the plane in the grass at Airhaven, where it would be tied down for a monthly fee, it was all I could do not to watch that airplane as much as I could afford the drive from north Dallas, where we lived, to the airport. It was close to the plant, so that made it easy when I was there to stop by and make sure N7885W was doing okay sitting there, waiting for someone to take her flying.

I decided it was time for me to start ground school and got Dad's permission to use the plane for lessons with Homer. I took my first lesson and began my instruction logbook when I was sixteen. Ground school was on Wednesday nights from 6:00 p.m. to 9 p.m. for six weeks, and I would drive all the way to Redbird for class. Most of the time Sandee went with me if she wasn't at Wednesday night church with her friends at Northwest Bible Church.

When Homer, who was teaching the class, found out Sandee was sitting in the car for three hours waiting for me, he demanded I bring her into the class. He was so right. Why didn't I think of that? Because I didn't think guests were allowed to attend, I guess, but it was stupid of me, and when she came in and sat next to me, it reminded me of cheating off her in school. But this was different. I needed to learn this stuff. She has always been a math whiz and a critical thinker, so it put me to the test not to make a mistake that she could easily catch, but I didn't want her telling me how to do it.

Some things never change. She liked telling me how to do things, and she still does, because that means we are "working on things together." Well, kinda, but let me do it. I'm the pilot here! She did not want to be a pilot, but she wanted me to be a great pilot, and her attention to detail has been a great model for me and helps slow me down when the chips on the table need to be stacked ever so carefully. I have always been a good multitasker, and that skill is a must-have if you are going to be a pilot and continue flying more complex and advanced aircraft.

After six weeks of those long classes, I went to the FAA and took my written test and passed it on my first attempt. Much more fun than an eight-foot pole vault. With Sandee at my side for this initial training, it taught me the value of appreciating someone else's interest in helping me achieve what I wanted to accomplish. **It was the beginning of understanding collaboration and how a team of two can overcome and dominate any obstacle.**

I began to fly Dad's Cherokee with Homer about once a week for a while, but then life got in the way and my lesson frequency went down. I was graduating from high school, preparing to go to North Texas State University in Denton, and I just didn't have the time or the money to keep taking lessons. Before things got hectic and my flying slowed down, Mom decided to take a try at flight lessons with Homer. She enjoyed it for a while and became a good copilot for Dad, but she didn't finish her private ticket and she didn't even solo. But she sat up front on our trips back to St. Louis, out to Taos, New Mexico, over to Hot Springs, Arkansas, and wherever else we flew.

Mom and Dad both smoked in the airplane, and Jay, Sue, and I were crammed in the back-seat bench designed for two people (Dad added another seat belt to the back seat), inhaling the secondhand smoke and trying not to puke. We had two air vents and three people. Sue got air- and seasick a lot. But we kept on trucking across the Texas skies and, whenever possible, above the cloud layer for smoother and cooler air. It was nice there, and I always remember the Cherokee flights when I am in the smooth, cool air above the clouds.

One routing trip during Dallas Cowboys football season was the Sunday afternoon flight to Lake Texoma Lodge. We would land on that narrow three-thousand-foot runway and walk to the lodge and rent a room for a few hours, only to watch the TV to see the Cowboys play. If the home games weren't sold out, they would block the TV coverage in Dallas, so we would fly out of the area just far enough and yet close enough to catch the TV feed. It was a ruse so we could go fly, but it served its purpose.

One time, landing there, I think we took out a landing light on the end of the runway. I know we took out a tire lining the runway over near Cedar Bayou, where Dad befriended a local landowner so he could land his Cherokee there instead of driving to the lake. He would circle overhead to let the owners of the marina know he was landing and would be ready to be picked up. He would land on the rough grass and dirt "runway" lined with tires painted white that was only about one thousand feet long and barely worked as a runway, until one time, it didn't.

Dad was landing—and I think he was solo because I wasn't there, or maybe he was with Homer, which was probably the case—when they drifted off centerline (there were no centerline markings—maybe some anthills or piles of cow manure) and hit one of the tires lining the runway. The tire bounced up, hit the horizontal stabilizer, and canted it backward, rendering the plane unflyable without some necessary repairs. Dad hired an airframe and power plant mechanic to travel to the tiny private strip and repair the airplane enough for it to fly, with an approved FAA ferry permit, back to Airhaven at Redbird for repairs.

Homer flew it out of there solo to avoid the weight of a passenger and made it to his destination. I have since flown over that long-abandoned "strip" and thought, *How the hell did he get in and out of there with a Cherokee?* It was a tight place to operate an airplane, but it was a challenge accomplished safely, but with damage. **The lesson in this is that you always need a margin of safety in business and in life, just in case your assumptions or execution are flawed.**

LEARNING TO HITCHHIKE WITH STYLE

During high school, our family, and consequently, Sandee and I, spent a lot of time at Texoma. My family joined other families at Tanglewood Lodge one time, and Sandee was back in Dallas, and I didn't have a car. But I had a thumb. I talked Dad into dropping me off at the little grass strip at Tanglewood to see if I might find someone flying out that I could hitch a ride with. I got lucky. Two guys arrived and untied a Cessna Cardinal and prepared it for a flight back to Dallas. They were probably locals, since it was a short flight. I asked if I could hitch a ride so I could get to Dallas to see my girlfriend. They told me to hop in, and that's when I got my only flight ever in a Cessna Cardinal RG. A very cool Cessna with no wing struts and retractable landing gear. It looked really cool in flight. Cessna didn't build a great number of them, but that day I only needed one.

We landed at Addison, and Sandee picked me up. It was great. I went from the lake one night back to my girlfriend by air delivery the next morning. Life was sweet. Very sweet. I just had to get my pilot's license. That wouldn't happen for a few more years. But if you can't be a pilot yet, get friends who are pilots.

During Christmas 1972, Sandee invited me to join her on a church youth group skiing trip to Colorado. She and Laura and the entire Sherman family were deeply involved at Northwest Bible Church, located at the corner of Northwest Highway and the Dallas North Tollway in Dallas. She was involved most Sundays and Wednesday nights when the youth would worship, have fun, and do Christian youth group activities. I would wait patiently for Sandee to get dropped off at her house on those Wednesday nights. There I was, waiting for her, sitting on her front step next to the window of her room. When she asked me to go on the ski trip with her and all her church friends, I was excited about the offer, but I had to talk my parents into it. They agreed to pay the $300 for the trip, which included the eighteen-hour bus ride, the church camp for housing, the meals, and other expenses.

I'll never forget the night we left, and the entire trip and its importance in my life. This was an opportunity to fit in with other teenagers, including my girlfriend, in a safe and fun environment, to get real-life lessons as told by solid church leaders and a peer group who I had some things in common with. It was exciting riding on the bus, sitting right next to Sandee all the way there. When the sun was rising after the all-night ride, everyone was excited to see the Rocky Mountains and was looking forward to learning how to ski and all the events they had planned. I had never been on a teen trip before, and the adventure is a lasting memory that I deeply cherish.

We went to a Christian camp near a small ski resort called Geneva Basin. Nearby was the camp we stayed at, and in the evenings, there were Bible lessons and singing and a lot of eating. I was not a believing Christian at that point in my life yet. I had been raised through the Methodist Church because of Dad's commitment for us to do so, but I hadn't heard the relationship message that comes with the Christian faith. I was a high school boy with a girlfriend and was a perfect prospect for a faith conversion.

During that trip, one evening after dinner, the youth pastor and I went to the little worship center and sat upstairs in the back row, and it was there that he led me through the prayer of salvation, and I accepted Christ as my Savior. I kind of knew what it meant, but as with all newborn believers, it is an unfolding process. When we got home from the trip, I was counted as one of the many who had accepted Christ on the trip, and almost as importantly, I felt I was part of a group of new friends, who had been Sandee's friends, and now I was part of that crazy bunch of guys but was never one of the popular people at Northwest. I was there for Sandee, and in the process, Jesus found me.

7

*Heading to college, getting dumped,
surviving with five jobs, getting a new girlfriend,
how to hitchhike, New Jersey, blinded,
getting a real job, parking lot sweeper,
Villa Capri Motor Hotel*

After graduating from W.T. White in May 1973, it was time to get serious about college. Sandee had already applied to and been accepted to Baylor University, a very expensive private school in Waco, Texas. She had some friends go there, and Si was stepping up to afford her a full ride to get her a great college education. I was not in the same fortunate circumstance and knew I would not be going to Baylor. It was a sad reality that we were parting to different schools, and she was on to other higher college experiences. I had to work and did not get to the fun part of college until I was a second-semester junior five years later, after she had already graduated.

Dad made a deal with all three of us kids, and it did not pan out, at least not for me. His deal was that he would put up an equal amount of money to what I would earn each summer to cover expenses at school. I wasn't able to make enough in ten weeks to make a hill of beans. But he piled on more beans, and off I went to school, broke. The money I had bought about half of my books and the dorm room for a semester. Every other expense was on me to figure out. That original concept was reasonable on paper, but only if I could make $1,000 per week during the summer. Instead, I made about $100 a week.

My first paycheck at O-I for a full day of work was about $14. So I didn't have much of a chance. But I planned on applying to school, then figuring it out.

Sometimes you have to have faith that you will be able to figure it out while you are figuring it out. It can be done; you just need to figure out a way.

I had applied to North Texas State University in Denton, Texas, just thirty miles north of Dallas. I was accepted in time to begin fall classes. It was a good school, the third largest in the state of Texas, and a lot of kids from White went there after high school, but I couldn't afford to live there or keep up with the social existence there, or anywhere else for that matter. I couldn't afford the dormitory, so I commuted my first year.

The thirty-mile drive each way to Denton wasn't too bad, though the gas bills put a dent in me, but I was able to keep my job at Kinney's Shoes at Northpark Mall. My schedule was brutal. I had 8:00 a.m. classes until 3:00 p.m., then drove back to Dallas to get to work for the 5:00 p.m. to 9:00 p.m. shift, then went home and studied until I fell asleep and began the same schedule the next day with a 5:00 a.m. alarm. I could not help thinking about how my life was changing and how reality was setting in and the real idea that, at this rate, I wouldn't be able to keep up with Sandee.

That proved to be true. She was on to the life of a Baylor Bear and joined a sorority, became a fraternity sweetheart, and met a lot of new friends. For the first year, from the fall of 1973 to the summer of 1974, I did my best to go to her functions at Baylor, and she did her best to include me, but it was not going to work out. I could not keep up the financial pace or the geographic challenges one hundred and ten miles away with a car that needed constant maintenance. It did not help that Sandee's first roommate was dating a rich kid whose parents were from Oklahoma oil money. He drove a Porsche, and I drove a broken-down Mustang. He had cash and credit; I had neither. He had the clothes and the swagger; I had myself and my drive to survive, and hopefully keep my Baylor girlfriend, but I knew it would not last.

During my freshman year at North Texas, I was driving all of the time, so I would make random trips to Baylor to see Sandee, but I simply was beginning to resent the school because it wasn't a place for me, but my girl was there, and I felt left out.

My parents were having marital problems, and Dad turned down another promotion, which would have moved the family back to the O-I home office in Toledo. After a crazy trip to London to discuss the move and to get away from the corporate noise to talk about it, Dad agreed, at the request of Mom, to leave the company to keep our family in Texas. That was a bad decision. After twenty-three years at O-I and at a growth apex in his career, Dad resigned from O-I. He helped justify it by agreeing to try to launch a competitor to O-I and create a blow mold company to produce plastic fifty-gallon drums, which are commonplace today, but not in 1975.

Dick Langdon, another family friend who worked on the customer and sales side of O-I, agreed to also leave the company and help Dad in the search for one million dollars to get things started. They traveled to the UK to look at a machine that would be moved to Texas to start the company. The machine cost $1,000,000. Dick and Dad didn't have the money and didn't know how to raise it, and that really caught my attention because I wanted Dad to succeed with the new company. They ran out of time and what little money they had. Dad had to take a job for Igloo in Houston in 1975.

When the family, including Jay and Sue, moved to Houston, I moved into Kerr Hall at North Texas. I was finally on campus, but my family was beginning to fall apart, and my girlfriend was in Baylor life in Waco. I remember going home to Houston to figure out how I was going to survive after the current semester at North Texas. A friend of my parents suggested I apply at a popular restaurant in west Houston called the Mason Jar.

When I came home for the summer in 1975, I applied and was hired that day. But before the summer and the job started, Sandee invited me to a spring sorority function that was in San Antonio. I had to find a suit to wear, find some pretty clothes to fit in with the Baylor elite, and make the drive from Houston to San Antonio. I didn't fit in, and I knew it. I was the out-of-town, had-been boyfriend. I didn't have the chops to climb into the Baylor private school social culture, and I didn't want to. It seemed fake to me. Get a job and earn it yourself was how I grew up. I was a working kid; no time or resources to party and wait for summer.

By the fall of 1975, Sandee told me, on the telephone of all places, that she wanted to "date other people." That meant she already had another boyfriend. And she did. I tried to talk her out of it. It scared me. We had always been together, and I felt a need to protect her from anyone else as she was my rock, my surrogate to a normal world outside a home that was crumbling around me. Now I was facing the humiliation of losing the only girl I ever had, who I had grown up with, without the resources to stop it from happening. And because I wasn't there, she already had a rich new boyfriend in place before I really understood I was being given my walking papers. Always have a replacement before you get rid of anything, I guess.

I learned this by going by her parents' house to see her one weekend, and a different car was in the driveway. I knocked on the door and was greeted by Sandee and her new boyfriend. I couldn't handle it. This was out of line. So, I grabbed him by the shirt and tried to get him out on the porch, where I could give him a fifty-five gallon of whoop-ass to remind him that he was making a big mistake. He chickened out, and I think I ripped his shirt.

Sandee's mother came to the door. I'll never forget hearing her say, "David, hit the road!" So, I did. I went to work for my waiter shift at Chandler Landing's Yacht Club in a completely bewildered daze. Like I had been shot out of a cannon and no safety net was at the landing site.

It took me a long time to get over getting dumped by my only girlfriend since ninth grade for a rich bum a year older than her, going through dental school. A dentist? Really? Is that all you got?

I leaned on all my friends for support, and I had to cover myself in work to make ends meet. I was just plain lost without her. In order to help myself, I began a chart I put on the wall of our dorm room. I was wanting to give myself some inspiration and personal determination to climb out of the loss and get back on my feet. I started to measure my happiness every day on a scale of one to one hundred, so I would have some tangible (if you can numerically measure emotion) way of seeing my way up the curve to whatever emotional recovery would be. I needed money, and I needed help, and I needed to stay in school as much as I could. So, I worked. A lot.

I returned to Houston from school that summer and started working as many shifts as I could at the Mason Jar. I stayed in touch with Mark, who was still at Texas Tech University, but he and Mona had broken up, and she had transferred to Baylor to hook up with Sandee, and Mark had moved back to Dallas.

Unimpressed with life as a Texas Tech student, Mark began his corporate work life. In the fall of 1975, I stayed in Houston and kept working at the Mason Jar, saving my money and living at home. I also worked at a start-up gym, selling memberships, anything for a dollar. By the time the spring semester started in 1976, I had enough money to move back to Denton to keep living with Randy in his parent-paid-for apartment while I worked on getting my head back into classes.

At one point, I was sharing my car with my brother. I had sold my Mustang to an auto mechanic school for cash. I then bought a canary-yellow 1970 Chevy Nova. I ended up sharing it with Jay, so 50 percent of the time I was hitchhiking or riding a ten-speed bike that I bought for $10 off someone's porch in Denton. My roommate in the dorm, Randy Smith, decided to move to an apartment. When he did, I followed him to that apartment as a roommate. The great deal was that he really wanted to live with his girlfriend Lucy, so he moved in with her without telling his parents. They kept paying his rent at the apartment I was living in, so I had a two-bedroom apartment to myself for half price. It was a very good deal, and I took full advantage of it. I needed it for the business I was about to start so I could survive.

I still needed to work. So, I began stacking work gigs. I got a job as a desk clerk at the hotel that was on the I-35 frontage road right behind my apartment building. I checked people in, and I checked people out. I took reservations and operated the old-time telephone operator's switch station, connecting each call mechanically by plugging and unplugging various lines into the station. Very circa 1940s, but it was the commercial business phone system still in existence in the seventies. I loved using it. Very task rewarding, connecting and disconnecting a call. There, check that one off the list. Oh, another one calling in; that connects over here. Got it.

The owner of the hotel was Ann Savage. She was a resourceful woman who had her whole family living in the back room with her. Her husband worked maintenance and worked at the steakhouse restaurant in the parking lot, also a part of the hotel. The Villa Capri Motor Hotel, it was called. I got a paycheck that didn't bounce every Friday. I opened a checking account at the nearest bank I could walk to, just off the highway at what is now a major intersection on I-35 in Denton.

I also went to the Denton airport to see if I could get a job there while I was also working at the hotel and going to school. I was hired as a line service boy, fueling airplanes, sweeping hangars, taking out the trash, running the inventory on airplanes parked at the airport, refueling the fuel trucks, washing airplanes; you name it, I did it, and I loved every minute of it. Except my schedule. It was a nightmare. I never took less than fifteen hours of classes because I needed to finish and get on with life. I had no girlfriend, no real money, was behind in school, and rode a bike most of the places I went. But I was still in school. I was going to finish my degree, and no one was going to stop me. Someone had gotten my girl, but they wouldn't ruin my life, and I was the one that I must rely on the most. I needed to figure it out, and piece by piece, inch by inch, I made progress.

I found it helpful to view progress in inches or millimeters if that was what it took to feed my sense of progress. The difference between hot water and a steam locomotive is a one-degree increase in temperature, and that is what I was going for. Find enough progress to create a whole new dynamic of power in my thinking and in my daily living. It is amazing how challenges can change you from the inside out. You wouldn't believe how much power is in you simply by believing you can do it. A person who never gives up is impossible to beat.

My classes were at 8:00 a.m. Mondays, Wednesdays, and Fridays and 9:00 a.m. on Tuesdays and Thursdays. During the week, my hotel shift started as soon as I was out of classes, usually around 4:00 p.m. until 10 p.m. Then I went to the airport for the night shift, sometimes until just before my 8:00 a.m. classes. I usually went to school in my dirty airport uniform. I flunked Spanish. I would fall asleep in class. Can you say "adios"? It was my 8:00 a.m. class, and I had to take it again the next semester.

I had so many weird things happen at that hotel. They should have a reality show on TV about working the night shift at the Villa Capri Motor Hotel. I had to lock the doors at night because of the riff-raff coming off the highway, looking to rent a hotel room with no money. One afternoon a young couple who had been living at the hotel—that's right, living at the hotel one day at a time—called down to my switchboard and told me they were getting married. Today. Right now. The bride told me that the preacher was on the way, and her parents would be there soon. Everyone showed up in less than thirty minutes, including the bride and groom, the parents, the friends, and the preacher. I, of course, was working in shorts and flip flops and became the wedding photographer, using a plastic Instamatic 110 Polaroid camera.

When the ceremony started, right in front of the desk where I was still answering calls, a truck pulled up to the front door. It was an eighteen-wheeler unloading supplies for the steakhouse in the parking lot. The truck doors were slamming, carts were rambling, guys were hollering at each other, unloading stuff. The noise was close by the glass windows separating them from the wedding party inside. I took a picture of the bride's father watching how they were managing the unloading process instead of watching his daughter getting married. I thought that might be a conversation photo whenever they developed the pictures that I took.

When the wedding was over, everyone left, and the couple went back to their room for their honeymoon, I guess. The only thing missing was the shotgun. But my desk operations never slowed down. Ann never knew the wedding had taken place as she was somewhere else when it all happened in less than an hour. I think she found out later, when the happy couple "checked out" finally. But nothing seemed to faze Ann, as she just kept rolling with the punches of running a motor inn on the side of the highway in a college town.

One night I got a series of wake-up call requests from several of our hotel guests. I wrote them down, room by room, and the times they wanted me to call them. The calls started at 4:30 a.m. and went to 7:00 a.m. During the night, I fell asleep at my post. I woke up at 7:15 a.m. So, I started dialing each room and told them it was their wake-up call. I got blasted by Ann for that, but hey, at least I made my 8:00 a.m. class. But Ann knew I was a struggling college kid and was dependable. She would ask me to do family favors for her, and I could usually barter a porterhouse steak from her that I could eat off for a week or so. I was always trying to figure out how to survive.

In those situations, you really learn to depend on yourself. No handouts. Figure it out. Fix it. Keep going, and don't give up.

And somehow I stayed in school.

I added to my airport and hotel jobs by getting weekend shifts working for Mark at Chandler's Landing Yacht Club in Rockwall, Texas. It was over an hour's drive from Denton. But most of the time, I did not have a car. So, on Friday afternoons, I hitchhiked the seventy-five miles to make it to Chandler's in time for my 6:00 p.m. to 10:00 p.m. shift. I learned how to hitchhike with on-time results. Rules of the road included trying to get a ride with someone with a CB (citizen's band) radio. The driver could usually show off by calling other "breaker one-nines" to get a pickup for further down the road. That worked great with truckers; they loved making that coordination work. "Breaker one-nine, I got a college kid carrying some hang-up clothes and a tennis racket, trying to get to I-30 East. East bounders, ya got your ears on?" they would broadcast to anyone listening.

"Yeah, I got ya, breaker. Where are you dropping off the preppy load? I can scoop him up on the haul eastbound," someone would respond.

"Well, I'll leave him at marker 167 under the bridge at the LBJ freeway. You cain't miss him; he's got on shorts, a ball cap, and tennis shoes, and he's carrying a couple of shirts along with his tennis racket. Not sure where the hell he's going, but he looks like he's going for fun." They would back build the storyline for me so others would pick me up. They would explain it on the CB radio. But I wasn't hitchhiking for fun travel. It was work, it was survival, and I was a hitchhiker.

NO CAR AND NO PLACE TO STAY

At the yacht club, I needed a place to stay after my dinner shift. For a place to sleep, I borrowed a boat from a club member when he was not there. I used the locker room showers in the resort to clean up before members got there. If the family I borrowed the boat from was using their boat when I was working, I slept on the floor in the locker room, using tablecloths as bedding and locker room towels for my pillow. The sauna was a suitable place to sleep after it cooled down. I have Mark to thank for the boat connection as he did the asking, and sometimes we both needed to stay on the boat.

I would work two double shifts on Saturday and Sunday, then hitchhike the fifty miles back to Denton in time for my Monday morning eight o'clock class. That semester the eight-a.m.-er was Sales Management. I could not miss a class, or it was a full letter grade off. If you missed three classes, the best grade you could get was a D. It was a lesson in Sales 101. **If you ain't on time, you ain't getting the sale.**

I only missed one of those classes all semester. It was a race to get back to Denton on Sunday nights. One night, out on LBJ, I needed a good handoff to make it up I-35 to Denton. A Volkswagen pulled over to pick me up. When I opened the door, the driver was Homer French! I could not believe it! My flight instructor was picking me up to take me to Denton. But instead, Homer drove me about five miles up the road and let me out on I-35. It was his exit to go home, and he did not have time to drive me to Denton. As his VW taillights disappeared in the distance, I had my thumb back out, trying to make it to class by morning.

A few minutes later, a big weird-looking truck with two guys in it pulled over to pick me up. I had my clothes hanging on a mile marker and had to go grab it while the shotgun rider waited for me with the door open. I jumped up in the cab with my clothes and my tennis racket (Mark and I would play tennis at lunch between shifts to break up the day a little bit) and we were off down the highway around midnight.

After a few miles, the driver said that we were going to make a stop, and he didn't say where or why. We pulled off in Lewisville, turned west, and drove a couple of miles before turning into a parking lot with a big-box store there. We drove behind the store into even more darkness and stopped the truck. Freaked out, I prepared to fight my way out with my tennis racket. The shotgun rider got out, then the driver got out, and I was sitting there alone. My class started in five and a half hours. I didn't have time for this. Whatever this was.

Then the driver climbed back inside and told me to reach over and close the door on the passenger side. I thought about getting out and just running into the darkness, but I didn't. When I shut the door, the shotgun rider guy appeared in the headlights with a broom and yelled, "Okay, you're good! Let 'er roll!"

The driver reached down and pushed some levers on the floor, and the entire truck began to shake. Then we started moving forward, lurching little by little toward the guy out front who was sweeping trash off the curb. Then I realized that I had been picked up by a sweeper truck, and we had to sweep this big-box store parking lot before continuing to Denton. What a relief! When we got done, we went on to Denton, where I had time to take a shower and change clothes before jumping on my $10 bike to ride to class. I did whatever it took to survive.

I got picked up hitchhiking by a county sheriff's deputy and his family in the middle of the night once. That was a comforting ride, and they were very friendly. For no extra charge, I got a good scolding from the deputy about the dangers of hitchhiking. I told him the dangers if I did not hitchhike, like dropping out of school. He took me right to my apartment door, and I was thankful.

I got picked up on a short hitchhike home from campus by a teacher, and when he asked me where I lived, I jumped out of the car at a stop sign to get away from the creepy guy. Another time, I got picked up on the highway by a Christian couple who were very nice and gave me a little gospel revival on my way home. That is always appreciated. I survived all those encounters, but it was all because I had no other way to get around much of the time.

I couldn't help thinking about hitchhiking in the night with my clothes on a mile marker while my girlfriend was comfortably gallivanting around with her boyfriend at Baylor. It was triple motivation for me to crawl out of this existence. When I worked at the hotel, from time to time one of my old dormitory roommates would drop by to see me. Chris Nichols and I were suitemates in my first semester at Kerr Hall, and I introduced Chris to Laura Sherman. They were dating, and Laura never lost touch with Sandee, but I did not want to hear about her or anything she was doing. I had moved on, so I did not really care. I needed to live my life and still needed to finish school.

In the summer of 1976, my parents moved to Middletown, New Jersey. Dad had moved on from the days at Igloo in Houston, where he was part of the development team for the Igloo cooler, called the Playmate. He had been fired by a guy at the top of the company because of some internal politics. When I found out, I drove to Igloo to find the guy. I never made it past the parking lot guard, but I tried to get Dad's job back for him so we could return to whatever normal was for our family.

When he and Mom finally landed in New Jersey, Dad was working for Midland Glass near Newark. Middletown was a fine community in a beautiful part of New Jersey. Dad bought the house without Mom ever seeing it first, which in my view is always a bad idea. But it was a cool house.

For a while during the summer of '76 our whole family was there together. Jay was working at a marina, doing the boating work lifestyle that he always loved, and Sue was working a summer job and tending to her horse named Joe. Joe had been relocated from Texas by horse haulers during the move and arrived by truck on a cold, icy day around the holidays.

I was there with Sue when Joe arrived. She backed Joe out of the trailer onto the ice and Joe was unsteady, but he figured it out. We had gone from Texans to folks living in New Jersey. Geez! We all missed Texas, and the drive from Texas to NJ was a bit brutal.

My first summer trip to NJ to live at home and get a job did not start as planned. I could not find a job that I wanted, and I didn't have much time to find the right one. I applied everywhere, even if I did not have the skills, interest, or training to do the job. I needed a paycheck. I applied to be a brake specialist at an automotive repair station. The hiring manager asked me if I had ever worked on brakes. I told him I did a lot of it. He asked me where, and I said in my garage. He asked me what kind of brake systems I was familiar with working on. I told him most of them, but some were easier than others. He wanted details. I had none. I was told goodbye.

I finally got a job at an apartment complex as a lifeguard. I got it through a contact my mother had from somewhere. It was a long drive from home to those apartments and was a very lonely job. One apartment complex pool had a bunch of parents who just stared at me. So, I tried to change things up and find some extra cash. I offered swimming lessons. I had never given a swimming lesson in my life. The moms brought all their children—babies and teenagers. One teenybopper took an affinity to me and wouldn't leave me alone. She even invited me to her family's apartment for her birthday. I decided to go because of the goodwill it would bring to my "classes." I was nineteen, and she was about fifteen, and it was awkward when she came and, without asking or being invited, sat on my lap with her arms around me like I was hers. We sang happy birthday to whatever her name was, and I left. About two days later, our next-door neighbor's son-in-law reached out to me. His name was Matt Freibaum.

Matt is a game changer in my life's story. Matt was married to the daughter of Dick and Joan Noble, who were very close friends of my parents. Their daughter, Janet Lynn, and Matt had been married a short time when Matt had a contract to run the Marlboro Township swimming complex, complete with five pools, a swim team, twelve lifeguards, tennis courts, and a snack bar. I had met Matt earlier when I came up for the summer, but we never really talked much. When I told him I was in a dead-end lifeguard job in an apartment complex, he asked me if I'd be interested in being his assistant manager and helping him run the Marlboro swim club. I couldn't wait to say yes! I started the next day.

Oh, what a summer that was. We worked seven days a week, and it was a blast. Matt and I got along great, and he became a mentor of mine and was a nice buffer between me and his father, Jack Freibaum, who was the main boss over the management contract. He was a piece of work, but Matt dealt with him, and I dealt with five hundred private members and their families and managed our lifeguards, which turned out to be some good fortune, as I met a girl who became very special to me, Terri Sue Miller. She was an identical twin to her sister, Kathi. Since we worked together every day, we got to know and enjoy each other a lot. She was an outstanding swimmer, qualified for Junior Olympics, and was recruited by Florida State University while Kathi was recruited by Auburn University. Their parents, Leroy "Bud" and Jean Miller, lived in Tinton Falls, which was exactly five miles from my parents' house in Middletown.

When I started enjoying distance running, I began to run to Terri's house and after a while could make the return trip for a ten-miler before going to meet Terri at the pool to work all day. We were there from 10:00 a.m. to 9:00 p.m. and sometimes later. For once, during that summer, things became fun and not the beating of survival that I had become used to at school. I had to teach her about country music and all my favorites, and she looked forward to getting to Texas one day. But for now, I had a swim club to run.

All the lifeguards reported to me, so I was making their schedules, assigning pool chemical and maintenance checks, and overseeing the required equipment and training we had to comply with under our contract. One time I was repairing a chlorinator and 100 percent chlorine accidentally sprayed into both of my eyes. I made it to one of our pools and jumped in to begin flushing my eyes with fresh water. They called an ambulance, and I ended up at home that night with both eyes covered and wrapped for twenty-four hours. Terri came over to help me make some dinner and thought it was funny to move some of the furniture around so I would trip over it. Funny, that girl.

When they took the bandages off my eyes the next day, I could see just fine. But being bandaged and not seeing for twenty-four hours was, well, dare I say, eye opening. Mistakes and bad things can happen very quickly, particularly when you don't really know what you are doing. So I went back to the swim club to change the procedures for fixing chlorination problems so that it wouldn't happen to anyone else

I was also in charge of WSI training. The Water Safety Instructor designation was necessary for commercial pool operations. This was the first time I was exposed to someone else's rules and regulations, and I was such a rookie, I didn't know what to worry about first, so I figured the safety and survival of all members had to be near the top of the list. That was something I could figure out how to manage. I had gotten my WSI when I was a Boy Scout, but I am sure it had expired or I no longer qualified. I ran the program and added some of my own techniques to keep the team sharp.

One of my maintenance guys, Arlen Forst, was a great kid. I loved Arlen. He helped me, and I helped him. Arlen had been hit by a car while riding his bicycle when he was a young boy, and his back was badly scarred from going through the windshield of the vehicle. He usually worked with his shirt off, and his back was a constant reminder of the dangers of everyday life. I had an idea that I needed Arlen's help with. I wanted to see if we could enact a simulated rescue, using Arlen as the drowning victim. I was interested to see if one of my guards would pick up on it in a sea of kids in a crowded pool. This one guard/kid spent more time talking with the girls out of the pool than he did watching the kids who were in the pool. His name was Neil.

I told Arlen to go into the pool at the far end and make his way slowly through the other swimmers and begin having trouble in the water right in front of Neil. He did an Academy Award–winning performance, only Neil didn't see it. He was clueless. So, I had Terri ready to dive in and "save" Arlen. When she dove in to get Arlen, I walked over to Neil and yelled at him to see if he had a clue what was going on. I told Neil to go home for the day, and I changed the rotation around to fill the gap of one less lifeguard. It was a wake-up call to everyone that this was serious stuff.

The responsibility of serving and protecting others, as in lifeguarding, requires a seriousness to the attention that it requires. You have to make finding those in distress a priority, as in a Big Deal, above anything else. If you want something to be a big deal, then make it a big deal.

It served another purpose a few days later when I was in trouble after a high-dive accident.

The other side of protecting others is to also protect yourself. It made great sense to reprimand a lifeguard for not seeing what he was responsible for seeing, but when we do something that will cause unintentional personal harm to ourselves, which then requires others to intervene and save you, then maybe that was something that shouldn't have been attempted in the first place.

I had been taking diving lessons and really wanted to learn a two-and-a-half somersault dive off the high-dive board. As I got closer to the full two-and-a-half turns, it started to get dangerous for this rookie. We were at the diving tank that was up on an elevated hill, and I had a couple of guards there working with us, including Terri. I attempted the best dive I could make but did not get the full rotation and hit the water flat on my face one-quarter of a turn short. It was more of a two-and-a-smash. I was barely treading water and could not feel the left side of my body. I needed help staying afloat.

Terri and another guard dove in and pulled me to the side of the pool, then somehow got me out of the water to sit at the edge for a few minutes. Just then, Arlen walked up the stairs to the pool to tell me someone was on the phone, calling about my car that was for sale. I looked at Arlen and said, "What car?" I couldn't even remember what car I had. I was really dazed.

I made it to my office and stayed there the rest of the day, and life went on for everyone there. This was another good lesson in sticking with what you know, but sometimes you don't know that you don't know until you try new things. Pro diving, along with pole vaulting, was also not in my future.

As the summer began to wind down, I began making plans to drive back to Texas to go back to Denton. Since the newspaper gig was doing well, I had ample shifts at the airport and the hotel, and I was bartending at Doc Holliday's on Tuesday nights. I figured I had time to start a side business of my own. I had a friend in the art department that had also gone to W.T. White, and we stayed in touch in Denton. I had decided that I wanted to start a company to sell pre-popped popcorn to bars on Thursdays and Fridays to increase their weekend beer sales. Salty popcorn needs a cold refreshing beer, and I worked up a sales pitch, including projections for their sales for each order of popcorn. That was the easy part; it was just a guess but made sense, and they were willing to try ordering from me to see if it did increase sales. The harder part, at least initially, was getting the popcorn.

I did not have full time use of my car as Jay was sharing it with me, so I found a popcorn distributor in downtown Dallas where I could buy exceptionally large bags of pre-popped popcorn. The vendor would fill the bags with popcorn and then shoot nitrogen in each bag before sealing it to keep it fresh. It was amazing. I could make one exceptionally large trash sack full of popcorn last a month, and it still tasted like I just popped it.

I opened a second checking account under the name of the Super Pop Popcorn Company. I ordered a car full of popcorn, and when it was my turn with the car, I drove to Dallas to pick up a load. Over a span of three weeks, I was able to fill Randy's side of the apartment with inventory ready to be sold. He was never there, so his bedroom became my warehouse. You could smell the popcorn outside of the apartment. I had Gayle Spraggins, my art friend, paint about ten different large tin canisters with different logos that would go to each bar or restaurant I sold to so they could rent the tin from me and purchase the popcorn. I charged $3.50 per week for the tin rental and $6.50 per week for a single fill-up of popcorn. That made it easy on Fridays to deliver popcorn and pick up a check for $10. With ten accounts, that was $100 per week I put in my pocket before hitchhiking to Rockwall to work at Chandler's Landing for the weekend. An extra $400 a month in popcorn sales was a stroke of passion and luck.

Sales kept increasing, and I had requests for more. I should have charged more and paid someone else with a car to deliver, so all I had to do was shake a hand and pick up a check. I should have raised the price until the customers quit buying it, then backed it down to where they would buy it. It would have been more than $10, but I could not take the risk that they might tell me to get lost. The other benefit of all that popcorn in Randy's side of the apartment was it was easy to snack on and reduced my living expenses for meals. I was living off popcorn and Shake-and-Bake chicken.

Everything was going great until Randy called me and said his parents were coming for the weekend to visit. We had to make it look like Randy did live there with me. I put all the popcorn in my room and anywhere else I could stack and stash it. Randy came by and put some clothes in his closet, spilled some toothpaste in the bathroom, cluttered things up, and I left so he could enjoy their stay. I never saw them. After they left, we went back to the normal popcorn warehouse arrangement, and I didn't see Randy again for a month, as usual. He did leave a gray suit in the closet that, at the time, was too big for me, but in a pinch, when I needed a suit, I wore it.

THE UNRAVELING OF A FAMILY

During the summer of 1977, Mom and Dad were on the cusp of a divorce. For the past two summers when I was working in Marlboro, I saw truly little of either of them for weeks at a time. Dad was working in Newark; Mom was doing her thing; Jay was at the marina; and Sue was with her horse. I was at the swim club every day, seven days a week, and I had three more semesters to go back in Texas. It was mono y mono, baby.

During that summer of 1977, one morning, Dad asked to talk with me before we went our separate ways for the day. We were in the backyard in Middletown, sitting on the picnic table not far from the back door. It was a split-level house, and for the short time our family called that home, we had compiled some nice memories. As Mom and Dad usually did, they were part of a neighborhood energy that produced crazy fun times. Peggy Gasmire later recalled that when the Gasmires landed in Middletown, the neighborhood was never the same. Like the riding lawn mower parade that neighbors competed on for awards. There were awards for best decorated, most agile mower, fastest mower, and on and on. When Jay was home from college, he stayed in the basement bedroom, so no one ever saw him unless he was in trouble with the parents of the next-door neighbor's daughter.

Soon after that discussion with Dad telling us that he and Mom were divorcing, we were not surprised to learn that Mom and a neighbor friend of our family, Peggy Rusche, had gone to a bar one night, and Mom met a bartender from England named Tim Foley. The family dynamics were coming off the rails. Our little family of five was scrambling each to their own home turf, without any huddle up among who was left to see if we were still a family. It was a terribly difficult time.

Tim had been a professional butler/attendant for affluent families in England, had a charming British accent, and a crazy, I-don't-know-what-to-do-next lifestyle, and I think that reeled Mom in. They were preparing to run away together, but we didn't know it until after the divorce that summer when we learned that she and Tim had gotten married and moved to Florida. Jay, Sue, and I were not invited to the wedding. We didn't even know when or where it happened. I was devastated by it, and so was Sue.

While that was all unfolding, Dad and Peggy began spending more time together. So that summer ended with Mom running off with Tim, Dad hanging out with Peggy, Jay enjoying many relationships, Sue hanging on, trying to figure out which parent to go with, and me heading back to school, always wishing Sandee and I had never broken up. Sue went with Dad, and they moved to Langhorne, Pennsylvania, when Dad changed jobs again. They were living there when I graduated from North Texas. If we had not had those few short years in New Jersey, and had I not worked summers there and gotten to know Matt Freibaum, the rest of my life would have been very different.

It is amazing how one new friend or acquaintance at just the right time and in just the right way can have such a dramatic, life-changing impact. Pay attention to these opportunities that God puts in front of you. It just might be the path to the road He wants you on. That is what my intersection with Matt produced in my life.

Dad wouldn't have met Peggy, and I wouldn't have begun a career in health care that I have now been in since 1979.

DIGGING INTO A MAJOR THAT WOULD LAST A LIFETIME

I changed my major one more time before my senior year, and it did not disrupt the timing of my graduation. I moved to Advertising under Professor Ernestine Farr. She was formidable and busted my chops every chance she could because she knew I would respond to it. She got me an internship at a prestigious advertising agency in Dallas called Glenn,

Bozell, and Jacobs. It was an impressive opportunity. I put on Randy's suit every Monday and found a way to get to Dallas for my one day a week as an advertising flunky. I was assigned to the Pearl Beer account. Perfect for a college kid.

We also worked on Tex-Sun Fruit Juices and OlinCraft Paper Products. We worked on all three, but Pearl was a favorite of the firm. I started working in accounting, with no accounting experience, not a single accounting class in college. Not sure how I got away with that. I changed majors so many times I outran that curriculum requirement. Once I survived the accounting work, they moved me in to work for Pete Mitchell, a rising star, as an account executive. He became my boss, and we got along great. He sent me to "Traffic," which is the department that schedules media buys and placements. It is where the best type of medium and best time and way to reach the customer target audience are decided.

When you saw an ad on TV that interested you, the traffic group knew that and sold that space at that time and for that product. It was genius, and I liked it, but I was only there on Mondays, and I did not get paid for it. A business model to consider: have part-time help. Do not pay them anything but the experience, and absolutely don't put them in charge of anything. But Professor Farr expected important things from me and got me placed there, and I wasn't going to let her down.

I wore out Randy's gray suit because I wore it every Monday and could not afford to have it cleaned. When my gig at Glenn, Bozell, and Jacobs ended, I began to interview with ad agencies in Dallas. Professor Farr got me in the door here and there, but it was getting harder to reliably make it to the interviews downtown without a car and wearing an unfitted, borrowed suit. I felt like a pioneer in the 1800s, sending letters or telegrams saying I might make it home in the spring of next year. Or maybe, if winter wasn't too rough, I might be able to be in town by late summer.

I had no reliable way of being on time and prepared for any important events. The kids from other schools with money were beating me to the punch. My brother Jay had an old pickup truck. Homer French had sold him a row of airline seats from an old Boeing 727, and Jay put them in the back of the truck as a platform for Skylab cruising. Skylab was a satellite that was losing its geo-referenced orbit and was scheduled to reenter the earth's atmosphere and disintegrate. Jay painted the words "Skylab Cruiser" on the side of the truck and drove his friends, mostly girls, around for fun. I had to borrow the Skylab Cruiser to go to an interview during a hot-weather month before graduation. It did not have air conditioning, and Randy's suit was beginning to fall apart from wear.

I drove to downtown Dallas for an interview with a prestigious ad agency. The interview went horribly wrong. I looked like a street person who stole clothes off a friend. Which is exactly who I was. I did not even get a second look. I drove the Skylab Cruiser back to Denton to work on my popcorn business and get ready for graduation. My family and Terri were coming to town, so I had to get my act together. But I didn't know what I was going to do after graduation. My school income at the paper was going to be gone, and I could not hitchhike to Rockwall anymore; it was wearing me out. So, I reached out to O-I to get shifts working in the warehouse on the weekends. Then, the neighbor's son-in- law and my summer boss, Matt Freibaum, called me again, and everything changed.

FROM THE WAREHOUSE TO A NEW YORK STOCK EXCHANGE COMPANY

Just a few days before all my graduation activities were to take place, including commencement and a big party at Club Schmitz in Dallas, followed by staying at the home of Homer and Chris French, I reached out to Matt Freibaum again. Matt had gone on from working at the Marlboro Swim Club with his father to bigger and better things, and he wanted to invite me to the company he had joined. It was Arnar-Stone Laboratories. He asked me if I would be interested in getting an interview. I didn't understand what the job was, really, but he did say something about selling drugs. Matt explained that Arnar-Stone was a division of American Hospital Supply Corporation (AHSC), and they manufactured drugs used in doctors' offices and hospitals. He asked me again, "Would you like to sell drugs?" I told him that I believed I could sell anything to anybody at any time.

He said, "I know you can; that is why I think you should interview. It is a great company."

When I had that telephone conversation with Matt, I was at the home of Homer and Chris French, and Terri had just left town after my graduation. A couple of days later I told her that I might have an interview with a big company for a nice job, but I would probably have to move from Dallas. She still had two years left at FSU but was very interested in how this job opportunity would play out for me, and potentially, for us. But there was a development that I had not anticipated that made all of this, in retrospect, a very difficult situation.

One night, before my last semester of school, during a dinner shift at Chandler's, in the middle of the serving rush of a busy kitchen, restaurant, and bar, Chef James yelled at me that I had a phone call. I was extremely busy, and who the hell would be calling me now? All my friends were here working with me, and I didn't have time to have a phone conversation. A few minutes later, as I recall, the call dropped, and I had not gotten to it in time. Chef James then told me the caller had called back, so on my way out the kitchen door with someone's chicken kiev with rice pilaf, I picked up the phone and said, "Hello?" On the other end, I got this: "Hi, Dave. This is Sandee."

I damn near dropped the dishes and the phone. I went blank for a few moments, then told her I had tables waiting on me and I needed to go. She asked me if I would call her back sometime. I don't remember what I said after that. I thought about that call for the rest of my dinner shift and for several days after, trying to decide if I should call her back. I was beginning the final semester of my senior year, after six calendar years to get a four-year degree. It was brutal, but I could see my college degree in sight. I had been bum-a-fied over six years because of how I had to live to stay in school. I certainly was not able to be a good rescue candidate for anybody.

I did call her back, but I did not step up to the plate to assume that role for Sandee. Instead, I looked ahead to getting myself established on my terms, pursuing a career that I could build on. I wanted skills. I wanted to experience a normal social life that I could support financially. If I had $40 in my pocket on Monday, I could make it last until Friday simply because I had no choice.

RELIEF IN SIGHT

After graduation in May 1979, Sandee had already been out of school for two years. I was about to start my professional debut and remained flexible while I considered where I might live and what I would do for work. Matt was able to arrange for my interview with Arnar-Stone Labs. It started with a field day to ride with one of their sales trainers in Dallas to give me an idea of what the job was. I spent an entire day calling on hospitals and doctors with trainer Pam Dybvad.

Pam was tall and a great runner. She wore big glasses, had a fun personality, and knew her accounts well enough to take me with her in tow for a full day. It was a very new experience for me. She had sales brochures and organizational systems in the trunk of her company car. She was nicely dressed and had a business card and a purpose for being there. Quite the juxtaposition for a guy like me wearing a rundown suit, with half a car, no brochures, and one Super Pop Popcorn card. I had been an army of one for so long, I couldn't get over the idea of wondering what I could do inside an established organization that paid me to sell and create more business. I noticed that the job she was doing was not all that different from what I had been doing in the five part-time jobs that I had my senior year, including my own company, leading up to my graduation.

There were products and services, paying customers, transactions, customer satisfaction feedback loops, repeat orders. Get more customers, again and again. Wash, rinse, and repeat. I could do that job. I could sell drugs to doctors. What could be easier? What is harder is selling popcorn to someone who doesn't even know they need it, having them pay for it, then doing it again the following week. On a bicycle. Sometimes it doesn't matter how you get things done, just that you did get them done.

Function over form in times of challenge is the smart person's approach to achieving lasting steps of improvement. There will be time for glamor and form later. At least the doctors don't also pay for the drugs. They write the orders, and someone else pays for it. The mission was to get them to write orders for Arnar-Stone's product line, and I was no stranger to what it would take to be good at it. I just needed a chance, someone to believe in me and be willing to pay me to do it.

I passed the field-ride test with Pam and interviewed with two other people before being sent to Chicago to go through the full interview day at the company headquarters. My hiring manager was Terry Crabtree, the district manager. His boss, the one I needed to approve my hiring, was Tom Erickson, the area manager. To this day, both are great friends and colleagues of mine. I went to Chicago, got handed from person to person, and two days later I got a call from Terry that they wanted to offer me a job as a medical sales representative. I had the choice of moving to Los Angeles or Oklahoma City, and I had a couple of weeks to decide. Once again, I was at Homer and Chris's house when I got the offer from Terry on the telephone.

For the past five years I had been making, with my own two hands, between $2,000 and $5,000 per year, sharing a car, sharing an apartment, working five jobs at the same time, hitchhiking, working nights and weekends, and mooching off just about everyone that I knew. In that past light, I listened to the "offer," which meant I could decide if it was good enough. Ha, that was funny.

Terry offered, "You are only in an entry-level position, so all we can pay you is a starting annual salary of $13,200 per year, a company car with all expenses paid, a quarterly bonus up to 50 percent of your salary if you hit sales targets, an expense account, and we will pay all your moving expenses to either LA or Oklahoma City. What do you think?" I asked him to repeat it because I was in shock and wanted to make sure that he was not kidding. He told me again and then asked, "Do you think that will work for you to get started in a couple of weeks?"

I said that I would love to work for Arnar-Stone and accepted his offer. I just could not believe that I had done it. I had a real job. And a car. And an expense account. And a sales territory, somewhere. And business in hand and more to grow. And the need for a new wardrobe. And the need to call my parents to tell them I still was not dead yet. It was awesome. I felt so good, so relieved, and so inspired to know that it could be done! Terry Crabtree set my start date as Monday, July 8, 1979, but I needed to tell them which territory I wanted to take. I really wanted Dallas, but it was not available, so I had to decide.

I don't remember how it happened, but Sandee came over to the French's house and I think we sat on the back porch. I updated her on my plans and told her I hadn't decided on California or OKC just yet. The allure of California was enticing, but Oklahoma City was the safer bet for me. I told her I would let her know when I had decided.

For the next two weeks, I did what I normally did. I worked. I got a few shifts at the O-I plant in Dallas, knowing it would be the last time that I would work there. O-I had a lot of memories for me, so it was a good place to say hasta-la-bye-bye to factory work. I was looking forward to being a medical representative for a division of AHSC. I got my last paycheck from O-I and started my professional work on July 8, 1979.

8

My big chance, girlfriend on the fence, a job but no money, moving to OKC alone, selling drugs, reuniting with Sandee

As I prepared to enter a professional career with a great company, I was quite sure that I would be unsettled and potentially overwhelmed by the opportunity. I had punched my way through college and earned my bachelor of arts degree with a business minor, but the only thing I had to offer an employer was that I knew how to sell. I could sell because I had to sell. But that was it. I did not understand finance, operations, legal, corporate compliance, fundraising, organizational behavior, business communication, budgets, three-year planning, cash-flow analysis, organizational chart development, and the list went on. So now that I am looking back on it, I was very realistic that I was not going to retire at age twenty-five the way some social elements suggest you can and should today.

Work is good for the soul. But personal development is good for your life. I was so glad to have the chance to shift the financial risk to an employer who would give me a chance to learn some of the skills I needed and pay me if I performed the job to their satisfaction. Instead of struggling to pay someone to teach me in college, I was now going to receive a reliable stream of income for the same. Just because I ran a little popcorn company, tended bar, sold advertising, waited tables, and did an advertising internship didn't mean I could do what was expected of me at AHSC. I was so honored and excited to start that job. The reason I got the interview was because of Matt; however, the reason I got the job is that *I asked for it.* Then *I asked for it* again. And then I *asked for it* again. *I practiced* the pitch I would take to interviews in Chicago. *I practiced* what I would ask and say during my field-ride day with my soon-to-be trainer Pam Dybvad. Life during my first twenty-two years was just a prep to really begin learning something about business and about myself.

Another very important element that I took with me from school was some very good friends. People who were also ambitious, fun, and dependable. They were smart people.

I highly advise you to hang around and acquaint yourself with smart people. Smart people are naturally curious, and they enjoy solving problems, which is what life throws at you from the beginning. Smart people are introspective and confident in their own intellect but open to dissecting issues and problems. They think in multiple dimensions and listen more than they speak. These are good traits and behaviors we all need a measured dose of, and you can find it, if they are your friends.

Regardless of what field you are in or what job or vocation or trade you have your heart set on pursuing, you will be far more successful, and more importantly, happier, if you stay in touch with smart friends. To this day, I am still in contact with three of my best friends from UNT. They are Chris Nichols (who was a dorm suitemate who married one of Sandee's and my best friends, Laura Sherman), Gene Massad (who I palled around with and flew two airplanes that his family had; he has been an airline captain at United for decades. He was the youngest 747 captain at United Airlines when he moved to the left seat), and Randy Smith (my roommate in the dorm and apartment who I bummed around with at the Denton airport and in all sorts of fun escapades. Randy is a financial whiz, just retired from Southwest Airlines as a captain, and developed the training facility for Southwest, including their simulator program and the building development. To keep his love for flying in the left seat, he is now training 737 pilots for American Airlines. I had lunch with him in my hangar recently, as he and his wife Terry are building a home in Fredericksburg, Texas, where we live today.)

Keep your friends. Have friends with high moral character who you can trust. Stay in touch with them and pay attention to how they made you a better person and how you can be a mentor friend to them. You will be glad you did, and it will pay off big as you get down the road in your life and have a few more miles behind you.

This should be a priority: keep developing high-quality friends. The next employer for me, AHSC, gave me friends that I am still working with today. I am not kidding. Such an excellent group of people who have all leaned on each other and helped one another from venture to venture. So, with my friends and family in my life, a clean slate, and no money in my pocket, I moved on to my career in medical sales, but I still loved a good bowl of fresh popcorn.

THE AMERICAN CRITICAL CARE (ACC) DAYS

I decided to move to Oklahoma City to take the sales position there. Before going to my initial two weeks of training at the Harrison Conference Center in Waukegan, Illinois, I had to get an apartment in OKC. But first I met my boss, Terry Crabtree, at his house in Plano, Texas, to pick up the prior sales rep's car I was getting. It was a baby blue Chevy Monte Carlo with a baby blue cloth seat with an FM radio. I was so happy to have that girly-looking car. It did not ping like it was almost dead. The tires had tread, the A/C worked, and the windows rolled up and down. I drove it to OKC to find a place to live and stayed at a hotel for two nights because Arnar-Stone Labs was paying for it. I was on cloud nine, although I still ate Cap 'n Crunch cereal for dinner in my hotel room because it was cheap. I was not used to anything fancy yet.

I found an apartment across from Deaconess Hospital in northwest Oklahoma City, at the Chandalac Apartments, rented my furniture from some cheap place, got moved in, then headed to Chicago for training. It would take me fifty books to write all the events, people, and successes that happened to work for AHSC. The people that came out of our division and the companies that were created from this group of people were nothing short of amazing. Those contacts are still my closest friends today. We had extraordinary success at Arnar-Stone, and I did not realize it until years later, as it is a frequent topic of discussion in our family.

I was lucky to know Matt Freibaum. If Dad hadn't taken a job in New Jersey, I would never have met Matt. But oddly enough, within the first year of my employment there, Matt divorced Janet Lynn and ran off with a young beauty from the islands somewhere. Then he left ACC, and I haven't spoken with him since. I guess New Jersey does weird things to people.

Shortly after I started in sales territory #5309, our division name changed to American Critical Care (ACC), a subsidiary of AHSC. AHSC was a NYSE company and had a great reputation. The market capitalization of AHSC was $3 billion, which was a huge corporation in those days and still is today. But ACC was one of the most profitable divisions because of one product. It was called Intropin, pronounced in-tro'-pin. It was the patent-protected chemical compound called dopamine. It was one of five different products we had at the time and was the anchor product/success for ACC at that time. Intropin was used in the ICU for patients in septic shock, which has nothing to do with electricity. When the body shuts down from infection, kidneys fail, the heart begins to fail, and bad things happen. Intropin, at low doses, could increase renal output without adding large volumes of fluid that could be hard on the heart. It could also be titrated (adjusted) to make the heart pump with more authority without increasing heart rate. It was the drug of choice for septic shock patients, and we were trained to sell and support it in our territories. My territory was all of Oklahoma and the panhandle of Texas.

I had one doctor in Lawton, Oklahoma, who used so much Intropin it represented a third of my Intropin sales. Companywide, Intropin sales were around $26 million, which seems tiny today, but the company felt huge to me. I was so happy there. My paychecks didn't bounce, and I was making a quarterly bonus. We had other products too that were added along the way during the company's development, including plasma volume expanders (Hespan), a life-saving drug used in cardiac arrest (Bretylol), an IV nitroglycerin drug with IV tubing setup (Tridil), a calcium heparin (Calcipirin,) and a microfibrillar collagen hemostatic product that stopped uncontrollable bleeding in surgery (Avitene).

In my first year, I qualified for Rookie of the Year and went to Chicago to be tested against two other top reps. One of them, Keith Metzler, was a medical student nearing completion of his medical degree. He was no match at the product knowledge level, and he won the award. Pissed me off. He couldn't sell anything; he just knew what all the big fancy medical words were and sounded more like a doctor. That taught me a lesson. ***Know the role, be the role, be the ball.***

Our product line also included a product called Isoclor. Isoclor was an antihistamine that didn't produce spikes in antihistamine that can cause intense drowsiness. We were trained that the way the pills were made, the outer coating dissolved at a uniform rate so that dose-dumping was less likely to occur. That is how it worked, and it did all that—unless you took more than one. We had samples that we would deliver to our referring physicians so that we might also see the doctor to "detail" our product to them. Detailers were sales reps that explained the details of their products and got labeled "detail men." I never liked being called that, and our company supported marketing us as medical representatives. I started as a Med Rep I. To get to the level of Med Rep II, I had to attain certain sales goals and demonstrate product knowledge.

In the home office we had many great people, and when we would travel there for training, we would find our way downtown to the blues clubs of Chicago. A club there called "Chicago Blues" was a favorite. I had still been playing some guitar and did not own one at the time but always loved a great guitar solo and really dug listening to blues. This club had the big names of blues musicians that carried the night sound—Big Time Sara, Pistol Pete, Willie Kent, and a host of others would play in this smoke-filled bar that was so small I don't know how more than fifty people would be in there at a time, but they packed them in.

OUR TINY LITTLE DIVISION HEADQUARTERS

The Chicago support/home office team for ACC was a huge cultural driver of our company, and the people there were solidly the best anywhere. I was more involved on the product sales and support side and got to know those people very well. I knew that I needed to learn what they knew as product managers and sales trainers. Sales was the lifeblood of the culture there, and they paid us well, and we were recognized for our achievements each year with a national sales meeting (NSM). I had never been to an NSM before! I had slept in my car in the parking lot after a good night of tips at Chandler's Landing Yacht Club but never slept in a five-star resort after a night celebrating at a national sales meeting.

The NSM, and the recognition that would take place on that one night per year, was a strong motivator for everyone. I wanted to be on that podium as a sales achiever, but mostly, I wanted to learn how to get there.

The sales training that we had at ACC was professionally developed and proved to be a very effective way of breaking down the sales process and the sales call. I began to learn about communication skills and the specific components necessary to take a prospect through the process of making him a customer. There is an exchange of ideas, needs, and wants, and it was our job to determine what they needed, then to fill the need with one of our products. It was not slam-it-down-their-throats-until-they-give; it was more relational than that, and it was professional. There is a difference between knocking on someone's door to hand them a squishy piece of fruit that they just must buy because it is so drippingly delicious (I've done that) and stepping into a physician's lounge, nicely dressed, well prepared for the discussion about plasma volume expanders for patients in the operating room right then and there. It not only required confidence to walk through that door in the first place, but you needed to be prepared in the event there was actually somebody there to talk to that might not yet be interested in you or your product.

You will not run into perfectly prepared customers searching for a roleplay with you. You need to listen and think. They will give you the clues to what is important to them, then you can address the need with a feature of your product.

I was finally learning about building trusting relationships in business and being patient for the measurable sales success. I was so used to running around at high speed to make ends meet in college that I did not realize my job now was a more strategic and tactical, and professional endeavor. I remember one time I was working at the University of Oklahoma Medical Center in Oklahoma City (OUMC), and I ran into a guy who was the sales rep for Eli Lilly Corp. He was a pharmacist by education. All Eli Lilly reps had to be pharmacists. I always wondered why they required that, but it made sense—they were credible because of their education before they needed to be credible in sales. At least that is my view, but I do understand the advantage of doing so.

The day I was working at OUMC I ran into him while he was sitting on a bench outside one of the main buildings at the hospital. Everyone knew Glen, including me. The sales rep society in any profession is a tight group of people. Everyone calling on the same people, competing for their business. Swinging for the fences every time at the plate and making a name for themselves in a proud and respectable way. Glen was the guy. I started talking with him and asked why he was sitting on that bench and not hammering the doors down to get some sales. After all, I was on my way to call on the ER supervisor (who tried to get me to join AMWAY) to set up some Bretylol in-service presentations. I did not have time to sit around, so how did he?

Glen calmly looked up at me and said, "Do you see those doors over there?" pointing to some obscure double doors nearby.

I said, "Yes, I do."

He said, "In seven minutes those doors will open, and thirty-five cardiology fellows will be walking out on their way to clinic." Then he asked, "Do you see that door over there on the other side of that courtyard?"

I nodded and said, "Sure do."

He said, "At one thirty today, there will be six surgeons walking down that sidewalk to go in that door for rounds."

We both paused and I think I heard a bird chirp, or a kid scream, or a dog bark somewhere, and I said, "So why are you sitting here?"

He said, "Son, you can run all over this hospital and chase the one elusive doctor, or you can know your territory so well that dozens of them come right to you in less time than it takes for you to park your car and walk over here."

I have never forgotten that concept.

Know your accounts, how they behave, where they go, what they do, what they eat, the name of their dog, and the kinds of shoes they like to wear. But mostly find a way to fit into their routine, not to make them fit into yours.

SINGLE AND GETTING STARTED —AND FINALLY OUT OF COLLEGE

During 1979 and rolling into 1980, I was adjusting to single life in Oklahoma City and settling into a travel routine throughout Oklahoma. Occasionally I would have friends come visit me in Oklahoma, and I was hanging out with Larry Moore, who was married to Sandee's first college roommate, Amy. He was the rich kid I spoke of earlier who drove the Porsche, liked soul music, and had a lot of money. Since I lived in OKC, and he and Amy lived in Edmond, we started getting together from time to time. Larry talked me into getting into tae kwon do, and we used to work out together.

Sandee and I started talking a little more often, and I was still in touch with Terri, who was considering transferring to the University of Oklahoma to be closer to me. The truth is that Terri did not want to get too much further from her twin sister at Auburn and couldn't commit to moving before she finished FSU. I completely understood that, and I was not lost without her as I had been when I lost Sandee, and I had my own fish to fry.

The last time I saw Terri was at a swim meet in Norman, Oklahoma, for a bunch of schools, including FSU. I went to the hotel to talk with her, and we agreed that it was too hard to keep it all together. She had her life, and I had mine. I gave her a kiss and told her how much I had loved her and wished her the best. She cried as I left, but it was time to move on, and we did. But we had a blast while we dated.

In 1993, I received a call from Terri's sister, Kathi. Kathi was married and living in Joliet, Illinois, and called me to tell me what had happened to Terri. Terri had graduated from FSU in 1980 and was married and living in Florida. In April 1985, she was riding her bike, training for a triathlon (swim/run/bike) on a major highway in Florida. It was a four-lane road with no shoulder, the news account said. She was hit from behind by a car traveling seventy miles per hour. She suffered two broken legs, a broken pelvis, a broken arm, and went into the windshield. She survived the crash, but the rehab was difficult, and how she did not die, only God knows. It sickens me to think about it.

I did not reach out to her after hearing the news from Kathi, but I'm very curious today if she fully recovered and has had a good life with her husband and family. Their father, Bud, died around that same time, so they had a pretty rough stretch in the late eighties. Terri did call our house, probably sometime before the crash, and she just wanted to say hi. Sandee answered the phone, and Terri and I talked for about five minutes. I appreciated her calling but had my life with Sandee. I have not spoken to Kathi or Terri since, and that was, as of today, more than thirty years ago. I really hope that she fully recovered and has had a full life with her family.

Sandee and I began having more contact with one another. By the end of 1980, I had my sales territory really rolling. Sales were strong, and I was enjoying traveling about 50 percent of the time. If I wasn't working OKC, then I was usually in Tulsa or Amarillo. When I worked in Tulsa, I would go there for the entire week and work the four main hospitals, St. Francis, St. John's, Hillcrest, and the Osteopathic Hospital. Our hospital products business required us to work closely with the hospital pharmacy department and their various committees. The Pharmacy and Therapeutics Committee, aka the P&T Committee, was my first frustrating sales blockade. If your product wasn't approved by the P&T, then you couldn't move product through the system even if the doctors were ordering it. You could have the greatest doctor loyalty, and it didn't matter if it hadn't gone through the P&T. This was not a fast process. It was slow and bureaucratic and chewed up a lot of my calendar. I finally figured out that rather than pushing it through the system and forcing them to put it on the P&T calendar, I needed a product champion that would pick up the battle with and for me.

Each hospital was different. Some needed clinical efficacy and trial data. Some needed testing on the floors and staff surveys of need.

Some needed more committee analyses, and some needed just plain alcohol. In Tulsa, my osteopathic pharmacy customers were a couple of cowboys and didn't quite see the world as it was at the time. They viewed it as personal opportunity shielded by corporate presence and prestige.

The director of pharmacy and the assistant director of pharmacy liked their three-martini lunches during the week. Once I figured out what they wanted and needed, it was my job to give it to them. It was the easiest P&T approval I ever got. And in record time! I just had to buy those boys lunch a couple of times per month and as much booze as they wanted before they went back to the hospital pharmacy. It was a really good account for me**. You must give the customer what they want!** Just saying.

One of our products was called Americaine. If a product has a "caine" in it, you can count on it having some kind of pain relief agent in it, such as lidocaine or benzocaine. Americaine was a cream packaged in a small tube and was primarily prescribed for episiotomy pain in postpartum mothers. An episiotomy is an incision the doctor cuts into the side of the vagina to expand the birth canal for larger babies on some deliveries. After the episiotomy is sutured closed, it can begin to itch soon after. Americaine was used as a topical ointment to stop the itch and relieve the burn. And it worked.

We were taught the lip test. This was a test where we had potential customers of all kinds dab some Americaine on their finger and apply it on their tongue and bottom lip. In no time, the lip and tongue were numb. It could be used on soft tissue because it didn't cause internal problems. The lip test made me a lot of money.

One of my hospitals, St. Anthony's in OKC, did not have Americaine on the formulary, where medications get added after the P&T committee approves it. I got to know the OB/GYN supervisor and did the lip test for her. She was interested in trying it. The P&T committee wanted some sort of analysis or data that would support recommendations they would consider approving. So, I created one. I put together a spreadsheet that would record the date, time, and use of the product, its results, and comments by the user, which were usually the nurses on the OB floor. I brought in the Americaine products to be used from the samples I carried in the trunk of my baby blue Monte Carlo.

I did an in-service for the floor nurses and had all of them try the lip test. I had slides that I put on the wall with a projector that showed the episiotomy application in all its vivid OB glory. And me standing there, telling them how to apply it. Now that's something I never thought I would do.

After a few weeks of perfect results, and a solid review of my "data," the P&T committee approved my product and added it to the formulary. We sold cases of it. St. Anthony's was the largest OB hospital in the state of Oklahoma, and I nearly won the Americaine Cup at the NSM that year. I could have won it, but I spent more time selling Intropin and Hespan and Isoclor.

What I learned about selling and creating a business from this experience was that you must make it easy for the customer to make the decision, and the only right decision, to use your product. You must make it so compelling that if they don't buy it, it will be a huge mistake. If they do buy it, it will be one of the best buying decisions they have ever made, and they will wish they had made it sooner.

It can be done for every product or service if you just know your product, know your customer and how it will benefit them when they buy, and know the drawbacks to them if they don't. Simple stuff, but selling for ACC in the professional environment allowed me the time and resources to figure it out without worrying about starving to death while hitchhiking in the rain in the middle of the night to make it to a sales management class. I loved my job, and I loved the company I worked for. It was fantastic.

MY SWEETHEART IN TEXAS

During 1980, I continued to make periodic trips to Dallas, but now I was going there hoping to see Sandee, not just to hang out with my brother or Mark. I was beginning to see an emotional pathway back into Sandee's heart. A few times when I'd be at her apartment, I would see letters from her old boyfriend and clear signs that I wasn't quite back in the family yet, and that was a bit of a bummer. But over time, we began to be Dave and Sandee again. We would grab dinner with her father, Calvin Coolidge Orr, whom she now had the chance to spend more time with, and she would include me in a few of those times.

Sandee really wanted Calvin to be in her life, and as a young, pretty, single female teacher living on her own, I think she found security in that. I think she also began to feel security with me and had moved away from her other relationship and was emotionally leaning into me. Not sure what happened or how the other relationship ended. I have always wanted to know more, but maybe it's not in my best interest. But the question remained of who broke up with whom, and that's what I struggled with in 1980.

BECOMING AN OKIE

My little apartment in the Chandelaque apartments was a one-bedroom with a small porch, and it was on the first floor. I knew my neighbors, and I liked living there. I had all my sales brochures and other sales tools neatly organized in the only closet that I had other than the kitchen pantry, and my dining room cubbyhole table was my office desk. At night, the light from the outside, marking the driveway into the apartment complex, was glaring and lit up my bedroom like a stadium. I started removing the lights to darken my room, but it also darkened that part of the apartment complex and the apartment manager didn't like it and told me to stop. So, I bought a comforter from Target and put it over my "drapery" in my bedroom, and that knocked the light down pretty good—at least good enough to sleep.

Then a friend of mine gave me a waterbed that I installed. I removed my other bed and set it up and used a water hose from outside, brought it through my window, and filled the bed up. Everything was fine until I slept on it. I did not know it needed a heater— otherwise it was like sleeping on a block of ice. I got cold, got sick, and hated that thing. So, I had to drain it back through the hose out the window, dumping about two thousand gallons of water into the parking lot in the winter, where it promptly froze, to every pedestrian's peril. What a mess, but that was life for me, living on my own in OKC.

My furniture was early Harlem. The couch was made of, well, I'm not really sure. It was a kind of cloth but was so hard and rough to the touch that it was very unpleasant to sit on. I couldn't afford to buy furniture and never really thought about doing so, but I did need a good stereo. I bought a Hitachi turntable with Cerwin Vega speakers, and it was one loud, concert-producing sound. I let that thing wail whenever I wanted to, and my neighbor friends never called me out on it.

I was making regular trips to the dojo to work out and was getting pretty good at karate, particularly the fighting. I loved the fighting and the idea that I could defend myself even against two or more people. Larry was already a brown belt, and I moved up through the ranks from white to orange to green to purple and was working on my brown belt. I would join Larry in his garage, working out on an eighty-pound bag that we would go after with hands and feet for two-minute rounds. We became good boxers and kickers. Our instructor was Tommy Williams, who was a ninth- or tenth-dan master instructor and was the welter-weight champion of the world in kickboxing. He had the world record number of knockouts with kicks to the body. His go-to kick was the spinning back kick and he taught us how to use it, but we were never anywhere near his level of anything karate.

Larry and I and the other students got used to getting hit and kicked in the face. I would not say that had always been a dream of mine, but it came with the territory. My interest in tournament fighting grew as a result, and I won the Oklahoma State Championship as an orange belt. I beat a guy about six inches taller than me, and I just worked his torso over and over instead of trying to reach his head with kicks. That was how Tommy won the Super Welterweight title of the world in kickboxing, with his signature spinning back kick to the body. Tommy was so excited when I competed in the tournament and defeated my last opponent during the point-fighting competition and won the championship that he ran out onto the mat and we jumped around together. I was the orange belt champion and was given a trophy that I still have today. I loved the competition and enjoyed standing across from a competitor, waiting for the ref to start the fight. I enjoyed the mental challenge of creating the want-to necessary to not be afraid of the guy. I also enjoyed believing that I was the better competitor without even knowing anything about him.

I was betting on me. I knew I would get punched and kicked, but I also knew that I could and would punch and kick him more. A lot more. When the ref would put his hand in the middle between us, he would begin the fighting match with one word: "Fight." Okay, let's get this party started!

DISTANTLY CASUAL AND AVOIDING ANOTHER SETBACK

While Sandee and I were keeping in touch but not really dating, as we called it back then, or "going steady," we found times for her and I to talk and just stay in touch. We had never left each other's hearts. I had a vision of getting her back and finding a way to have business success to support our hopes and dreams. It was one day at a time, turning one brick into two and learning hard lessons along the way.

9

Proposing to Sandee the wrong way, her parents' mixed reviews, wedding plans, building our first house, cutting off our electricity, DINK

Late in 1980, with my early career going great, Sandee and I were seeing each other more often. I invited her to visit me for a weekend in Oklahoma City. We had a great time finding nice restaurants and spending time just talking. I was falling in love with her all over again, and it was time to consider what was next for us. At the end of 1980, I was making frequent trips to Arlington, and she was making frequent trips to Oklahoma City. I remember during one drive I was making down I-35 to see her for the weekend, it hit me: I was ready to propose to her, and I was going to get my girl back. I can show you on the map where I had this feeling and made my personal commitment that it was the right thing to do, and I better get to it, or I might lose her again. I will never forget that moment, and when we drive I-35, I usually point out where I was when I made that commitment to myself.

On one trip Sandee made to visit me, we were driving in Edmond, about twenty minutes from where I lived, and we came across a cute neighborhood in the country called Kelly Park. We were not engaged and had not been talking seriously about it yet, but I knew we were both thinking we should be making plans. The homes in Kelly Park were Fox and Jacobs–type starter homes and were small.

We found a house on a corner cul-de-sac lot that was just getting started. Although we were not married yet, I agreed to move ahead with making the financial commitment to buy it with the intent that we would be engaged sometime during the building process. I signed a contract to purchase it for $60,000. I did not have any money, but I figured I'd worry about it later. Sandee jumped into action, thinking about materials, colors, appliances, and the rest.

Back in Arlington, she purchased on layaway a refrigerator costing $800. She agreed to make four monthly payments of $200 each and we weren't even engaged yet, but I knew she was ready for me to pop the question. She had been hinting to me that Valentine's Day 1981 would be a good time for making a commitment, and it would give her time to plan a move to Oklahoma and find a teaching job in Edmond before the school year started in the fall of that year. I had every intention of proposing to her that Valentine's Day weekend until I made a very bad decision.

Larry called me about two days before I was to drive to Arlington to see Sandee for the weekend when she was hoping/expecting me to propose. He offered me the chance to go snow skiing in New Mexico that same weekend and said we would be back the following week, and I would have time to propose a few days later or even the next weekend. Spring skiing was magnificent, he said, and we should not miss it. Sometimes friends give advice that is primarily in their best interest and completely off track for your plans and priorities, and I fell for it. It sounded like great fun to Larry, so it kinda sounded like fun to me, so I called Sandee's school and asked if they could get her out of class and put her on the phone. I should have hung up and stuck with my plans before she got on the phone. Larry was looking at me, grinning like, "We'll have a blast."

Today it sounds like something comical from *Seinfeld*, but there was nothing funny about telling a potential fiancée that she would remain potential for a couple more weeks. When she picked up, I told her that I was going skiing with Larry and would come down the following weekend. That was a very stupid decision on my part. She was devastated and had every right to be, although we had not agreed I would propose that weekend. Shouldn't it be a surprise? I thought so, but not necessarily Sandee. I have learned over more than forty years that she does not like surprises of a meaningful nature. She likes to be part of big events and involved with the details leading to those events. She is an extremely good planner, and I came across like the moron I was. I had not even bought a ring yet. I had been shopping, but I wasn't quite prepared for the proposal event. I decided to cancel the trip with Larry and head to Dallas that Friday.

By Sunday afternoon, before it was time for me to drive back to Oklahoma City, I proposed to her at her apartment. I gave her a pretty, heart-shaped box that contained the key to the new house I/we were building together. The following weekend, over Valentine's Day, I presented the wedding ring to her that I had purchased from Odom's Jewelers in a mall in Oklahoma City. I gave it to her at dinner at a restaurant in Addison called Andrew's. It was a decent restaurant, and we were sitting upstairs at a table where we talked about all the events to come. It is a very pretty ring, and it took nearly every penny I had, and some bank credit, to purchase it.

I liked the ring and was excited to give it to her, but I did not handle my proposal, in retrospect, in a way that Sandee would have preferred. I had the chance to redo an event like this when I upgraded her ring for our twentieth anniversary during a trip to France. But for now, we were engaged, and I could not believe at the time that we had come full circle and were back to being Dave and Sandee, Sandee and Dave, you and me. It was exciting and still very much is!

It was the following weekend that we told her parents, Ruth and Si, over dinner in Dallas. Si had a bad back and could not wait in lines very long, so we had to scrap our wait at the San Francisco Steak House and went next door to Steak and Ale.

During dinner, we told them that I had proposed and wanted to have their blessing to be married. Shock of shocks on the face of Ruth, and a mighty smile and lifting of his drink for a toast from Si. I'll never forget his reaction because years later he was struggling with dementia, but in this place, in this time, he was very happy Sandee was getting married. It was the complete opposite reaction we thought we would get from each of them. I do not know why Ruth was so shocked. I immediately thought that she was disappointed that it was not someone else that was marrying Sandee, given things she had told me before. Her shock turned to joy in just a few minutes, and everyone was excited. It was official: we were making plans to be married in June 1981.

HOW WILL I PAY FOR ALL OF THIS?

The bonus plan at ACC was a very motivating construct of immediate cash for the quarter but rolled a portion of each bonus into the fourth-quarter bonus as an incentive to keep building sales and achieve a hefty sum at the end of the year. It also produced a cognitive commitment to stay in the company, at least until the end of the year, but I never considered leaving; I had more money to earn and more to learn. I wanted a promotion into sales training but needed to focus on our wedding, finishing our first house, and getting Sandee moved to Edmond to join me after our wedding.

The first half of 1981 was a blur. So many big events in our lives and a huge change from where I had been just two years earlier as I was trying to figure out my career path. Now I was finally getting married to Sandee and had a great first job. We closed on our first house on, if you can believe it, April Fool's Day 1981. I bought it in my name since we were not married yet. I took advantage of bond money that had been issued for local economic development at the staggering rate of 9.9 percent. It was the best mortgage rate to be found on the local market. We were on the back end of the Jimmy Carter presidency, and there were high interest rates and a busted oil economy in Oklahoma. I only had to put 5 percent down, which was $3,000. Of that $3,000, I paid $1,000 in cash and put the other $2,000 on a credit card. Now I had a note on Sandee's wedding ring of $2,100, credit card debt of over $2,000, and a monthly mortgage of $678. Good thing I was making a salary and building my bonuses. A bonus that would dry up in 1982 after achieving high sales numbers, only to have my quota raised as a result. Somehow, Sandee still reminds me of that year, and she is right to do so.

When we got married, my base salary had been raised to $19,000 per year, but my bonuses were getting hard to achieve. Sandee was making more as a teacher at Sequoia Middle School than I was as a sales rep with American. But together, we had a good income. I just wanted to get a handle on growing my income through more bonuses and promotional advancement. DINK—double income, no kids is a productive time indeed!

WRAPPING THINGS UP WITH SHOE POLISH AND A LOT OF RICE

We were married on June 20, 1981, at Walnut Hill Methodist Church in north Dallas at 8:00 p.m. It was a beautiful wedding, and Sandee was beautiful in every way. Mark was my best man, but we renamed him the worst man. Mona was Sandee's maid of honor, and my siblings were in our wedding party. Sandee is an only child, and we included her closest friends in her party, including Mona and Laura and my mother. My parents had been divorced for a couple of years, and I do not think we saw Mom very much, largely because she had set up home with Tim Foley in Key West, Florida. They did fly out to Dallas for our wedding. But just as was customary, Tim, who we really didn't know, did weird things: he left twenty-four hours after they got to Dallas and left Mom there to do all the family wedding moments, including pictures and lunches and the rest.

My mom did very well and looked very pretty in her blue dress and makeup to fit the occasion, and I'm glad she was there and is in our wedding pictures. Dad was also there and paid for the rehearsal dinner that was held at Tupinamba restaurant, out on the outdoor patio, where the jets landing at Love Field made a loud entrance into our conversations as they arrived for landing. I thought it was a nice ambience for a couple who always enjoyed aviation. I also loved it because I had not been flying in a long time because I simply couldn't afford it, and I didn't have the time since I got out of school. I was finally at a place in life, at twenty-five years old, where I didn't have to worry about holding five jobs, traveling the way I had, and barely getting by all the time. I could just worry about me, Sandee, and ACC. But I missed flying and had every intention of getting back into it after we were married, because I knew it could be done.

We spent our wedding night at the Fairmont Hotel in downtown Dallas as a gift from my brother Jay. The reception, which was pretty but very low-key, was held in the atrium of the Summit Hotel on LBJ in Dallas, complete with champagne fountain and a wonderful wedding cake. We didn't have a band, but it was nice. Sandee's father, Calvin, was also there, and we got nice pictures with him. During the day, I spent the night with Mark and Bob Shapard at Bob's house next door to Mark's parents' house. When I woke up on the couch that morning, Mark, Bob, and anyone else were already gone. They left early to decorate my company car for the wedding reception that night. I was left alone for the day. No car. No lunch. No friends. I did nothing.

I guess that is fair play since I didn't handle the proposal sequence and style in a more romantic and appropriate fashion. By the time my car pulled up for us to leave the reception, you could hardly recognize it. By then I had received a new company car, one that I chose when they retired my baby blue Monte. This car was a maroon-colored Pontiac Grand Prix, complete with electric windows and a gray Landau top, which was the popular body style of cars back then. No wonder they were gone all day long. The car was so covered in white shoe polish you could not tell what color the paint on the car was. The interior was filled with white rice, so much white rice that when we stepped into it there were three or four inches of rice on the floorboard and at least that amount when you turned on the air conditioner. Rice would come spitting out the vents like a machine gun.

There was so much written on the windshield, I could not see where we were going while we drove to the Fairmont downtown. When we got there, we pulled up front and center to the hotel at about midnight. When I stopped the car, two of the hubcaps fell off the wheels because they were also filled with rice. There was rice everywhere. It was very embarrassing at the time but is funny as hell now.

Sandee couldn't find the hotel confirmation when we were checking in, so we had to open her suitcase on the floor of the reception area at the Fairmont and start pulling out all her fancy, honeymoon-type outfits, to find it. There were people there enjoying watching this never-to-be-forgotten moment. She found it, and we got our room key, but before going to our room, we decided, at the suggestion of the staff, to grab something to eat in the restaurant because they were closing. By then the *Dallas Morning News* paper had been printed and delivered to the hotel for the next day, and Sandee's picture and our wedding announcement were in it, and we hadn't even been to our room yet. We enjoyed a hamburger and fries, which we shared together along with more champagne and finally called it a night. It was a wonderful wedding and reception, filled with so many memories with our friends.

After staying at the Fairmont, which Jay paid for, it was time to go on the fancy honeymoon I had planned and paid for. Not. We went to Lake Texoma and stayed in crummy little cabins at Caney Creek Lodge on the Oklahoma side of the lake. We spent so much time growing up on that lake, it seemed like the right place to honeymoon, and it was the only place I could afford. Sandee was really good about it, and we had a nice time making our own meals and grilling on a little portable grill that we took there. But then, enough was enough, and we had to upgrade our honeymoon experience. We checked out and headed to Arkansas!

That's right! Hot Springs, Arkansas, here we come, without a reservation for a place to stay or any real plan in sight, which was not and is not Sandee's style, but she went with it. We made the beautiful drive to Hot Springs. Winging it can be a fun, spontaneous plan some of the time. But a real plan, in advance, with details thought out, always is the best and most predictable way to keep her happy and looking forward to the journey. I learned that early on and have been committed to providing that sense of security in our life's plans.

We had a blast along the way, talking about how we would get dressed up and go to a fine restaurant, have a great steak, rent a boat, and maybe sit out fishing on the dock. And that is exactly what we did. We stopped for gas and beer at a local service station and asked the clerk there where the best steak place was in Hot Springs. They had Busch beer, which is what my dad drank in St. Louis, so we picked up a six-pack. The clerk made her recommendation. "It depends on what kinda of steak you two lovebirds want. If ya want ya a sirloin, youse gonna have to pay a little extree. But ya cain't go wrong going to Western Sizzlin'." Thanks for the tip!

We checked into a little place that was on the lake and had a fun lake-style room, but fortunately it was a measurable upgrade from Caney Creek, which did not need much to be a vast improvement. We made reservations for dinner that evening at Hamilton House. I remember sitting there at dinner under candlelight with Sandee, enjoying a glass of scotch, then a bottle of wine, and looking into her beautiful eyes and feeling so glad we were married. This was a moment of which I had dreamed for many years. I felt secure in our future. I finally had a little bit of class, which I couldn't have previously afforded, and now here we were, full of hope for our future.

The next day we rented a boat for half of a day and enjoyed the lake like it was our own. After three days, it was time to drive back to Dallas before going back to our home in Edmond, and our life together was off to the races. For perspective in today's world of wedding credos that say the honeymoon needs to be over the top and paid for by the groom's parents (who decided that rule?), we paid for our honeymoon, and we did not have the money to do so. All in all, including the side trip to Arkansas, gas, meals, drinks, boat rental, and bait, we paid less than $1,800. Pretty efficient for two broke lovebirds wandering around Oklahoma and Arkansas. Less like Bonnie and Clyde and more like Tom Sawyer and Becky Thatcher. But we had a blast.

When we finally made it to our new house in Edmond, Oklahoma, after our honeymoon, I felt obliged to carry Sandee across the threshold of our front door. She was surprised when I just scooped her up and opened the door, stepped into the doorway, and asked her to turn on the lights of our new home. It was a very meaningful moment, one filled with "let's get this dream life started" intentions. I told her to "light this candle" and to switch on the lights. When she did, nothing happened. The power had been turned off because I had not paid the electric bill before all the wedding events.

The first decision we made as a couple was that Sandee would manage all the bill paying, and she has done so every month since June 1981.

10

More DINK, working hospitals, our first dog, my first solo flight, getting my private pilot's license, the Johnny Carson Show

By late 1981, I had my sales territory at ACC back on track and I was on the way to nice bonuses for 1982. My salary had been increased to $19,100, and Sandee was making about the same as a teacher. I recall that she was making more than me in base salary, but combined, we were in hog heaven with a double income and no kids yet.

The ACC product line did not grow for a few years, but we had good products and there were plenty of sales needs in my territory. The company launched a joint venture with American Edwards, the flow-tip catheter division of the corporation. The Swan-Ganz flow-tip catheter was positioned in the heart by a cardiologist in the cath lab to measure cardiac output. The catheter went through a vein in the leg, and it was pushed along its way to the heart, where the tip would be inflated in the pulmonary artery. The inflation would create blood back pressure, measured as pulmonary wedge pressure, or PWP. That measurement showed how effective the heart was as a pump and was referred to as cardiac output.

The heart has two mechanical ways it creates blood pressure. The first is how hard it pumps, called contractility, and the second is how fast it pumps, simply called heart rate. Depending on the cardiac and pulmonary health of a patient in measurable terms, the treatment plan and drug regimen could be determined. It was state-of-the-art in its day but has since gone the way of the buggy whip, which is surprising to me, but technology in the field of imaging and other monitoring and measuring systems has reduced the need for more invasive procedures. Our job at ACC was to support the American Edwards sales reps in the cath lab and OR. The Edwards reps also sold sutures and was a very cool type of sales. I was around it but wasn't responsible for it.

As a result of the time we spent on Swan-Ganz, it took time away from other products that I was getting paid handsomely to sell. For the first four years in my territory, I was able to win various incentives and received award recognition at the NSM on several occasions, which was very motivational to me. It was so motivational that I began a monthly newsletter I would send to reps in our region. It contained selling tips, discussion about medical terms, and suggested ways of selling the corporate hospital contract programs we were also responsible for. There were about thirty different divisions under AHSC, and there was a solid effort trying to get every hospital system in the US on board with the entire AHSC product line by division.

ACC was the smallest division, having come from being a small, laboratory-based company originally known as Arnar-Stone Laboratories, Inc, when I was hired. Our lead product, Intropin, only had sales of $26 million but was so profitable it got the attention of "XO," which is what we called the home office of the corporation. As a result, they wanted to expand our ACC sales force and were looking for leaders to train and manage the group. We had one hundred and three sales representatives when I was in my territory, and they were located all over the US. We had two sales training courses for our new hires. The first was for in-house training for two weeks, followed by six weeks in the field. Then another three weeks of training to learn the more difficult products, before going back into the field as a fully trained rep. The training was superb, and I ascribed to its concepts of the systematic selling technique, called SST.

The "system" called for a specific dialogue algorithm that helped the sales rep connect with the prospect in a way that was meaningful and useful to the prospect. It included open probes, closed probes, confirming probes, trial closes, and other types of dialogue that, if followed, worked extremely well. We became very good at it, and looking back, I still use the SST system in business dialogue today. It was a great system and still is. Sales isn't and doesn't have to be complicated. It is essentially two or more people agreeing to a change in behavior, using a product, with the respective roles agreed to such as who does what, what happens next, is it acceptable, and if so, the customer pays the bill. And the process repeats.

By the time 1983 rolled around, I was asked to travel to other regions to help new reps get set up in their territories and help them call on accounts. It was an incredibly fun job as a regional sales trainer, and I was able to keep my territory in Oklahoma and all the sales credits and bonuses that took place while I was training someone else. I still got paid.

TRAVEL FOR BUSINESS IS OVERRATED

Traveling to anywhere from Oklahoma City was not easy. I had to fly to Dallas first, then fly to my training destination, then begin my workday when I arrived. It was a physical beating to travel to the West Coast, and that was primarily where they sent me. Always look into the future to see where your career path might take you geographically. A dream location one thousand miles away may be fun for vacation but might be an exhausting, repetitive grind if you're told to go there frequently for work. But it was good training, learning how to develop reps and learn about different sales environments other than just what I would run into in my own territory. The travel was brutal and continued for the next thirty years of my career. That was how we did business. No cell phones, pagers or computers, or Internet. Nothing to keep us connected and driving the pace of business other than landlines and 1-800 numbers to call.

The technology of the day was the simple use of a "Daytimer Organizer." It was a condensed paper calendar system for your personal and business activities, but the most important technology we had was the OAG. The OAG was the "Official Airline Guide," and it listed every flight of every airline to every city in the US. If you had an AOG sticking out of our briefcase, you were a road warrior. And I was. I had an annual subscription to AOG, and sometimes the information was right and a lot of times it was not. We learned how to flip our outbound and return trips to purchase two tickets at once and get the benefit of a lower-priced ticket because the trip was over a Saturday night. The trip really was not over a Saturday; we just used the outbound on one ticket to one destination and used the outbound from the other city as the return. We had all the tricks of the travel trade figured out, but it was still a beating.

Because I flew commercially all the time, I began to miss my flying lessons. I had not flown since college and during my days working at the Denton airport. I remember one time that I rented a school airplane for the weekend so I could fly down to Waco to see Sandee. I did not have my pilot's license, but my good friend Gene Massad did. Gene was a college suitemate of mine, along with Randy Smith, at Kerr Hall. Both Gene and Randy became airline pilots. Gene flies 747s for United Airlines, and Randy flew 737s for Southwest Airlines. We called Gene the "bunless wonder" because he didn't have an ass. He said it was because he moved it all to the front. Yeah, right. He had all the lines, I tell ya.

Gene had been a private pilot since he was sixteen and had full access to his dad's Cessna 310 and a Piper J-3 Cub that was part of a flying club in Lewisville. Gene and I had flown his 310 to Laredo, Texas, when he and I were living together for a summer in Dallas. We flew to Laredo and landed at an airport we thought was our destination. It wasn't. We landed at the wrong airport. We taxied back, took off, and found the correct airport in Nuevo Laredo. We spent a couple of days there going across the border and buying starving-artist value-priced paintings and large ceramic animals and Mexican shirts. When it was time to fly back to Dallas, we loaded the airplane full of this stuff and headed home. The Mexican swag stayed in our apartment at Greenville and LBJ in Dallas and reminded us of the great time we had.

I was fortunate to have friends who were already pilots, and Gene was one of them. So, Gene and I flew a school Cherokee 140, N1750T, to Waco, but I was in the left seat and Gene in the right. To keep the costs down, I turned off the master switch after we took off so that the Hobbs meter would not run until we turned the master switch back on when we needed to use the radios. When we got back two days later, we had put only .4 hours on the airplane, and it only cost me $12 plus the avgas to make the trip. I was severely reprimanded for it by the flight school chief pilot and told not to do it again. Okay. I just couldn't afford to rent it for "book rates," and I figured since I was an employee of the school and flight line, I made the executive order to give myself an employee discount. At least I got to fly and see Sandee because of it.

SELL OR FLY—SHOW ME A SIGN

Back in Edmond, on my way to work my territory one day, I was sitting in traffic waiting to turn left at an intersection that sat at the end of a private grass landing strip. I looked left out the window just in time to see a Cessna barreling down the runway right toward me with its bright landing light on. It looked very cool, and I remember it vividly. He lifted into the air, put up his landing gear, and flew right over the center of my company car with a roar. Huh. Instead of turning left and heading to my sales territory, I turned right and headed to the Guthrie County Airport. I was getting back in the cockpit to stay this time.

SELLING AN INCREDIBLE SURGICAL PRODUCT

In late 1983, our division bought a new product from Alcon Laboratories. It was called Avitene and was the most dramatic product I carried, among a solid line of products that were strikingly advantaged in the marketplace. Avitene was a microfibrillar collagen hemostat, used to stop the most unstoppable bleeds in surgery. Avitene was used when nothing else would work, and I was able to spend time in surgery providing instruction to the surgeon and the sterile team on how to use it. It was an exceedingly difficult product to use correctly, but when done so, it worked.

A microfibrillar collagen hemostat works like this. It is made of small particles of collagen. Collagen is a naturally occurring tissue in the human body and can promote clotting because of how the molecule is built and shaped to give it a porosity that can grab and hang on during the clotting process. I am no scientist, but that is how I remember we explained it. More importantly, we demonstrated it.

This one-gram jar of Avitene was like a miracle weapon. "Okay, Ferdie, she's still bleeding. What else ya got over there that we should try?" a surgeon might say.

The scrub nurse replied, "Well, we got this powdery stuff called Avitene that is supposed to stop anything. Wanna give her a whirl?"

The surgeon, wanting to be the hero while Ma Flanders was dying on the table because the bleed would not stop, said, "Open a jar of that stuff and dump it right in my hand so I can work with it."

Then the mistakes happened. They didn't change to dry gloves; the Avitene was handled with wet and bloody latex gloves, and it stuck to everything but where the bleeding was happening. Reminded me of the scene in the John Wayne movie *McLintock* when Maureen O'Hara is tarred and feathered and running down the street out of control with the whole street of observers laughing at her. Just like that scene, the OR would be in a bit of, shall we say, panic, because now the doctor was completely out of control, trying to get a hold of the bleed, and the Avitene powder was sticking to everything.

Enter David Gasmire, Medical Representative I, to the rescue. Kind of reminds me of the opening scene of the Netflix movie, *The Ballad of Buster Scruggs.* In the movie, the hero, a singing cowboy, all dressed in white, riding a white horse and playing a white guitar, rides into the scene singing prophetic words of wisdom with an echo in complete harmony. Yep, that was me, sort of. The key to using the $50 (in 1983) one-gram jar of Avitene was a dry surgical field, with only dry gloves, and a dry sense of humor. You could not get flustered when this thing, as our sales brochure said, "Adheres tenaciously to anything moist that it comes in contact with."

Yeah, buddy, it did. If the scrub nurse and surgeon changed their gloves every minute or two while they shaped the product and prepared it for aggressive placement on the patient's wound, then changed gloves repeatedly, there would be virtually no mess, no wasted time, no embarrassment, and no dead patient. I loved selling the product.

I had a friend that I met in karate. His name was Byron Goff. He had a job he did not like and was always asking me about mine, and one day he asked if I could get him in to see a surgical procedure. I asked my best surgeon customer, Dr. Nate Grantham, a thoracic surgeon who I had been in surgery with dozens of times, if I could bring a friend in to a case because he was considering selling products in the OR and wanted to see if he could handle it. Dr. Grantham told me, "As long as he stays with you and does not get in the way, you can bring him in. We have a case at 7:00 a.m. tomorrow at Presbyterian Hospital."

I said, "Yes, sir, I'll be sure it is managed appropriately."

The next morning, I got Byron into scrubs in the doctors' surgical locker room and lounge and met with the anesthesiologist to let him know Byron would be there with me. He was fine with it if I didn't lose track of Byron. As the case had gotten started and the patient's chest was open and the team was working on bypass grafts of his heart, I brought in Byron. Dr. Grantham looked at me and didn't acknowledge us as he was busy in the chest of this man. The music was blasting rock and roll. It was about fifty degrees in the OR, and everyone was gowned up, including me and Byron. I brought Byron to the head of the patient outside the sterile field, and the anesthesiologist placed Byron right where he could see everything. I was standing behind Byron and in front of the anesthesiologist, who was on a four-legged rolling stool.

Byron was looking around the room, and I asked him if he was okay. A minute later, he was looking away from the surgical field where the patient's heart was not beating because they had gone "on the pump" so they could work on the heart while it was motionless. The scrub nurse squeezed a lap sponge full of blood back into the chest of the patient, and that's when Byron passed out. I caught him before he hit the ground and wrapped him up so he would not take any IV lines and other patient connect equipment with him in the fall. Byron landed on me, I landed on the anesthesiologist, and all three of us rolled about five feet away and hit the cabinets on the wall in the OR.

Without missing a beat (get it?), Dr. Grantham stopped to watch the commotion that I was responsible for, and said, "I think your friend should sell shoes." And he went back to work. I will never forget it. No harm, no foul, but **I learned my lesson about surgery: it is not a place for everyone, but I really enjoyed it.**

EARLY SEEDS OF OUR AVIATION JOURNEY

Sandee was enjoying her teaching at Sequoya and made many good friends there. She would be up early each morning and was usually out the door before me unless I was flying out to go train someone in a distant land. The day that I went to the airport to inquire about resuming flight lessons had turned into a morning routine that sometimes meant that after Sandee headed to school, I headed to the airport for a flight lesson before heading to Oklahoma City to sell drugs. She would give me a hard time about flying and not working—she wanted my bonuses, so get to it, fella! When the first credit card bill came in with about $2,000 of flight lessons on it, she hit the roof. We had to have a squaring off about it and figured out a way to stagger the lessons out over a few months so we could afford it. Flying is not cheap, and you have to plan for it and deal with it.

We worked it out, but we had to go slow because we simply could not afford it. Anything centered in true passion and desire has a corresponding solution to getting it done, no matter how long it takes or what sacrifices need to be made to achieve it. It is up to you if it gets done. Or not.

FLIGHT INSTRUCTORS AND JOHNNY CARSON

Crabtree Aircraft in Guthrie, Oklahoma, became my flight school and airport hangout from 1983 to 1986. Glen Crabtree became a good friend, and my instructor, David Crater, and I flew for my student ticket, my private license, and my instrument rating. We usually flew the school's Cessna 152, and for the instrument we did all the air work in the 172. David was an interesting guy, and you get to know your instructor very well when you live in the cockpit for hours on end. David was an ordained minister and a very clean guy. Did not smoke, drink, or cuss. I could not make him cuss. Even with all the lessons that I gave Bob Lepine, a national talk-show host, who finally learned in his school-aged years to throw out a few expletives now and then, I could not get David to cuss.

We had him over for dinner one night, had a nice bottle of scotch and some wine, but David did not partake in either. He was not married and lived the life of a starving flight instructor. Years later, I received a tragic call from my secretary at the time that David had been killed in a crash in California on the Mexican border. He had moved there to fly for the border patrol, and the word on the crash was that they were doing low-level recon at night and hit the top of a rock outcropping. That story has been disputed. His family and others close to the crash speculate they were shot down by drug runners and the feds do not want us to know of it, but that is unproven.

I was shocked to learn my friend had been killed. It still bothers me to this day. David is the one who soloed me, got out of the airplane and told me to go fly by myself, and watched me from the ground until I completed my three takeoffs and landings. I miss him. He would love to know that I now fly my own jet.

Although I had to frequently travel to southern California, there were memorable times that, for one reason or another, made it worth the hassle. I never did get used to the time change going out there, and the grind was getting to me. On one trip, I was scheduled to spend a week working with a fellow rep named Pat Newton. Pat was a young, good-looking SoCal kid who loved living out there. He would show me some of the cool things they did in California. His favorite was to try to find a girl during delays in a traffic jam. He would wait until all the cars were stopped dead, and if he saw a pretty girl in the car next to him, he would put the car in park, get out, run over to the pretty girl's window, and ask for a lip-smacking kiss. Those pretty SoCal guys can probably pull that off most of the time, but in Texas they might get their asses shot off. I thought if he did get his ass shot off, at least I could catch an early flight home.

One day, we had lunch at Universal Studios in Burbank. After lunch, we were heading down the elevator in a crowded post-lunch exodus of people. Pat and I were talking about country-western dancing. A lady on the elevator overheard our conversation and said she was a country-western dance instructor. I thought to myself, *Yeah, right. In California? There is no way.* Well, as it turned out, way! Not only did she teach dance lessons, but her day job was working at NBC studios in the On Air programming studio. On Air would develop and film the promos of new television programs coming out soon on the network. Her job was to coordinate all of that, and oddly enough, her name was also Pat. She said that if we did not believe her to just show up at the NBC studio gates at 4:00 p.m. and she would let us in and show us around. We were supposed to be making sales calls, but it was too much of a temptation for this Texas boy to pass up. She was probably lying, and I was a sucker again, but we had to find out.

At 4:00 p.m., Pat and I pulled up to the guard gate and gave our names to the guard attendant. I figured he would draw his gun and shoot us, or at least Pat. Nope. He said he had been expecting us, opened the gate, and told us where to drive and look for special parking near a door in the back. We did that. We found the parking spot, got out of the car dressed in our full suits with dapper-looking shoes and neckties, and stood outside the door. It opened, and another guard welcomed us inside and told us to go up the stairs to On Air Productions. We did that too. And I will be damned. We walked into On Air and there stood the other Pat! She was excited to see us and told us we needed to hurry to another part of the building.

A couple minutes later, we found ourselves standing backstage with Johnny Carson. His guests the first time (yes, we did this trip twice) included Liberace and Joe Williams, a jazz singer at the time. This was in 1982. I shook the hand of Doc Severinsen and talked with Liberace. It was really cool.

They kept Johnny away from everyone as he prepared to walk out on the stage from behind the center of two curtains. NBC Pat got us two seats, and we sat ten feet behind the set, directly behind where Johnny would sit interviewing his guests. There were two TV monitors, and the guests had to walk between us and the TV to go to stage center, waiting for a guy to pull the curtain apart while Doc's orchestra played a snazzy introduction of the next star.

I was amazed that this little lady got us in there. The second time she got us in I had the chance to pour coffee alongside and speak with Robert Blake, the childhood star in *Our Gang* from 1939 to 1944. He played Mickey. In 2005, Blake was tried and acquitted of the 2001 murder of his second wife, Bonnie Lee Blakley. In November 2005, he was found liable in a California civil court for her wrongful death. He died on March 9, 2023, at the age of eighty-nine. Doc Severinsen is ninety-four years old. They were part of the glory years in Hollywood.

NBC Pat was great to us, and Sandee and I invited her out to Oklahoma the next year, and when she visited we had a blast. I wonder what ever happened to her. But she was the real deal, and we had a lot of fun. And we sold drugs between the visits to NBC studios. We would watch the recorded show later that evening, knowing we were behind the curtain and the whole stage setup.

FINDING A CHURCH HOME

In 1984, I was doing more sales training than I was selling in my own territory, so I was beginning to be away from home more than I really liked, but I did not really notice it because I was trying to get a management job. Sandee had become interested in finding a church home, and her close friends at school were members of a Baptist church in Edmond called Henderson Hills Baptist. We began to visit there and began to know more people and participate in social events that Sandee wanted to attend.

When it came time to join the church, the pastor asked me if I had been baptized, and I told him just the water drops on the forehead as a baby. He said to join Henderson Hills, that it required immersion baptism, and that I needed to do so to join the church. So, I did. I was baptized at Henderson Hills, making good on my prayer of salvation spoken years earlier at a ski camp in Colorado. Sandee and I were members of Henderson Hills Baptist Church.

BREAKING THE SURLY BONDS OF EARTH —A SOLO ACHIEVEMENT

By Christmas 1983, I was preparing to solo in a Cessna 152 at the Guthrie Airport. It was December 23, 1983, when David got out of the airplane and watched me complete the pattern three times. By May 1984, I was preparing for my private pilot check ride. I had started flying my dad's Cherokee, N7885W, in 1970 at the age of fifteen. Now, thirteen years later, I was finally getting my private pilot's license. I took my check ride in May the following year with examiner Buddy Haines. You never forget the names of your instructors or your check ride examiners. I can forget the name of someone I met this morning but still always remember the names of my instructors and examiners. It is easy to remember people who were a part of the significant events in your life. When I think of them, I can remember every detail.

I think that's what happens when we focus on those moments, the ones greeted with such anticipation that they never lose their inspiration. In aviation, there are few things more satisfying than achieving a new pilot rating, an advancement of duty and responsibility that can never be taken away. I was so thrilled to pass my check ride. I recall my examiner telling me in the cockpit when I had demonstrated the last required flight maneuver, "Well, since you are a new private pilot, fly me home." When we landed, friends at the flight school took out a pair of scissors and pulled out my shirttail, promptly and unceremoniously cut it off, and my instructor, David Crater, signed it. Cutting the shirttail off new pilots is a tradition dating back decades.

With my private "ticket" firmly in hand, I called my good friend Larry Moore and asked if he wanted to go for a ride. And we did. We went up for about an hour in a Cessna 152. He was my first passenger. I will never forget it.

The first trip that Sandee and I took in a rented Cessna 172 was to St. Louis, Missouri, to reunite with a close family friend, Betty Lowry.

Soon after we were married, we adopted a cute little dog from the local animal shelter. She was just a mutt, but in our experience, mutts can be awesome pets. She was a mix of cocker spaniel and dachshund. I'll bet that was a party. We named her Ginger. Ginger was a little green around the edges when she flew with us, but she never got sick. On the way to visit Betty, we stopped in Rolla, Missouri, to visit my best childhood friend, Bill Merten, and his wife Charlotte.

I took Bill on a short ride around his town in the Cessna, and it was fun to fly with a friend I had known since second grade. I only had about seventy hours at this point, so I was very green and at the most dangerous time of a young pilot's career. You have the license but not much experience. We went on to St. Louis during a SIGMET for a storm front entering the area. A SIGMET is code for significant meteorology, or in other words, harmful stuff is coming.

We landed as the winds changed, and I got my first lesson in wind shear. We took every inch of a four-thousand-foot runway to get on the ground and stopped. We waited for better weather for our return three days later. We had rented a plane, taken a trip with Ginger, and we returned all in one piece. It was the first of many trips for Sandee and me together. Now it was time to begin thinking about a family to join us and Ginger.

I began my instrument flight training soon after getting my private ticket. I continued to rent airplanes from Crabtree Aircraft in Guthrie, Oklahoma. Glen Crabtree and I became good acquaintances, and I looked up to him for the business he built, which included the flight school, a small fleet of rental airplanes, a maintenance shop, and a sales office. He shopped in Trade-a-Plane for low-priced deals on used airplanes.

Being around all these airplanes owned by others made me begin thinking about owning my own airplane. I found one in the newspaper that I was interested in and bought it before Glen found it in the paper. He was always looking for a deal. I told him that I had found one I was trying to buy, and he put me in touch with his banker, who made the loan process easy for me. I appreciated his favor even though I had cut him out as the middleman. After all, I found it; why should I pay a middleman? I could barely even afford it anyway, but I bought it.

Our first airplane was a 1968 Piper Cherokee Arrow. It had retractable landing gear and had the same 180 hp engine my dad's plane had, so it felt very normal for me. It had crummy radios like most used airplanes of its day. I recall it had one radio, a Narco Mark 12, normal steam gauges and the like. But it was a smoker's airplane, so I had to clean it inside and out after I got it back to my Guthrie tiedown slot out on the grass next to the taxiway. When I bought it, I did not know to have a mechanic do a full inspection on it, as I didn't know that would be a wise thing to do. I was so excited to buy my first airplane that I approached it like buying a car.

Again, the first version of anything you do is typically a bag of mistakes. I paid $10,500 for her and picked her up coming out of the maintenance shop in Stillwater, Oklahoma, after she had a propeller overhaul. When I bought her, the previous owner had already begun an overhaul on the propeller. I did not even know what a prop overhaul was until the mechanic who completed the work, but not a full inspection, explained it to me and showed me what they did before I flew it home.

When I got her in the air for the fifteen-minute flight back to Guthrie, that prop began surging and making funny noises but finally smoothed out. I guess when you're an old girl like her, she takes a little bit of movement to get the kinks out, or at least that is how I got myself off the hook emotionally from realizing I did not know as much as I thought I knew and not as much as I was going to learn while owning airplanes. As of this writing, I have owned and operated twelve airplanes, from single-engine pistons to turboprops to our own jet today. I have learned a lot, but as with many things in life, I wish I had more experience on the first one.

A tool in the hand of the inexperienced is just a tool, and it is the experience that determines the fate of both.

I had a blast flying that airplane. I received my instrument rating from David Crater and Buddy Haines again and flew one of the IFR airplanes (instrument flight rules) for my instruction. One time Sandee surprised me with a rental of that airplane. When I got home from a trip, she had my golf clubs loaded, the rental agreement signed, and fooled me into thinking we were taking some friends flying. She used one of my customers, the head of pharmacy for Presbyterian Hospital, Mark St. Cyr, as a scapegoat for me thinking we had planned something with him and his wife.

When Sandee and I got to the Guthrie Airport, everyone knew about the ruse but me! Crater knew, and so did Crabtree! It was a surprise because it was my birthday weekend, and Sandee had arranged for us to visit our friends Mona and Randy Hines in Austin. I had to change gears for a few minutes because I was so surprised. Very clever, Sandee. We have learned in our forty-plus years of marriage that I like surprises, and Sandee does not. I have adhered to that premise and reinforced that premise by re-attempting other surprises that didn't work, such as buying her horses, swimsuits, lingerie.

I am firmly in no-surprises mode these days. I can only take beatings with a restaurant menu so many times when she tells friends these surprise stories. But she keeps the surprises coming, that is for sure! We took off for Austin, and the airport was reporting IFR skies requiring an instrument approach to the parallel runways for multiple takeoff and landing operations.

The only problem was that I was a couple of hours away from taking my instrument check ride and not yet legal to fly in the clouds solo. Well, for where we were and the conditions, I determined it was safe to shoot the approach. I shot the instrument landing system (ILS) among scattered clouds into the parallel runway with a Southwest jet landing on the other side at the same time as us. I could have ducked under the ceiling and gone to visual flight rules, but it was easier just to shoot the approach in and around the scattered layer of clouds, which gave us some visibility, so that is what we did.

It was a legal approach. It felt like a visual approach. If it had been overcast, we would *not* have shot that approach, but the weather was good. I treated it like a visual approach with instrument backup, and we arrived safely. We had a wonderful time on the weekend. Nice trip, Sandee! I will return the favor without surprising you.

We tried flying the Arrow to see her relatives in Gatesville, Texas, one evening, but because of the weather we turned around when we were over Dallas and flew back to Guthrie and got in the car and drove the six hours instead.

Even though I was an IFR pilot, the Arrow was not certified for instrument flight, so we drove and still had a great time with Sandee's family once we got there. We kept Cherokee Arrow N4934J on a tiedown at the Guthrie Airport until I decided to trade the Arrow for a 1954 Bonanza 35 with the V-tail. Long story, but Sandee did not like that airplane, and in hindsight it was a bit too much vintage for both of our tastes. Older is fine in wine and art, but not on bent and shaped aluminum.

We had issues with that airplane. We had to make an emergency landing on a piece of concrete on a guy's ranch east of Dallas in the middle of July 1985. The engine was overheating, the electrical system had fully discharged, and I couldn't get the landing gear down without hand cranking it. The crank was on the floor in the back seat, and I could barely reach it and fly the airplane at the same time. It was an old system, and without the electrical system working, I could not get three green lights telling me the gear was down all the way. I had to trust that it was down.

I told Sandee to crack the door open in case the gear was not down and we belly landed. We did not want that door stuck closed with a buckled wing sitting on the pavement instead of the three-wheel landing gear. I could see our shadow as we crossed the "runway," and the gear looked down. When we flared, with the runway getting shorter in front of us, the wheels rolled onto the runway and we came to a stop. We turned the airplane around and taxied back to find the landowner on a tractor, already removing fence posts in his driveway so our low-wing Bonanza could taxi to his house. When we shut down and got out, we met a man who lived there who was not only a pilot but was also an aircraft and powerplant mechanic (A&P). We could not believe it.

I apologized for the surprise visit. He lived in Dallas and had come down to his ranch for a little bit, just in time for our unexpected arrival. God is great all the time. He made some adjustments, charged our battery, *and* gave us some fuel so we could make it all the way back to Guthrie without needing a refueling stop. We sent him a check a few days later, as I recall. We landed in Guthrie at night with all lights on and the landing gear fully deployed, so life was good once again!

Nothing like learning lessons in an old and experienced airplane. Airplanes with a lot of hours on them at the hands of pilots unknown have a mystery to them that creates a sense of risk to fly them. They are mostly perfectly fine, but you have to watch them and learn early in a flight if there are problems. Experience is the teacher, but fate is also the hunter. So you have to be on your toes one minute at a time. I have stuck to newer models since. If you fly long enough, you will have pesky surprise situations that require training and creativity to deal with, as I later learned.

11

A career change, Natalie is born, leaving Oklahoma for Dallas, James Burke "Kingston" the legend, first true start-up company, two houses, one income.

In 1984, our company went through a Reduction in Force (RIF). When I learned about the RIF, I was stunned. I was in Tulsa when I got a message to call my area manager, Bill Ward, who told me to get to Dallas that night because he needed to talk to me. I was sure I was going to be a casualty of the RIF and lose my job. In a RIF, a company sheds its nonperformers or other expensive people to save money and try things differently.

When I got to Dallas, I met Bill at Tupinamba's restaurant, which I thought was going to be a weird place to get fired. Instead, he promoted me. My boss at the time, Jerry Lyden, and a handful of reps and managers had been terminated, and Bill wanted to reassign some of the district and area responsibilities under new leadership, including me. Bill promoted me to a region of the Midwest down to Oklahoma and included about seven states. I named it the "Western Plains Region" and got to work right away. I was now reporting to Bill, whom we all called Buzz.

Buzz and I became absolute best of friends, and we worked our tails off, but we partied a lot too. We had area meetings in some pretty swank places, such as the Biltmore Hotel in downtown LA. It was at that meeting in 1986 that Mr. Bill Ward, Buzz, announced to our group that he was leaving the company to work for a start-up in Dallas called United Dental Care.

We rode together in first class back to Dallas later that day. I got the full story there, and I just could not believe anyone would ever leave American. We were there in its best glory years, but it would now be different with Buzz no longer at the helm of our area. I had some career thinking to do as it was my first experience with a company forging ahead with new plans that created a lasting effect on everyone involved, including me.

AMERICAN HOSPITAL SUPPLY CORPORATION MAKES A LANDMARK CHANGE

By 1985, AHSC was going through a lot of changes, trying to navigate its size and strengths among the big boys of health care. Baxter Travenol, one of American's strongest competitors, was lurking around the water cooler, trying to buy the larger AHSC. AHSC maintained its position as leader in the health care industry until being acquired by Baxter Travenol in a merger on November 25, 1985. Founded in 1920, by 1964, American sold products and services to nineteen of every twenty hospitals in America. American also employed one out of every forty-six workers in America. "While the tremendous success enjoyed by the AHSC was a result of the corporation's strong leadership, the growth of the hospital industry also played a vital role increasing sales for American," according to the AHSC biography published by the Northwestern University Archival and Manuscript Collections at the time.

It was all a shock to me because after seven years I had a management position with a great company, and I wanted to stay with ACC. With the parent corporation preparing to be purchased by Baxter, they anticipated an employee exit. I got a call from my new boss after Buzz left, who offered me a stay bonus of $40k and a chance to move to the home office, which was being moved to Wilmington, Delaware, for a chance to be a product manager. But there was no way I was going to the East Coast, and Sandee and I really wanted to get back to Dallas at some point. And to make the world even more exciting, three months before the announcement that AHSC was being sold, Sandee surprised me with a planned weekend getaway in Tulsa. I had flown in from somewhere on a Friday, and we hit the road, driving to Tulsa to get away from it all. We checked into a very nice hotel after dark.

We hadn't been in our room five minutes, and there was a knock at the door. In came a waiter, pushing a cart with champagne (Sandee's favorite for forty years), chocolate-covered strawberries, cheese and crackers … and a balloon attached to the champagne. With the waiter still in the room with us, I finally read the balloon, and the waiter was hanging around to see my reaction. The balloon read, "Congratulations on your New Baby!" It was a game-changer and a moment to always remember.

The waiter asked me what I thought about the moment, and I said, "It is time for you to go! I am excited, of course!"

We ordered room service for dinner and just enjoyed the game-changing life experience. And, true to Sandee's form of making big deals, big deals, we had a great weekend and launched into our next phase of our first baby. Sandee had many dreams while she was pregnant, and in one dream, she pictured a baby in her arms and bringing a little girl home to be introduced to our dog, Ginger. Sandee woke me up during the night to tell me this dream. She introduced the baby as "Natalie," and lo and behold, we had a little girl on February 23, 1986, and we named her Natalie Sue Gasmire. When she was born at Mercy Hospital in Oklahoma City, I was still at ACC; however, we were on the cusp of making a job change, which really made life exciting, and we were planning to move back to Dallas.

Bill Ward called me while I was in Key West, Florida, during our last NSM at ACC, and asked if I would be interested in interviewing at his new start-up company, United Dental Care, and meet with his CEO, the one, the only, the infamous, the conqueror of all things, the Mensa, never forget anything and kick your ass with both hands and one foot tied behind his back, give it up for James … Burke … Kingston!

We always called Jim "Jim" to his face and in conversations with him. But he was more commonly referred to among his senior team simply as "Kingston." His name brought shivers and shakes to all who knew him. When Buzz asked me to interview, I was so excited at the prospect of working with him again, I carved out a day during the meeting to interview on the phone with Kingston. Six weeks after Natalie was born, "JBK" was my new boss, and Buzz already had six months under his belt at UDC.

Two days into the job, I thought I had been hit in the face with a basketball. Buzz was the VP of Sales, and I was the director of provider relations. I did not even know what that meant, but we were moving back to Dallas. With little Natalie in tow, just six weeks old, we headed south on I-35. Sandee was still recovering from surgery and the trauma that a new mother has just after getting a first baby home. I left for Key West with the crazy meetings, parties, and the boozing it up with friends as we celebrated another great sales year. She was not happy with me but excited to be heading to Dallas.

After her mother left after helping Sandee with Natalie for a week or so, my wife was home alone with a crying baby and recovering from a cesarean birth. I did not blame her for the frustration and the difficulty adjusting to this new life with Natalie and a move. She also was going to quit teaching, and it was hard leaving her friends. We were both adjusting. We could not sell our house, so we rented it out. It was during the oil crisis of the mid-1980s, and gas prices were almost seventy-five cents a gallon, and home mortgage interest rates were 10 percent. It was tough times, particularly in Oklahoma, where oil and gas reigned king.

We rented a house in Plano just to get started there. I was working in Dallas for Kingston before we moved, so I was staying with Ruth and Si while we looked for a house to rent. We found one, and I made a deal with the landlord, gave him the telephone handshake, and told him we would come by after work to give him the deposit and sign the lease. When we got there, he had already leased it to someone else who got there before we did. I was livid but kept my cool.

Ruth, Natalie, and Sandee were in the car when I came back out to tell them we still didn't have a house. "Are you serious?" Sandee said. We just drove off and kept living at Ruth's. It all worked out with a different house that we rented in Plano until we had the means to buy another house. But we still needed to sell our house in Edmond, Oklahoma, in order for us to pull it off financially.

OKLAHOMA WAS A GREAT PLACE TO LIVE AND START OUR CAREERS

Life in Edmond, Oklahoma, was low-stress and a lot of fun for both of us. We would take occasional flying trips when we could afford to rent one of the school planes in Guthrie. According to my most recent statement from the Social Security Administration, my reported earnings had gone from $2,400 per year when I was a senior in high school, working summer and weekend jobs at the O-I plant in Dallas, to $8,404 in 1979 when I was working while finishing my degree at North Texas. In 1980, my first full year out of school, not married and living on my own, I reported earnings of $17,730. Of that, $13,100 was my salary at ACC, and my sales bonuses were $4,630. That was a pretty penny back then.

To me, it was a relief from living like a twenty-two-year-old pauper. I was twenty-three years old when I graduated in the spring of 1979 and moved to Oklahoma City before Sandee and I had gotten back together. I enjoyed and really dove into learning how business in a large health care products company worked. I knew how to sell because my life had depended on it for the previous ten years. But now,

I was beginning to see that I had no business experience that could be leveraged into anything meaningful any time soon. There were corporate programs that had been rolled out at ACC, and I began to connect some dots about how business could be aggregated into increasing sales volume and protection from competition, both in the marketplace and in the mind of the customer.

There were other large manufacturers of products that we competed with, so we were not the only game in town, but it sure felt like it for the first seven years of my first professional career as a Medical Representative II, then a regional sales trainer, and finally a region manager. All of that experience also came with complete autonomy with my schedule and where I spent my time. I was left alone as long as my territory or region was at or ahead of our sales budgets. I can only remember two tough years. They were 1981 and 1982.

Those two years were when we got married. After a good sales year in 1980, my sales quota was raised to a level I did not overachieve, so my earnings were flat. We had enough money, but we also weren't saving anything. When we moved to Dallas, and I went to work for Kingston at United Dental Care (UDC), life was getting pretty serious. I was a new father, we had a load of debt with a house we couldn't sell in Edmond, Oklahoma, and we were living in a house that was not what Sandee and I really wanted—but it worked for the time being. I was working insane hours, including weekends. I was making $48,000 per year, but the company car was gone with the ACC job.

We were on our own, but we had the help of Ruth, who constantly visited after Natalie was born. The economy was so bad at that time, having gone from feast to famine for everyone. During the feast, home values soared, and the mortgage companies jumped on it with a product called "negative amortization." It allowed new home buyers the opportunity to purchase a home beyond their means by capturing the predicted increase in the home's value and adding it to the amount of the loan. The concept was that inflation in the home's value would be more than enough to cover the higher balance owed when the house sold sometime in the future. Mortgage interest rates were nearly 10 percent, and inflation was staggering at the time.

For perspective, I am writing this book during and just after COVID in 2021–2022. The Russians invaded Ukraine the day after Natalie's birthday in 2022, and gas prices are over $7 per gallon on the West Coast. Inflation is being reported by our government as nearing 10 percent, but many essential goods and services are much higher than that. The references today to past decades of inflation most often point to the years I am writing about here. I have the perspective and personal net worth to endure today's troubling times, but back then I felt like we were in a rubber raft with a lot of holes in it, with one paddle and no bucket to keep up with the troubling water. Our experience with negative amortization made the situation worse, and I had no idea how to dig out.

It all worked fine until it did not. The way we found out about the fine print on our mortgage was when we had an offer from the people who had been renting our house for a year (their golden retriever was hit and killed by a car in front of that house, which was on a one-acre cul-de-sac lot). We had built and bought that home for $102,500. The value of homes had now plummeted to the famine part of the economic cycle. The only savings we had were in that home equity. But there was no equity. Because of negative amortization, the balance owed on the home was now $113,000. We accepted an offer of $80,000 for the house to get out from under it.

When some Oklahoma homeowners were mailing the keys to the mortgage company and leaving their houses behind, we chose not to do that. Although I did try asking the mortgage company to make us a deal that we could live with to get the loan paid off. I was working for Kingston, and I was traveling through the Dallas Love Field airport when I grabbed a pay phone (yes, we grew up on pay phones and landlines) and called the mortgage company to ask them to help, or I would mail them the keys. Sounded like a reasonable threat, although we were not going to just walk away from the debt.

The loan officer told me she was shocked that I even called her to ask! Then she promptly and directly told me no. We decided to sell the house and drum up the $35,000 it was going to take to go to closing and get the house behind us. I was willing to get another job, although I do not know how I would have fit it in because of the hours I was working for Kingston.

Sandee's mother stepped in to help. She was by then a vice president at InterFirst, which today is Bank of America. It was convenient that she also headed up a new program called "Loan by Phone." It was pretty unheard of to call the bank on the phone and get a loan, sometimes within a couple of days. Ruth helped us—no, let's say she saved us—by cosigning on a loan from the bank that we were now obligated to pay, or she would be responsible for the balance. That was not going to happen. I did not want to stiff my mother-in-law. Bad idea.

The house in Oklahoma was sold. We had no money, were $35,000 in debt, on a single income, with a very young Natalie and the job title of director of professional relations, whatever that was.

THE UNITED DENTAL CARE STORY

"ALWAYS REMEMBER THE OLD YIDDISH SAYING, THE FISH ROTS FROM THE HEAD DOWN."
—James B. Kingston

I had an office. I had never had an office. There were no computers. It was 1986. All correspondence was handwritten, then manually proofed, then edited, then put in the regular mail. Stamp machines and copiers were the necessary artillery for office work. Mont Blanc pens were the status symbol of the successful businessperson. Some background on what was going on in health care at the time is necessary here, and this viewpoint helped shape my thinking about what, metaphorically speaking, the next lemonade stand or popcorn company should look like.

I had always thought about what customer need could be understood, fixed, and sold to. Joining UDC was a huge risk for me. I knew how to sell, but that was it. I had no training in finance, accounting, corporate transaction law, contracts, quality assurance, and risk management. My job at UDC was all those things and more.

Our business model was very forward-thinking. As with most things, the West Coast of the United States tries something, then, if it works, it drifts east and lands somewhere in Texas. This new health care model was an HMO. A health maintenance organization. Until then, I was a product guy. I could sell anything that I could hold in my hand. At UDC, the only thing I could hold in my hand was my No. 2 mechanical pencil. I had to learn and understand the concept of service. No physical product.

I was hired to build another foreign concept, a dental care delivery system. Our "product" was in the field of health benefits with large employers. What was changing the delivery and cost in medical care was beginning to be developed in the field of dental care. I could not see the vision of this for a while. It took a few years to grasp the idea that we were building something that people did not yet know they needed. Employers were looking for ways of reducing the premiums for themselves and their employees. We were creating a new economic and delivery model in dental care. We knew what benefits would result for the company; after all, that is why it was developed in the first place. Now we needed to talk the market into believing they needed what we had. It was sales. Period. And that is one reason Kingston took a chance with me, to get things moving, to get the early pieces in place so we had something to take to the paying marketplace. I have always been comfortable with the concept of a start-up because I know it can be done.

There were several ways to build this dental HMO product, including reducing the amount paid to the provider of the care, putting more of the financial burden on the company to help employees, or finding a way to share the risk with the employees. In any case, Buzz oversaw sales, and I oversaw the dental care delivery system. What that meant for Buzz was that he and a couple of sales reps that he hired were calling on large employers in the Dallas Ft. Worth area to get them to offer the UDC dental network of providers, aka dentists and dental specialists, such as oral surgeons, periodontists, endodontists, and orthodontists.

The proverbial listing of dentists in the UDC offering fell upon me. I was in charge, with no help early on, of recruiting dentists to discount their fees to fill their unscheduled and available chair time and turn that into cash from UDC. It was a system termed "capitation." After a dentist would hear my pitch, and because HMOs/DMOs were still unknown and not understood, they thought it was more like "de-capitation."

Here is how it worked. UDC had contracted with an actuary in Atlanta named Bob Gold and Associates. I had never heard of an actuary. Pretty simple, but an actuary takes large volumes of experience data among a population of people and forecasts what medical or dental needs and costs might "actually" be expected to occur. From that, we could predict the amount of care people would need and what they would spend for their care. The conceptual idea was to pay the dentists in a way that was affordable for the employer and "members" (HMOs have members but also just happen to be the patient).

We would pay the contracted dentist a monthly fee (capitation) for each member/patient who selected his/her dental practice. From this list, Buzz could market the network of available dentists to employer groups and other buyers of our plan. The dentist would get approximately $5 per member per month, plus would charge for services according to the fee schedule he or she agreed to accept from the patient.

The concept of a copayment was just beginning to be understood by the consuming public, and the dentist agreed to charge the fees.

But the dentist would not get any additional payment from UDC, and that is where the concept of capitation became decapitation for the dentist. The dentist would need to have a large list of members that selected him/her so that the monthly per-member fee was worth making the open chair time available to HMO patients. Most of the dentists I worked with hated it. I had to do a lot of explaining to keep them from bailing out on us. It would cause the employers all kinds of problems if there were only two UDC dentists left to serve their five thousand employees and their families. UDC was very forward-thinking in this regard, and Kingston trusted and demanded that I get and keep a dentist delivery system.

It was not easy to ask dentists to fill a practice with patients who largely had never been able to afford dental coverage, and many had never been to a dentist and needed a lot of work done. There was large adverse selection going on with these patients, and the dentists figured it out and complained a lot. To me. And to the patients themselves. And they complained to the employers that bought the coverage the dentists were contractually bound to deliver.

The capitation concept was too early for the delivery system that I put together, and I spent much of my time talking and training the dentists to enjoy the crummy economic sandwich I was asking them to eat. The patients loved it. The employers tolerated it. The dentists hated it.

Funny thing about the psychology of paying something for services rendered. In my experience at UDC, having been the one to write the benefit plans themselves and determine what the patient would pay at each visit, it is clear that patients who had *any* fee to pay appreciated it more and were better patients than the ones getting the same procedure done for no charge. There is an entitlement thing that happens, and I saw it and had to deal with it firsthand. Someone who gets a dental cleaning and must pay even $5 will show up on time, have brushed their teeth, and treat the visit like what it is—an investment in their health.

The patient that shows up with no charge for what will be done is a different breed of cat, and I saw this example in practice while I was recruiting a dentist in Toledo, Ohio. I was in the waiting room, and this woman was chowing down on a bag of Lay's potato chips when they called her name to provide a no-charge cleaning. Geez, I hope she brushed her teeth.

There you go: pay for something, and you will act with self-respect. Get it free, and you probably couldn't care less.

I learned through my UDC experience that there are only two ways to grow a market. The first is to directly *compete* with other "strategic" companies already doing the same service or selling the same proven product with zero customer orientation. Just make it or serve it and sell it faster than your competitors. The other way is to *pioneer* a new concept or idea to a market that does not yet know it needs what you can provide. That is what I ran up against with the dentist recruitment. It was hard for them to ignore all their training to just "hang a shingle" after dental school and believe the patients would magically show up without much effort. Instead, I was asking them to work harder for a lot less than they wanted, but at least they would be busy.

I had to put salt and pepper with some mayo to make that message go down without it coming back up. But I was able to convince one hundred or more dentists and their staff to think giving away free cleanings, $6 fillings, $3 extractions, and other money-losing services was a good long-term strategy for them. The bottom-line business problem that we had was that we claimed to be the "First Prepaid Dental Plan in Texas." It made us feel good to say it, but it did not give me bragging rights during dentist recruitment. They did not want the first prepaid plan or the last; they hated managed care, and that is what UDC was. The companies and patients wanted it if their dentist was on the list—then they were fine with it.

I guess, as with most things, either you're pitching or you're catching, and there are pros and cons to both.

I remember one time I decided to ask Kingston to better support the dentists that I had contracted with by giving them more money. In Dallas, where we first started, I had put together a delivery system of more than one hundred dentist and specialist locations. When an employee/member would make a dentist selection at enrollment, the $5 monthly fee began going to the selected dentist. However, if the member did not yet select a dentist, the $5 fee went into a No Dentist Selected pool of money held by UDC. The dentists did not know about it, and actually, if they did know about it, they would not understand it. They got paid for their patients, and they did not look deeper than that. They just knew about patients who had selected their practice and received a monthly capitation for those patients, then charged them a reduced fee per the coverage of services selected by the employer.

So, I went to Kingston in the weekly meetings I had with him every Monday at 7:00 a.m. In his office. Each day at 7:00 a.m., he met with one of the three founding members of his management team. Me, Bill Ward, and our CFO, John Steen. I had Mondays. It stressed me out every weekend for seven years. I went to Kingston to ask that we use the No Dentist Selected pile of money for a few of my best dentists to keep them happy and quiet and to make my job easier by not having to replace another dot on the map.

Kingston put down his pencil and stared at me. The red flushed up his neck and into his face. He continued to stare at me and said, "Fuzzy thinking, David. Very fuzzy thinking." He always called me David. Then he would call me Young David, as I was the youngest on the team. Then, without blinking, he asked, "Do you know what you are asking here?" I told him that I thought so. And that is when I got my first private equity lesson, explained to me in quite easy-to-understand terms.

He went over how the company was capitalized, what the three-year plan was, and how our spending and building of the business would impact each investor. We discussed my stock options and how they worked. He gave me the perspective from the top, and I was, in my inexperience, viewing everything at the pragmatic bottom, trying to exist from day to day.

I had not yet evolved into a thirty-thousand-foot thinker with that view from the top that I needed, which only comes from experience, to understand the impact of my short-term-thinking decisions.

I did not really understand this way of looking at a business. I was still reactionary and all over the board, responding to things that I thought were out of my control. Jim was an expert operator at the systems and algorithm hierarchy of needs—Mensa smart, but lacking people skills at the reporting level. But he was great to my friends and family, and it was incredibly challenging keeping up with his business intellect. I had a gold mine of intellect and experience at my doorstep with Jim, but I did not fully appreciate that for a while. I was overwhelmed by him.

TRYING TO KEEP UP

I can say today, with certainty, that had I not been taught and focused by Jim for the seven years I reported to him, I would not have had the experience and skills that I needed as I moved through my career of starting and building meaningful companies at the CEO and chairman levels that I have now been part of since 1995. His Kingston-isms were legendary, such as asking the question, "What will kill us next?" for purposes of planning and problem avoidance. He would ask me, "So, what are the drivers of our business?" and then he'd say, "The fish rots from the head down," which was his way of saying, "It's your fault if it isn't right."

When I presented a problem to him that I needed help thinking through, I was so intimidated to ask him that I would lose sleep the night before. Sometimes he was so infuriated with me when I did not understand some things, mostly financial, that he would give me that red-faced, slight smile, slight stink-eye, where I was hoping he was working patiently with himself to give me a chance. I am sure he was thinking, "Do I shoot him right here or in the parking lot while he carries his belongings out of the building?"

Or other times he would be sitting there eating his famed apples—he was always eating apples in the office—and shrug his shoulders, stare at me, and say, "Chewing bunnies." Which was his way of saying, "Do not worry about it; we will figure it out." He was a conundrum of a man. For some reason, I was his go-to guy. But I built him a delivery system second to none in DFW, and he knew it. He wanted me to learn more finance and operating skills, so he invested in me by sending me to a financial class for non-financial people, and that helped connect a lot of dots for me. I had no accounting or math classes in college. Not sure how that happened, but I changed majors two or three times and somehow, I missed those classes that I wished I had taken now that I was working for Sir Kingston.

Over time, he began to trust me with more responsibilities and began to trust my intuition on growth initiatives and how to treat people in order to expand the business outside the state of Texas. He would have me be the front man on deals because he knew he would piss someone off and blow the deal, and he knew that I would handle it to get it closed. I could build relationships, and that was not Jim's leading strength. He was too far ahead of people intellectually, and he strained at the patience it took to wait for people to catch up.

One very Kingston-type story that Buzz and I have told over and over is how Jim was so detail oriented and frugal with company money that he would keep a tick mark sheet on the refrigerator in the break room in the office to keep track of how many Cokes each person was drinking so he could take twenty-five cents out of our paychecks for each Coke we had taken. He was so into the details that it made it hard to go on vacation. I had a secretary by then, and she would call me while I was on vacation and say, "Jim is looking through all our dentist contracts. What do you want me to do?"

I'd say, "Don't worry about it. The fish rots from the head down!"

When I got back, Kingston would give me the results of his operating inspection of my department. Ultimately, I was rewarded with a title change to vice president of operations, COO. My first big step into the C-suite. I was asked to expand operations into Austin, San Antonio, Houston, and Ohio. I also learned a Kingston-ism the hard way during a private dinner with about a dozen of my favorite dentists who I put on a professional panel to advise me on dental practice stuff that we needed to know to help support them. We catered a dinner in our office conference room. Kingston sat at the head of the table, and I sat on the other end.

One of the dentists asked Jim who UDC considered the most important constituent to the business—the dentists? Jim shook his head and said, "No, the first most important people in our business are the employers. We need them to capture more members/patients." He continued, "Do you know who the next important people are to our business?"

One of the dentists chimed in, "The dentists?"

Jim calmly said, "No, the next important is the broker network so that we can get access to the employer groups. Do you know who the next most important group is to our business?"

Another dentist answered, "The dentists?"

Jim dipped his head again and softly said, "Well, no, it would be the benefit managers inside the health plans that we call on." Then Jim asked, "So you know who is last on the list of most important constituents?" The room was silent. Then Jim, with energy and a high voice, answered his own question with, "The dentists!"

I will never forget that night. And he wondered why I had a tough time keeping dentists. He viewed them as mechanical beings, putting out the production and expecting them to not make a mistake. If they did, because I built that network of dentists, it was on me to fix or replace them.

Perfection can be a goal, but realistically it is not attainable. Strive for continued improvement and be realistic with expectations; it is more beneficial than momentary perfection.

I also learned to discern what results were to be celebrated and those that were just perfunctory and part of the journey that had many more miles and years to go. A good example of this was when Kingston taught me a lesson in dealing with a state government and how to tell the difference between success and eye-rolling necessity.

Jim, Bill, and I flew down to Austin from Dallas to go before a review board to assess the viability of our business and consider our application for a license we needed in order to get local municipalities and to be credentialed to participate in managed plans that were coming to Texas, such as Cigna. We had a great tie to Cigna, but not with the state of Texas yet. Our founding chairman was a legacy in health care. Jack Anderson was the guy who put INA Health Plans and Hospital Affiliates together to become Cigna Healthcare. He was brilliant, but like Kingston, was a harsh critic, and he scared the fool out of all of us at board meetings where we gave management reports to the full board.

John Steen was so scared of Jack that he would take "calm pills" before the meeting started. I had never been in a corporate boardroom, and it took a while to get over the feeling of being a poser and not deserving to be among the business elite.

I guess it comes from not having the self-confidence or the experience that qualifies you to feel essential to the enterprise. But if you are there, you matter, so act like it. Don't act surprised to be there. Present yourself as someone that belongs in that boardroom. You have a role to play, and you are there to contribute to it.

I said something in a meeting that made no sense to Jack. He looked around the room and asked, "Can somebody please tell me what he just said?" He was probably right, and I couldn't even remember what I said because I was so nervous. But the reality is that, even in boardrooms, people are people first. The boardroom could be a water cooler for that matter. It isn't any big deal unless you make it one.

I thought Jack was interesting. His lore preceded him, from driving into the parking lot in his Bentley, to remaining silent for extended periods of time while he thought about what was being said. But he was very social, and if he had interest in knowing you better, he would make mild gestures of friendship. And for some reason, Jack asked me if I wanted to play golf with him and John Steen. When we played, Jack commented that my club head covers needed replacing, which I avoided because they were $20.

The next day, Jack left a set of *used* club head covers he had in his garage on my chair in my office. That's how millionaires keep from becoming hundredaires. Used anything has its place and economic advantages. Jack had a liking for John because John's brother, Don Steen, was also a health care icon. Don had founded so many companies and at the time was the chairman of United Surgical Partners International (USPI). Don Steen and Jack Anderson had been down many roads together. John was Don's younger brother, and Jack gave him a shot at working for Kingston as chief financial officer. So, John, Bill "Buzz" Ward, and I were all peers, trying to learn from these icons, who most people thought were rough and hard-charging, but they got results for the investor.

The three of us got along great and leaned on each other for support every week. We tried to laugh a lot, and Kingston did not like some of our antics. Buzz and I dealt with Kingston by getting a smidge of levity into our routine every now and then. Once, we skipped out in the afternoon to go to the afternoon matinee because we needed a break. We were the only suits in the theater, which was filled with kids and moms, and me and Buzz. Yep, we saw the matinee of *Ernest Goes to Camp*. We went back to the office a couple of hours later and kept on working. Jim didn't ask us where we had been and didn't even look up when we returned. He did not say anything.

Geez, it was weird, but we built a phenomenally successful company in a difficult, pioneering atmosphere. And Jim deserves all the credit for leading a solid team in his own way and pulling us all together to get it done. It might not have been the way I thought it should be done, but he was the expert, and it became a time of being taught in my career. I didn't know that I needed to know what he could teach me. Looking back, I wish I would have had that self-introspection and a confident approach to grab all the nuggets of wisdom he was dishing out.

JUST KEEP GOING

All the years I worked for Kingston seemed very tense and trying for both Sandee and me. She was a new mother and was able to keep the homestead under control even with the pressures that came with all that we were going through. Sandee is a very organized person, and she kept things on track. Before we left Oklahoma for Dallas, we decided to sell the Bonanza because we could not afford it anymore. When we did sell it, which is a whole other story, Sandee made me sign a one-page statement that I would not buy another airplane for ten years! I signed it because I agreed we would not be able to afford one again, even in ten years. But it also did not prohibit me from renting from time to time to stay current.

Kingston sent me to Houston to buy a business there, and he wanted to go with me. He sat in the copilot's seat, reading a *Wall Street Journal* while I flew him to Houston. We came back later that day. He never said a word. That was Jim. Renting was more affordable, so that is what we did. It was 1986, and other than occasionally renting an airplane, we did not fly much, until 9/11 happened in 2001. We have owned at least one personal airplane ever since that attack on America.

My grandfather Charles Gasmire with my great grandfather John Fredrick Gasmire c.1910.

My beautiful mother Ellen Louise Holdeman Gasmire in 1958.

The 10-arm Michael Owens automatic bottle machine c. 1913.

My first golf lesson at 3 years old in Toledo in 1958.

My dad Richard (Dick), my brother Jay and me in my grandads fishing boat on Lake Woodlawn in Brighton, Michigan 1962.

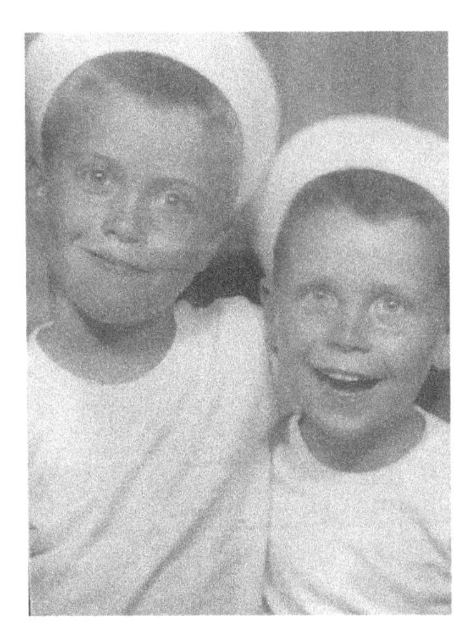

My brother, Jay, and I as goofy happy brothers in 1962.

Learning to hunt with my grandfathers .410 guage shotgun somewhere in Missouri in 1963.

Sandra Anne Orr in drill team at T.C. Marsh Junior High School in 1969 where we first met.

Sandee and I when I fell in love with her the same year I began flying in 1971.

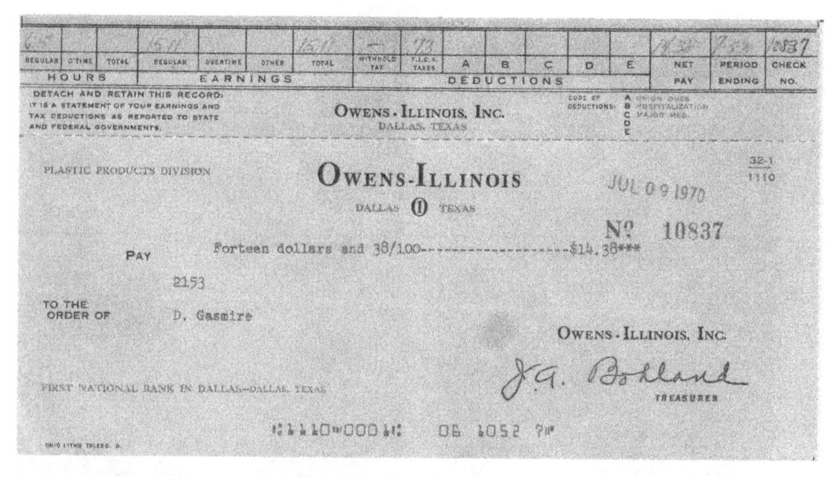

HOURS			EARNINGS				DEDUCTIONS							NET PAY	PERIOD ENDING	CHECK NO.
REGULAR	O'TIME	TOTAL	REGULAR	OVERTIME	OTHER	TOTAL	WITHHOLD TAX	F.I.C.A. TAXES	A	B	C	D	E			
[illegible]			15.11			15.11	—	.73						[illegible]	[illegible]	10837

DETACH AND RETAIN THIS RECORD: IT IS A STATEMENT OF YOUR EARNINGS AND TAX DEDUCTIONS AS REPORTED TO STATE AND FEDERAL GOVERNMENTS.

OWENS-ILLINOIS, INC.
DALLAS, TEXAS

CODE OF DEDUCTIONS: A UNION DUES B HOSPITALIZATION C MAJOR MED. D E

PLASTIC PRODUCTS DIVISION

OWENS-ILLINOIS
DALLAS TEXAS

32-1
1110

JUL 09 1970

Nº 10837

PAY Forteen dollars and 38/100-------------------$14.38***

2153

TO THE ORDER OF D. Gasmire

OWENS-ILLINOIS, INC.

J.G. Bolland
TREASURER

FIRST NATIONAL BANK IN DALLAS—DALLAS, TEXAS

⑆1110⑉0001⑆ 06 1052 7⑈

OHIO LITHO TOLEDO, O.

My first real paycheck for $14.38 in 1970. My dad told me to never cash it so I would always remember where I started. I never cashed it.

A Jim Kingston photo of me crossing the finish line at my first of six White Rock Marathons in 1987. I broke the tape in 3 hours and 48 minutes.

Sandee and I on a cruise with our family in 1998.

Bill "Buzz" Ward, Tom "TA" Blake and me at the finish line after a cold and rainy White Rock Marathon in 1988. We finished in 3:32.

Riding my favorite horse "Yello Cat" at our Flying G Ranch in Fredericksburg, Texas.

Jay, Dad and me at the Flying G Ranch built in 1891.

NASA Flight Director and my boyhood hero, Gene Kranz, with me at the Odyssey Healthcare Support Center in 2004. He is famous for the true story of Apollo 13 and why we named the company Odyssey, after the name of the crippled space craft which completed its intended journey. Very "hospice".

The day we publicly listed Odyssey Healthcare on Nasdaq, on my dad's birthday October 31, 2001. Pictured are Dick Burnham with his family daughters Krista and Kara, his wife Sally, with Sandee and I. It was a big day and created a lot of change on every front.

Playing golf with Phil Mickelson at Colonial Country Club pro-am in 2003. I qualified by tying for first place in a private golf event. Phil and I were tied with birdies after the first hole, then my normal game happened.

My dad, me, my sister Sue Ellen and my brother Jay.

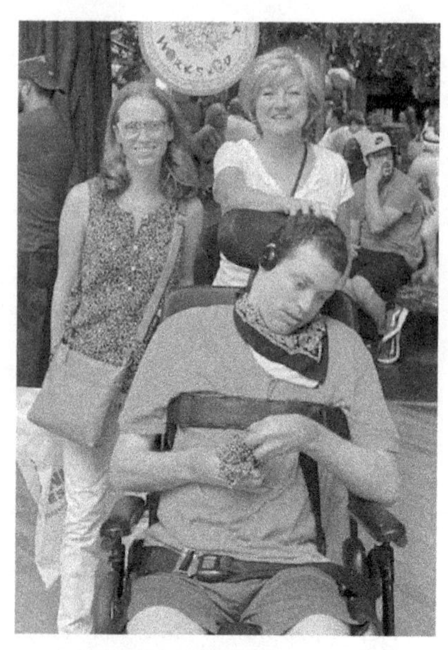

My niece Samantha Gasmire, sister in law Denise Gasmire and my special nephew Ty Gasmire.

My mother in law, Ruth Winkler, at our ranch. Ruth was a wonderful "Grannie" and we all love and miss her so.

My lovely daughter Natalie, me and son Charlie.

Sandee and her mother Ruth on Mother's Day. Wonderful ladies who changed my life beginning in 1969.

Me with my mother Ellie at the beach near her home in Jupiter, Florida.

Some of my closest friends and business colleagues at Luckenbach, Tx.
From left to right: Woody Grossman, Bill "Buzz" Ward, Me, Andrea Bohannon Lou Bock, Mark Brooks, David Fitzgerald, Tom "TA" Blake and the infamous Jerry Lyden.
These are great friends and colleagues of mine.

Three decades of pilots, Charlie, me and my dad on the day Charlie first soloed on his 16th birthday in 2006.

The Flying GT's professional studio promo picture in Dallas.
We were on a roll!

One of my mentor jet pilots, Captain Parker Madill, and me with my Citation M2 on the ramp at Addison Airport in Dallas, Tx.

My best friend since 9th grade, Mark Thompson, and me flying somewhere in my Citation M2.

Charlie, our daughter in law Corey, our grandson Caleb, daughter Natalie and granddaughter Collins on Easter 2023.

My brother Jay, my sister Sue Ellen, Peggy and my dad "Dick",
with me enjoying a marina in Florida.

My sister Sue Ellen, my step mother
Peggy and my step sister Mimi at Peggy's
90th birthday party in N. Ft. Myers,
Florida in 2023.

My son Charlie flying as First Officer
in the Citation as we journey to Toledo,
Ohio, doing research for my book
in 2022.

My business partner, Woody Grossman, and me,
when I received a Lifetime Achievement Award from Three Oaks Hospice in 2023.
The previous recipient was Dick Burnham. I was in good company.

Flying in my Piper Super Cub with Charlie in his Cessna Skylane in formation together at sunset over Enchanted Rock in the Texas Hill Country.

12

Charlie is born, my first of seven marathons, the Oklahoma City bombing, leaving United Dental Care, entering the hospice business, roughing it on church mission trips

We stayed in touch with our friends in Oklahoma after we had moved back to Dallas. Francis Leonard was a teacher that Sandee had worked with, and they became very close friends. They had a lot in common with each other. They liked homemaking, sewing, gardening, lunches together and with other friends, and their faith in Jesus. Francis was a lot of fun. She never married, so she did not have children of her own but spoiled her nephews and nieces. One of her brothers was an air traffic controller for the Federal Aviation Administration in Ft. Worth, and I always enjoyed talking with him about all things flying. Francis also had another close brother who worked for the US presidential front detail, securing protection for the president of the United States, and he was based at the Alfred P. Murrah building in Oklahoma City.

On April 19, 1995, Francis's brother, Donald Leonard, on his day off from work, decided to stop by his office on the top floor of the building before meeting his son for a round of golf. While he was in the building only a short time, it was precisely when an American terrorist, Timothy McVeigh, destroyed the building with a truck bomb. Donald Leonard was one of one hundred and sixty-eight men, women, and children who died in the truck bomb attack. Years later, Francis volunteered to lead visiting and solemn tourists through the memorial built in downtown Oklahoma City, where the building once stood. She was a wonderful woman and friend. Always up for a great laugh and baked wonderful cookies. I have the last cookie she ever made for me still frozen in our freezer.

We lost Francis to a tumor in her pancreas in 2021, and it was a huge loss, especially for Sandee. They were great friends. She fought the cancer for a few years, and we had the good fortune to visit her a few months before she died. In 1990 we traveled to her house to visit for a couple of days. While we were there, Sandee got together with her teacher friends to have lunch or dinner or make something at Francis's house. On this trip, we had gone out to lunch and as dessert, the waiter brought a big cake. I thought, *Why are we getting such a huge cake? I love cake, but this is a bit over the top*!

Sandee was holding the cake so I could read what was written on it. Natalie was a cute, well-behaved four-year-old who was deeply involved with every event that took place. Ever the expressive, precocious little girl, she could be counted on to be front of house, in the middle of the action. We had Natalie all to ourselves for four years and all the fun experiences that go with a first child. She had learned so much in a short time, and she was prepared to take the lead in being an influence on her first sibling one day. At least that is what I thought.

Natalie was standing on my right, looking at me as I read the icing script. It read, "Congratulations, Daddy Dave #2." I do not know which look was more priceless, mine or Natalie's! Her look was one of "oh, really? Not just me anymore?" What a great surprise for all of us. It was memorable for all three of us to be with Francis and Sandee's friends. I was in happy disbelief that our second child was on the way while we were building UDC.

On April 9, 1990, Sandee had been up for several hours, wondering if she was beginning labor. We did not know if we were having a boy or girl, so it was very exciting. What was also exciting was waiting for Kingston's reaction that I wouldn't be coming to work because we were having a baby. Sandee woke me up and said that she thought we should go to the hospital. She was timing her contractions and was hoping not to have a C-section like with Natalie.

On the way to Presbyterian Hospital from our home in Plano, I decided since it took all day with Natalie, I had time to pick up a paper, some coffee, and maybe an OJ. I went into a 7-11 and got what I needed for the day while Sandee timed her contractions in the car. I told the store cashier that we were having a baby today and he said, "Well, you better hurry!" I said we had plenty of time and got in the car to join the rush-hour traffic on Central Expressway on a Monday morning at eight thirty.

By the time we got to the ER, Sandee was nearly in full labor and her water broke about ten minutes after we got into a maternity room next to labor and delivery. Things really sped up from that moment on. The nurse handed me some scrubs and said to get dressed. Sandee was a trooper, and I look back thinking what an idiot I was. I thought I had it all under control because we had been through it before. But I put Sandee and baby at risk to some extent.

Never forget that the professionals who do what they do don't need the help of those who do not.

By 10:00 a.m., we were in the delivery room, and Sandee was pushing like crazy. About 10:15 a.m., this little boy came into our world! We were surprised and excited to have a little girl first, and now, a healthy little boy. The doctor asked if I wanted to cut the umbilical cord, and I still remember the tension of the cut and how it felt just like cutting a soft hose with a pair of scissors. By noon, Sandee was sitting up and eating lunch! Everything went perfectly!

Sandee wanted me to name him, and I took my time in doing so. I came up with Charlie because of the family legacy of the name Charles, particularly his great grandfather. We officially put the name of Charlie on his hospital crib before coming home. I called Ruth to tell her and Natalie, as Natalie was staying with our next-door neighbor.

Ruth said, "A baby boy!? How wonderful."

I told Natalie, and she simply said, "A little boy" in a sweet and loving way. She was a four-year-old big sister, and she was, and still is, very proud. It was a magical experience. After a few days, I went back to work for Kingston, knowing I would never forget Sandee having Charlie that week, and it gave me respite from the hard work of building a company!

As I said before, Jim was a conundrum of a man. He was intensely smart and intimidating for us on his executive team because, as a perfectionist, working with those of us who were not perfect, he would get frustrated and angry. But I will say, he hung in there with us and didn't fire anyone on our team, including me. I could not afford to get fired and was constantly worried about it. For his purposes, we were willing to learn and endure, so the professor came out in him, and he taught us things, but he was not going to give you more than a couple of tries at something—you needed to keep up.

Though he kept us so on edge at the office, and I mean, he really stressed us out, he was the complete opposite when out socially or entertaining friends at his house. He was a magnificent chef and loved to cook. I am not talking about cooking a steak or grilling a piece of chicken on the grill. He would prepare gourmet dinners of rabbit or veal or homemade pasta, and to top it off, provide a wine pairing to match the food. Even the way he cooked and entertained was intimidating.

One time, he invited me and Sandee, and unbelievably, my brother Jay and my best friend Mark Thompson, to his house for a gourmet dinner with him and his family. He invited us over at 6:00 p.m. for cocktails and wine while he worked on this gourmet display of best-in-class cuisine. He had printed out the schedule of every temperature and time that he needed to follow to produce the Kingston-perfect product. He asked that we be ready to dine at 7:00 p.m. so that our meal would be picture- and palate-perfect. The only fly in the ointment was that Jay and Mark were driving back from hunting in south Texas and were late. Very late. Extremely late. I think they arrived around 9:00 p.m.

Although I know Jim was livid and extremely disappointed his meal would not be what he wanted it to be, he gracefully delayed dinner until they arrived. I spent two hours trying to keep the red on Jim's neck from making it all the way to his face. Dinner was spectacular that Saturday night, and we left well after midnight and were thankful for Jim and Jessie's hospitality. Two days later, I was in Jim's office for our standard Monday meeting at 7:00 a.m., where he picked up from where he left off and continued to stare at me and say, "Fuzzy thinking, young David, very fuzzy thinking." Just another day at the office working for Jim Kingston.

Jim was an avid photographer. And he had a ferocious appetite for reading books. Very much a Renaissance man. He loved Stevie Ray Vaughn and was sad when Stevie died in a helicopter crash in 1987. He and I talked about Stevie's music during one of our Monday meetings.

You just never knew what to expect from Jim. I had become an avid runner to deal with the stresses of life at that time. I told Jim that I was able to think about solving problems while running, and things became clearer to me on long runs. He responded with, "Do you think we can put a treadmill in your office so you can start thinking more clearly?" That was Jim.

By this time, I had become a very active long-distance runner. I found that it helped me think, and it became more than a hobby through the years. I continued to reflect on goal achievement and always remembered the Olympic runners who could actually *race* at full marathon distance. So, step by step, I began thinking of putting myself through the test. I found that setting collateral goals for myself that supported and even improved my ability to achieve other goals was a very helpful endeavor. So I set my sights on running 26.2 miles.

My first of what became seven marathons was the Dallas White Rock Marathon in pleasant weather on December 6, 1987. The furthest I had run in my training was fifteen miles, so I knew I was under trained for the full 26.2 miles. I knew I could make it, but it would not be fun after fifteen miles. I finished the race in three hours, forty-eight minutes, and sixteen seconds.

A week later, Jim surprised me with a black-and-white photo he had taken of me when I crossed the finish line. I did not even know he was at the race. He showed me about twenty pictures he had taken of me running and explained how he decided on the two pictures he framed. One was of me with my arms over my head, screaming as I crossed the finish line, and the other was of me and Jay hugging shortly afterward at the finish line.

I am still so appreciative of Jim going through the effort to memorialize this special event with a Kingston photograph. He took the pictures from afar, and I never saw him. The picture of me crossing the finish line is on the wall of our gym at our home at the ranch. He was very thoughtful about knowing what people liked, and he paid attention to what other people's individual interests were and joined them with his interest in photography. That, in my view, is outstanding relational leadership. He was tough when it mattered and kind when it mattered most.

Jim would also celebrate Christmas in his own way, as he did with everything else. At the time, he was an agnostic and made fun of me during Easter but actively participated in the Christmas season by dropping off gifts to his top managers on Christmas Eve. Each gift was specific to the person that he had carefully thought about so the gift would be extra special to the recipient. Again, a genuinely nice and considerate Jim Kingston. His wife Jessie would invite Sandee and Natalie to birthday parties for their two girls. The trend in birthday parties back then was to play duck-duck-goose on the floor of a McDonald's restaurant. Nothing fancy, but the girls loved it and we participated when we could. But sure thing, on Monday morning, it was game on in Jim's office.

One time, Jim and I were in his Saab 900, going to recruit a possible dental director, F. Lynn Williams, DDS, in the Lakewood area of

Dallas. Jim liked to smoke cigarettes in his car with the sunroof open. He would drive to a meeting such as this and stare straight ahead with his Wayfarer sunglasses on, cigarette in his fingers, and give you advice or demands, which were the same with Jim. On the way to meet Dr. Williams (whom we hired; he reported to me, and we got along great), Jim told me that I was expected to dress more conservatively and that my suspenders needed to go. What? They were very stylish at the time, but he did not care. So, I ditched the suspenders. He was in my grill what seemed like all the time. Looking back, I am glad that he was. It reminded me of my dad being on my case growing up, and that helped me get through it. I was not a stranger to adversity.

By the beginning of 1992, I had grown weary of the grind at UDC. The kids were growing up, and I was gone much of the time, building delivery systems in new cities. The trigger that launched me to change jobs came after a call I received from Jim while I was in Austin on a Monday morning. I had arrived at 7:00 a.m. and was at the office before 8:00 a.m. Jim would not let us travel on company time and made us travel early mornings or late at night, but he was not going to pay us to be on a flight during the day when we could be working. That wore me out.

He called and asked me what I was doing in Austin and said that I needed to be in Cincinnati. I explained my purpose for being in Austin, and he vetoed that and told me to fly to Cincinnati that moment. So, I did. I flew back to Dallas, went home, repacked a bag for the week, and arrived in Cincinnati that evening.

A couple of weeks earlier, I had been reading the paper on a weekend and saw a classified ad looking for an executive with my skill set and experience. It was much of the new P&L skill set that I had learned from James Burke Kingston over the past seven years. I had no idea what the job was. It was an ad placed by a recruiter on the East Coast. I cut out that ad and put it in my wallet. A week later, on that flight to Cincinnati, I reread the ad and decided I would call the number in the morning.

The next morning, Kingston called our office number to see if I was there promptly at 8:00 a.m. I picked up the phone (I was the only employee in Cincinnati at that time) and Jim and I had a conversation. He called just to see if I was there on time. I was so micromanaged, I was forgetting what my job was. I pulled out the ad in my wallet and called the recruiter.

That call led to profound changes in my career and life that I would never have imagined. It was such a fulcrum event in my life; it was on par with Dad being promoted and moving to Dallas twenty years earlier, where I met Sandee and became a Texan.

As I contemplated making a change, I began to realize an important aspect of my life and my journey through it.

Everything that I knew by then about business had been taught by someone else who already knew what I needed to learn.

When I was surviving with small efforts in college, it did not take much experience to do what I was doing. My survival only took creativity and determination. But eventually, I needed to learn more than the things that were basically only concepts in college and not the real world of business and life. In college, you learn what someone wrote, but quite frankly, many writing professors do not know how to run businesses themselves. They can talk about it but have never done it. Sure, everyone can fly an airplane. Just go fast and pull. It does not work that way.

I know this to be a fact because I was asked to be one of the speakers at Baylor University in the Hankemer School of Business in the Entrepreneurship Program. I was asked to teach a couple of classes on "Harvesting your Business," which really meant making money at the exit. They brought me and other executives of successful companies in to teach the class because they had not done it themselves. I taught that class each semester for five years. Some of the students were interested; some were not. These kids did not have context for what I was teaching, so I modified it each time to get to the point of teaching at least one pragmatic, actionable fact they could take with them. It was fun for a while, but when I was asked by the university to donate/invest in an angel fund, I turned it down. The school did not invite me back to teach the next semester. So much for business school.

In business and life, there is much to learn, and you hope to be taught by someone who has the patience and who will be generous with their time and intentions to share those skills with you.

I have learned that a college education does not guarantee you business success any more than being given recipes makes you an executive chef.

Until someone shows you how and holds you accountable for the results, you will never really know every aspect of what goes into a business. A common mistake at the board level is to load the board with financial people without any operating experience in that business other than the CEO. In my view, the board needs to consist of the four skill areas I believe are crucial for the performance and protection of the company and the capital invested.

The areas requiring board member expertise at a minimum include finance (including capital markets and debt), compliance and governance (following the rules), operations (trains running on time with profitability), and development (sales).

Before I went to work for Jim Kingston to help start and grow UDC, I only understood sales. I was good at it, but by the time Jim was done with me, I could manage a profit and loss statement, raise capital, discover and complete acquisitions, and recruit great people. I got a street-level MBA degree with Jim, and I am very appreciative of his willingness to stick with me and teach me things that I rely on today in the businesses that I start, run, and oversee. Some of the macro concepts that I learned and have committed my leadership style to include:

- NOTHING happens until somebody sells something.
- Communication is culture.

- Understand and feed what drives the business.
- Lead from the front and anticipate what might kill you next.
- When raising capital, don't take a nickel more than you need.
- When investing capital in great companies, offer more than they need.
- Treat your employees with respect, as you would treat a good friend.
- Don't hire anyone that you wouldn't invite to dinner with your family.
- When providing guidance, guide down, don't guide up.
- Be transparent about problems in the company and be out in front of them.
- Reward in public, reprimand in private.
- The fish rots from the head down—take responsibility.
- He who writes it, likes it.

Thank you, James Burke Kingston.

Now it was time to take the steps to get to the next level and find my next mentor, but as importantly, become a mentor to others, teaching them what Jim had taught me. That next mentor was Richard (Dick) Ramsey Burnham, who became, and still is, one of my closest and most significant friends.

LEAVING UNITED DENTAL CARE

I knew when I was dialing the phone to talk with the recruiter that I had made the decision that seven years was enough. It was time to move on. The working lifestyle under Kingston had to go. There was no work/life balance. Of course, in the eighties, there was no such thing as work/life balance. I had never thought that was a virtue until we began having children. I needed to move on for my own health and for my growing family. It was the right decision.

I had put a dental delivery system together that got this start-up company on the map to positive cash flow. I was able to relate to this company from the aspect of starting from nothing, although I had arrived after the seed financing by our board and investors had been in place. But I was on the start-up crew, and I was wonderfully comfortable with the risk that went along with that.

When I joined the company, I had no idea what an "exit" meant. In these terms, it means the transaction for the initial investors to get their money out of the company. I had not had that experience yet, so I left before the initial public offering that transacted three years later. I could not have stayed three more years and kept my sanity. But fortunately, on September 21, 1995, the company, led by investment banker Alex Brown & Company, completed its initial public offering of common stock, issuing two million three hundred and seventy-five thousand shares at a price of $22 per share. The net offering proceeds were $48 million.

The company continued to grow during the two years after I left to work for Vitas. Then, one day, Jim Kingston called to ask if I wanted to participate in the friends-and-family pool of stock options that were available at a strike price of $2. I could then sell the shares at the IPO price, which meant a handsome profit from the growth of the company. It was my first experience with stock options. I had corporate stock at American but not options.

It was genuinely nice of Jim to do this, and I remember the phone conversation very well. Since I had put the delivery system together that got the company where it was, I was glad he was doing me this favor. I participated in the round and made enough money to help me and Sandee pay the down payment for construction of a new house in west Plano. We spent all of it on that house. If I had known then what I know now, I would have borrowed money, sold every unused asset, and bought as much of that stock as possible, but I did not.

I appreciated Jim calling me. Years later, he called me to see if he could invest in Odyssey Healthcare; unfortunately, there was not room for Jim to participate with his investment. I feel bad about that today. It was a vote of confidence that he would call me to ask. Jim never called anyone, but he called me three times. Once to see if I was in Austin. Once to see if he could talk me out of leaving UDC, and the third time to ask if he could buy stock in the company that I cofounded with Dick. The fact that I survived those years working for Jim is very gratifying, and today I think of Jim as a great business mentor. I hope to connect with him again one day over some duck and a glass of wine, when I can ask him, with confidence, "Did you miss me?" I still get nervous and jittery when I think about him.

LIFE AT HOME AS WE MOVED AND RAISED OUR KIDS

Sandee was working as hard at home as I was for UDC. While I was head down in the day-to-day effort at work, Sandee was in search of a church home for us so we would have a church to raise our kids in. She was also taking great care of herself with Jazzercise and running a hectic pace that really showed off her organizational and managerial skills and instincts. When we landed back in Dallas, we visited several churches and found Hunters Glen Baptist in Plano. We visited on a day when there was a visiting guest pastor, and they had just moved into a new worship center.

I remember that day well. We put Natalie in childcare while we were in the worship service. We knew she was safe there, as we adjusted to turning our daughter over to complete strangers to look after her. The fear of something happening to her in childcare at the church was an unnecessary stress, and their attention to the little ones turned out to be better than acceptable, so we began attending regularly. We began meeting new friends, who are some of our best friends still today—Bob and Julie Reach (Julie and Sandee met and found out they have the same birthday in the same year, May 1955. They have been best friends ever since); Ron and Tena Kolb; Allan and Ginger Brown; and all their kids that became friends with our kids. At first it was only Natalie as a baby, but by the time Charlie was born and we were preparing to begin the next company after building our Vitas Healthcare hospice operations, we were fully involved with our church, and we knew the parents of the kids our kids were hanging with.

"IT IS IMPORTANT TO SURROUND YOURSELF WITH GREAT FRIENDS, BUT EVEN MORE IMPORTANT TO SURROUND YOUR KIDS WITH OTHER KIDS WHO HAVE GREAT PARENTS."
—Sandee Gasmire

At Hunters Glen, we had many other fun and close friends, too numerous to mention here, and our pastor, Dr. Kim Hall, and his wife Martha, were among the best. Kim was a fantastic Bible teacher, and we looked forward to his sermons. Kim also baptized Natalie and Charlie. Our kids adored Kim Hall. We all did, and he led our church for twenty years or more. I joined a church planting ministry started by Steve Thompson, and Kim and I were asked to be trustees. It led to amazing trips overseas.

Kim, Steve, and I traveled to London to meet with pastors from Russia and other areas of eastern Europe, and I had the chance to run around London with Kim. He loved to travel, and deep in his heart he wanted to live out of a backpack and spread the gospel to other pastors who he could teach to do the same. However, he was the lead pastor at Hunters Glen and had to devote his time there. He was a teacher but not a manager, and he had a staff to oversee the administrative details. Every church has issues where there is more than one person involved. That is a fact and just the way it is. People have egos and power motives, and Hunters Glen was no different.

Kim was a funny guy. He could impersonate Elvis Presley like no other and was interested in music and guitars. He would call me from time to time to tell me about a funny schtick he heard on the radio with one of our favorite radio personalities. Such a great Bible teacher, and a lot of fun and a dear family friend.

As Natalie and Charlie grew in age through middle school and into high school, Sandee enrolled both of them in choir for several consecutive years. Sunday nights, both of them were at church, practicing with the choir, even when the Dallas Cowboys were playing football. It did not matter what other social events were taking place; they made it to choir, where they enjoyed most of their friends. Sandee accompanied them there so she could also run several different girls' groups, such as Mission Friends (for the younger girls) and Acteens (for the teenage girls). Sandee treated it as a full-time job.

She also accompanied the choir on mission trips, which required long drives. Out to New Mexico, Arizona, Louisiana, and other places, during the heat of the summer. One time she was driving one of five or six church vans full of choir members, and she was so tired from sleeping on the hard floor in the church. The mission workers were there to help, sharing a bathroom with fifty other people, and living the sweaty, never-ending workday, only to not sleep well each night. The night they headed home from Arizona, Sandee was exhausted from the lack of quality and quantity of sleep, along with everyone else. She drifted off just enough to slightly leave the roadway in a construction zone and woke up just in time to regain control of the van. Freaked her and everyone else out.

It was a dangerous trip, and I wasn't happy that Sandee was a designated driver to come home. But actually, it was good she was in the left seat. She kept the vehicle from careening out of control full of church sponsors and kids. A driving narrow escape for sure.

The next year, the trip was to Chicago, and I was not having anything to do with her driving with our kids and all the others all the way to Chicago and back. So, I secretly bought everyone round-trip air tickets on American Airlines, so no one had to drive. In my view, it was a solid investment, and I was able to do it at the time.

Sandee was such a solid contributor at Hunters Glen, as were many of our friends and their kids. Those kids all grew up together, and there were many times our house would be filled with those same kids. Then they would go to one of the other parents' houses to have fun there. We always knew where they were and felt good about their physical and moral safety. You become who you hang around with, and it is especially true for children and young adults. We would not trade any of our days at Hunters Glen.

All four of us participated in the annual Easter musical that was a Passion Play of sorts, telling the full story of Jesus Christ. Allan Brown played Jesus one year, and he was hard to be around when he thought he was Jesus! He did great and portrayed the agony of the crucifixion in a dramatic and moving way. As levity would have it, Allan has a Kentucky accent, and when he delivered the line, "You will see me again," he did so with a thick Kentucky drawl. Allan was great. He made a great Jesus.

13

The BIG change to hospice, meeting Dick Burnham, losing Calvin Coolidge Orr, cutting loose in hospice, running marathon #7 and trying to qualify for Boston, the beginning of Odyssey Healthcare, Inc.

My first interview for the general manager job with Hospice Care, Inc, was with Dick Burnham at a hotel in Irving near the DFW airport. I was introduced to Dick by the recruiter I had called from the ad in the paper. Dick had worked at Baxter Travenol, the competing company to American Hospital Supply, which eventually bought American. When he and I met for the first time, we instantly hit it off on all fronts—he could talk fast, I could talk fast, he knew how to sell, I knew how to sell, he was enthusiastic, and I was too. It was such a relief to talk with someone who wasn't trying to bust my chops but was looking ahead to some great things if we could make our partnership work. I had enough experience from my days at ACC and UDC to know what I was talking about. My experience was beginning to leverage to bigger responsibilities, and I was excited to meet Dick and have the prospect of having complete profit and loss responsibility for a business in health care.

Hospice. I had heard of it before; in fact, when I was in OKC, I ran a 10k race that was sponsored by St. Anthony's Hospital and their hospice. And more importantly, Sandee's biological father, Calvin Coolidge Orr, was on hospice, and we were participating in his care.

Calvin Coolidge Orr. Sandee's dad. Calvin and Ruth married in the fifties and had a stillborn son they named Bruce. Bruce would have been Sandee's older brother. As a result, Sandee was raised a single child and was the sparkle in the eyes of both Calvin and Ruth. Calvin and Ruth were divorced before I met Sandee in 1969, and Ruth remarried Silas Winkler, Sandee's new stepfather. When I met Sandee, I only knew Ruth and Si and hadn't met Calvin. But Calvin was in and out of Sandee's life over the years, and he was a very nice guy. He had a gambling problem and smoked a lot of cigarettes, and both caught up to him when he was sixty-three years old.

Calvin was on hospice for lung cancer and spent time at his home in east Dallas and at our home in Plano. During the last month of his life, he and I had some very personal conversations about his life, my life, and the future for him and all of us. During his last two weeks on hospice, he was admitted to a nursing home in Plano. Both Sandee and I were with him when he passed away quietly on November 14, 1991. It was very sad, and Sandee had just lost her father, who wasn't a large part of her life until she was an adult.

Si was a wonderful stepfather, and I could see how he cared for Sandee and Ruth, but Calvin was her dad. I was honored to have been there with her, just her, me, and Calvin as he took his last breaths. We talked with Calvin a couple of hours before he died, and I'll always remember that.

During Calvin's time on hospice, he was encouraged by people on the hospice team to do whatever he needed to do to prepare for the end of his life. Calvin passed on his attention to organizational detail to Sandee, and they began inventorying all that Calvin had, right down to the nails, nuts, and bolts he had, which they counted together and put in little envelopes with Calvin's handwriting. "11 nails and 4 hooks." Then another one, "13 small nails and 8 big hooks." It was therapeutic for them to do that together.

Before Calvin died, he told us that his hospice home health aide was so important and helpful to him. He just raved about how she cared for him, giving him baths, putting lotion on him, and taking care of him from day to day. Calvin also mentioned a volunteer who would come by to talk and spend quality time when we were not able to be with him. Overall, it was an extremely healthy and much appreciated hospice experience.

MY TURN TO MAKE A DIFFERENCE

The job I was interviewing for with Dick was to take the reins of the hospice company that cared for Calvin six months prior to his death. I had the real-life experience of hospice services as a family member before I became the general manager of Hospice Care, Inc, which changed its name to Vitas Healthcare, Inc, not long after I arrived. I started in the job of general manager in Dallas, with full P&L responsibility, in April 1992.

The culture at Vitas was striking compared to what I had just come from at UDC. Vitas was huge but was not very well run compared to the locked-tight culture I lived at UDC. UDC was small by comparison but was managed overly well. I spent the first two months at Vitas just following people around to see what we did.

At Kingston's suggestion the day I left UDC, I did not make any decisions for the first month and didn't make any changes for at least the first two months. It was great advice. If I had run Vitas the way we ran our people at UDC, everyone would have walked out. In hospice, the people who make up the interdisciplinary team are very caring and less concerned about form than substance. It was a valuable insight that I needed to understand about these very special caregiver professionals. They marched to the beat of patient advocacy and not so much corporate vision and direction.

My initial observations were that they were disorganized, easy-going, and unpolished from a UDC and Jim Kingston perspective. But they were great people who had the love of caring for others deeply embedded in their souls, and I wondered if UDC had gone too perfectionist and intensive. It was productive for me to learn business, but very hard on the people delivering the service. There is a balance to all things, and I was getting rebalanced to a more normal and socially acceptable work- and mission-based environment.

The teams in hospice can do what certainly most people can't and won't do. Care for dying people. I had to give them a break and try to understand this culture. I could not Kingston-ize my new team. To make it even more challenging, the corporate founders, Esther Cauliflower and Rev. Hugh Westbrook, were the ancestors of the Medicare hospice movement and were the drivers of legislation that created the demonstration project for hospice care from 1980–1983.

In 1983, hospice was added to the Medicare benefit. The CEO that ran the company was Duke Collier. Duke had been in Washington with the law firm Hartson and Hogan and was involved with the development of the legislation that put hospice on the map. Or at least created funding for hospice, which most of the world had not ever heard of or understood before. Because Vitas was the pioneer in hospice, they set the norm for the culture that I inherited when I took the job in Dallas. I had been given the responsibility of one hundred and seventy-five employees, caring for three hundred and fifty patients on service every day and approximately $20 million in revenue with earnings of three to four million just in Dallas. My job was to lead this group to grow the company, which, for me, was just Dallas. The corporation had locations in FTW, where the general manager, Laurie West, was a superstar, and she helped answer questions I had early on as I settled into the company. There were also locations in Chicago and Florida, and that was it.

The drivers of the business were new patient admissions and length of stay. We received a daily rate from Medicare and for approximately $160/day today, we would provide the drugs related to the terminal diagnosis, the home equipment and medical supplies needed, and an interdisciplinary team providing intermittent care, which included nurses, aides, social workers, chaplains, volunteers, and bereavement staff. I had a lot to learn.

PUTTING IT ALL TOGETHER

I could get my brain and arms around the business and was making improvements on the admissions side of the business, essentially the sales side, but I was really slowed down by the culture of the company. If people weren't doing what I needed, after several attempts and discussions to get the performance turned around, and I wanted to get rid of them, the company, more often than not, would have me and Dick send them to the corporate office in Miami, where "they might be happier." Fine! Take them and you can deal with them. Bless their hearts.

Darn it, I had a business to run, and the lack of productivity and accountability was an exceedingly difficult problem. My nursing managers would have frequent meetings with me to tell me what they wanted, union style, and usually included messaging that if I did not cooperate with them, they were going to riot. I learned to listen and try to get them to see things from the point of view of growing to care for more patients. We needed to keep what was important, quite frankly, important!

I had Dick as a sounding board and confidant, so he would come over to Dallas from his office in Grand Prairie, and he and I would walk over to the Galleria for lunch to discuss everything. He was great. We vented to each other but always found the humor in things, and that was a relief compared to what I experienced at UDC. I had to pinch myself every night when I got home that I was getting paid to do this work. It was a real study in human behavior, group behavior, communication, and teamwork, not to mention the financials. There were no spending limits in the company. That emanated from Miami and became a culture that was hard to change quickly.

Think about it. A pioneering business that went from no revenue as an industry to a fully paid Medicare benefit available to anyone over sixty-five that qualified under the hospice admissions guidelines, with healthy but not extreme profitability, helped create the spending culture. It is said that if you are a Medicare company and it is time to vote in elections, if you want to vote your wallet, vote Democrat because they like to spend money. It is true. Hospice, from a public policy point of view, is a large part of the answer to the out-of-control acute care hospital costs. In one view, it is the purest form of managed care (capitation in the dental business was managed care). The government, and other private payers, pay a daily rate that is a tenth of the hospital daily rate, and the hospice keeps that patient from returning to the hospital.

During the thirty years I have been in hospice, as an employee, a CEO, a chairman, and an investor, this basic premise has not changed. The rules and requirements have changed with the growth of the industry, but the fact remains that people want to be cared for at home, and the payers of care do not want people to return to the hospital because it is significantly more expensive.

At the time I started at Vitas, the industry represented about 2 percent of the Medicare budget and had about fifteen hundred Medicare certified hospices in the US. Today, hospice represents nearly 13 percent of the Medicare budget, with over four thousand Medicare-certified hospice agencies. So, at Vitas, we were still pioneering the concept of hospice. My staff even refused to refer to the company as Vitas, as they just wanted to call it Dallas Hospice. Dallas Hospice was not even a real company; they just referred to themselves as Dallas Hospice, and that's what they had the market calling them before I got there. As if they were the only game in town. We were not the only game in town, and it got even more competitive from year to year.

Competing in hospice is a very different animal. Because the Medicare rules of participation are the same for everyone, you cannot change the services being offered and you can't change the pricing. The only way to get growth in a competitive landscape is to provide better service. Period. And that is where my days at UDC came in handy. We had to decide what level of service we needed to deliver based on what our customers expected. Pretty simple stuff, but my Vitas staff wasn't buying it. They had their way, and that was it. So, I started firing people. I reassigned people, I shelved people. I transferred people, and I started to apply productivity standards with the help of Dick, big time. He and I figured out the number of visits the staff needed to make and how many staff we needed.

When I rolled out the productivity standards model to my staff, they began calling it the "P" word. They hated it. I needed them to do it, or I would not be able to grow the company. Without being able to serve and care for more patients with the staff we had, we couldn't accept new patients. I had six full-time sales reps who were beating the bushes for new patients, and we were getting them. I explained my dilemma to the CEO of the corporation at a meeting in Florida. I explained to the corporate group that I had a manager I wanted to get rid of and why. There were murmurs of "he can't do that!" "Oh, the staff there must be miserable with this guy."

Duke slammed his fist on the table and yelled, "Dammit, if he says she needs to go, then she needs to go. You can proceed as requested, David."

I nodded to Duke and did not say a word. I appreciated him backing me up, but it was such a culture shock that we were not holding people accountable, and it was very frustrating to me.

I got Dallas fixed, and we grew the patient census to more than five hundred in about eighteen months. That is when Dick and I decided to expand our geographical coverage and go to new markets. We opened in San Antonio, and we were very successful there. We became profitable on a cash flow basis in less than six months. As a result, we started another one in Sherman Denison. We were off to the races until we got thrown the yellow flag. Dick and I had gone on a trip to find more Texas markets to develop with start-up operations. The network of hospice operators back then all knew each other. We found that out the hard way.

Dick and I went to Orange, Texas, outside of the Houston/Beaumont area, just looking around and calling on a hospice or two along the way. He and I would play off each other as we walked into a hospice office, cold calling and just asking if we could talk to the manager or whoever would talk with us. It worked for us then, probably harder to do today.

We unwittingly walked into the wrong hospice. It was in an old building that, as I remember, was attached to a church or some other building. The manager there sat down with us because she was very curious to find out why in the world these two cowboys from north Texas would wander down to her neck of the woods asking about hospice. When we told her we were from Vitas, she lit up and said that Esther Cauliflower and Hugh Westbrook were her very close friends. She asked how Esther was doing, and Dick told her that she was not as involved with the business because she wanted to spend more time with her family, which was completely true. She asked why we were in Orange, and we told her that we were doing some work to determine where our hospice services could be expanded. She did not like that. She said they were managing all the patients just fine, and there was no room for another hospice. We knew it was time to leave.

About two days later, I was in our new office in Sherman Denison when I got a phone call from Hugh Westbrook while I was on another line talking to Dick. Dick said, "Hey man, Hugh or Esther is about to call you and chew your ass out, because I just got mine chewed out by them. Call me after you talk to them."

I said, "Dick, Hugh is on the other line. I'll call you back."

Dang it. I picked up the phone and said hello to Hugh. He and I always got along, and it was not a bad conversation. He just wanted me to know that we were not going to grow and expand the company to compete with any of his friends. He said to give him a plan of where we should expand to, and he would consider it. I thought, *Consider it? We can triple the size of this company in a couple of years if you just let us do it!*

Dick's conversation with Esther was a different matter. When she heard that Dick had said she was not as involved with the business anymore, she hit the roof. Pretty funny now, but it caused a big stink back then.

A couple of months later, Dick and I attended a national manager's meeting in Orlando, on Disney property. The meeting lasted three days. On the last day of the meeting (this was before cell phones), I learned from someone else that Dick had been fired, had already been given a ticket home, and was on his way back to Texas. I could not believe it. I tried calling his house and got his answering machine. I connected with him from a pay phone at the airport as I was about to board my flight home from the meeting, and he told me the whole scoop. He was out, and a guy named Chuck Dowling was taking his place. I was still with the company but now was getting a new boss to replace Dick.

I was blown away. The next day I had a meeting with my new supervisor, who told me I was now assigned to some other corporate projects and that my Dallas office was being consolidated into FTW and would be run by my colleague, Laurie West. I was very okay with that. I wanted to grow the company, and the day-to-day fight with sales and clinical was a beating that I was ready to move on from. I am a growth guy, and that is where I wanted to be.

LEARNING MORE PIECES TO THE PUZZLE

Chuck got me busy negotiating the national contract for medical supplies and working with inpatient hospice unit negotiations in California after an acquisition there and in Florida. Chuck and I got along fine, but I had my eye on my own hospice company and Dick did too. He was already gone from Vitas, and I needed to decide what my plan would be, and we did not know if he and I would hook up on a new hospice company for a few more months.

After Dick unceremoniously left Vitas, he and I had started working on two different hospice company development plans, independently. I called Jim Kingston to ask him if he would look over my plan and give me some guidance. He did just that by writing all over it in his signature red ink pen so I could see where my fuzzy thinking was. It helped me quite a bit as I moved from draft to draft. I then took my plan to a potential investor, one of the investors at UDC who was also on the board.

I took the plan to Ken Newman and met at his office in Denton, Texas, to have some dialogue about it. He told me that he would like to find a way to work together, but he never would commit to me after repeated calls to speak with him. A few years later, I ran into him at a restaurant in New York, and he told me he wished he had invested in the company. I am sure that was an understatement. The company reached a valuation of over $1B, and he had passed up the opportunity to be a founding investor. Again, **sometimes you are the bug and sometimes you are the windshield.**

BIG PLANS FOR A BIG COMPANY

One of the key things I did when I was starting the other hospice locations was to keep track of everything that went into a start-up, including how long things took and what they cost. I also had to inventory the compliance and certification steps and requirements to get the initial Medicare survey, as well as the costs required for the overhead in the regulations. This was brass-boots start-up stuff that had to be planned for and worried about. The drivers of the business as a start-up in the first few months are compliance, compliance, compliance. If you are not compliant with the rules of economic engagement with Medicare, they will not comply with paying you, so you work for free and have all the costs to pay in the business. Compliance.

I finally landed on a single-unit operating model that I thought could be an effective, easy-to-understand investment thesis to begin speaking with potential investors. This part was going to be very new to me. Dick and I collaborated on a combined plan that originally was called "CareFirst," as a placeholder for a future company name. It was not important yet, but would be soon.

On September 25, 1995, I resigned my position at Vitas Healthcare Corporation. I told my boss that I had other fish to fry, and he completely understood. Chuck and I had a lot in common, business wise, but I was not willing to stick around when I knew I had a bigger vision. The Vitas culture drove me crazy. The important stuff was not the important stuff. That. Ain't. Me. So, I left to join Dick in doing it ourselves.

THE ART/GAME OF RAISING MONEY FOR A HOSPICE COMPANY

Dick and I both agree that after years of raising money in hospice, there is a screenplay to be written with all the interesting, humorous, and intellectual experiences we had. We did not have to start from scratch, looking for interested parties to join us in the investment. We had been referred to two private investors that had been looking for a duo like Dick and me to get into the hospice "space," as they called it. David Steffy and David Cross became the founding fathers with us and introduced us to a handful of investor prospects.

Our first meeting was in Palo Alto, California, at Three Arch Partners. We flew out the night before, on our own nickel, and met with Mark Wan, a founding partner there. Their offices were on the famed and storied Sand Hill Rd, where much of the venture capital world worked and thrived. It was just down the way from Stanford University. They helped lead the first round of investment and introduced us to Ellen Feeney at Weiss, Peck and Greer in San Francisco, and Annie Lamont at Oak Ventures in Connecticut. Annie is married to the governor of Connecticut, Ned Lamont.

These three firms ponied up the initial $3 million it took for Dick and me to start our first two locations. While we were negotiating the money with these folks, Dick and I were crisscrossing the country in search of our first location. After narrowing it down to Indianapolis and Pittsburgh, we flipped a coin. It landed on Indianapolis, and that first year, beginning in January 1996, was the coldest winter in history in Indiana. All the while, Sandee was at home, taking care of and raising Natalie and Charlie, while I lived, once again, out of a suitcase.

Dick and I tried to ease the travel burden by renting our hotel rooms by the month and setting up shop there instead of renting an office. We interviewed and worked at the Marriott Residence Inn on Founders Road in north Indianapolis. My room was the official office. Room 921. That room number became famous with a God-led event the night we went public in New York City five years later.

Mark Wan at Three Arch, along with David Steffy, became very helpful handlers for us. They helped teach us the art of raising money, but also took financial advantage of us since it was our first "real" solo venture. You got to pay the piper, and we learned the hard way about such things as dilution, fees, and risk. After our first couple of days of meetings with Mark, he joined us on a trip to Chicago to begin meeting with other potential syndicated investors that he wanted us to practice on. He knew the other firms and people that he wanted in our deal, but he wanted me and Dick to get some experience in the big leagues first before pitching to them.

We caught an early flight from San Francisco to Chicago on a United 747, and we sat upstairs in the bubble in first class. I was liking this gig, but we needed to get our first round of investment before we could enjoy it too much. We also needed a name for the company to replace the already used name of CareFirst.

During the three-hour flight to Chicago, there was a movie. Mark suggested we watch it. It was Tom Hanks in *Apollo 13*. It had just been released, and I had not seen it yet. I was sitting next to Mark, and Dick was in the row in front of me. During the movie, there was a scene that stood out to me, and I thought they had given us the name for our company. In the scene, one of the ground controllers, who is reporting to Gene Kranz, the flight director (who later became a real-life friend of mine), played by Ed Harris, said, "The Odyssey is dying …" and that did it for me. Odyssey.

In our hospice business plan, we would be employing different team members, just like NASA. We would be caring for human vessels who had a life-limiting illness and useful life limit, just like the Odyssey spacecraft. We would have to work together to assist people/patients in completing their life's journey, like the NASA mission of a successful landing on Earth. The name fit perfectly and was a symbolic representation that we could build our culture around. I suggested the name to Mark, and he liked it. Dick liked it too. So began Odyssey Healthcare Incorporated. Now we needed money and a logo.

After several trips to visit different people, we were in Palo Alto at a very plush restaurant in the Redlands, outside of Palo Alto. Dick and I were having dinner with David Steffy and Mark Wan and enjoying the decompression that came with thinking we had the investment commitment. We had been working almost three months on finding our first two cities and finding the money, and now we could see it coming together. The purpose of this dinner was to close the deal and get a verbal agreement that the company would get the funding we needed from Three Arch Partners.

We were dining in a very nice restaurant. David and Mark were very savvy about fine wine, and we were enjoying the best during this dinner. In fact, Mark's partner was Thomas Fogarty. Tom Fogarty has, to this day, one of the premier wineries in California, and has been in business since 1981. So, Mark knew his wine and had his own wine cellar, with more than five thousand bottles aging in it. (One day later we had dinner at Tom's winery, and I sat next to the lady running the five-billion-dollar Ford Foundation. She asked if I had ever run a public company. I told her no. She said, very curtly and without emotion, as she sipped a fine glass of Fogarty cabernet, "Don't screw it up." Fine words from the head of the Ford Foundation.)

While enjoying our conversation and our wine, the topic of who knew who came up. I was sitting across from Mark, and Dick was sitting across from Dave Steffy. Just the four of us, reminiscing and crowing about all the influential people we knew. At one point, I mentioned to Mark that I knew Glen French, the CEO of American Critical Care.

He lit up and said, "Yeah, I know him too! Doesn't he have a son?"

And when I said, "Yeah! And his name is Glen French too!"

Dick burst out laughing before fully swallowing a mouthful of deep red 1990 French Bordeaux. He blew it out of his nose and mouth across the table and hit Steffy right between the eyes and down to his chest. It was a shotgun blast of wine of epic proportions. There went the money.

It took a waitstaff of about four people to clean up the carnage. They had to replace the tablecloth, the food, the wine, the silverware, and if they could have, they would have replaced Steffy. He was in bad shape. He needed a stretcher. To make matters worse, David was catching a flight home after the dinner to fly back to southern California, where he lived in Newport. I remember him wiping his glasses clean for about fifteen minutes, quietly laughing and shaking his head. His "boys" had just ruined any chance of getting the Three Arch money, and somehow, he found a way to laugh about it. Dick was selling, selling, selling his apologies. The only saving grace was that he hadn't taken out Mark. Since it was just Steffy, it was friendly fire, and well, stuff happens.

After we left the restaurant, Dick and I found a mall that was still open, and they had a Nordstrom's. We bought a new shirt for Steffy and had it overnighted to his house. The next day, we flew back home to Dallas. About a day later, Dick received a call from Mark Wan that their investment committee had approved our investment, and between the three firms, we would have a starting bankroll of three million. When Dick called me to tell me, we both began singing "we're in the money, we're in the money" and decided that should be the theme song to our Raising Hospice Money screenplay that we often talked about writing. Maybe we still will. But first it was time to go to Indy and begin the journey of Odyssey Healthcare, Inc.

Before the actual money hit our business banking account, we had to work through the process of a term sheet. A term sheet spells out the financial aspects of the deal, who gets what, the related limitations and covenants, and ultimately, who has the largest ownership. For this first round, Dick and I were in Detroit, waiting for a term sheet from Three Arch and the others (Weiss Peck and Greer; Oak Ventures) to come over the hotel fax machine. I remember standing at the front desk, waiting for it to print off so Dick and I could find a place to sit down and digest it all.

When we got our first look at it, it was not what we were expecting. It had fees for this, fees for that, dilution language that we did not completely understand, and it felt like we were being played, because we were. Kingston taught me a very important precept: "He who writes it, likes it." And here we were, reading a document that someone else really liked. Kingston also taught me to "only take money you really need and not a penny more." This term sheet was trying to shove a lot of money down our throats so they could effectively own 80 percent or more of the company.

We eventually got it worked out, but I know we were taken advantage of somewhere in the deal. I know that because I did the same thing to others once I had this little tidbit of how-it's-done-when-you-know-more-than-the-rookies information and experience under my belt. It just comes with the territory. It's like airline pilots. Give me the one with the gray hair because he has seen it all and knows what matters, when it matters, and how to survive when the shit hits the fan, so to speak. Either way, we got the money and we got started.

MY LAST MARATHON

In 1995, I had the opportunity to try and qualify to run the Boston Marathon as a forty-year-old, which put me in the youngest year of the forty to forty-four-year-old men's age group. My qualifying time also increased by five minutes, which was what I needed, if not more, to qualify for Boston. I trained like never before, knowing that at forty years of age, it was going to be difficult to run another sub-3:30 time. My new qualifying time in the older age group was 3:25, and I did everything I could to get faster and stronger to run that pace of seven minutes, forty-nine seconds per mile.

Buzz, Tom, and I had run twenty miles at a 7:30 pace before, but my new qualifying time meant I needed to hold close to that pace for the full 26.2 miles, and the last 6.2 are brutal. It is you against you. Mental training has to dominate the day. The endless droning on in training, mile after mile, does not get you to Boston.

In addition to running forty to fifty miles per week, I had to include speed and hill training, during summer in Texas. I joined a running club at White Rock Lake. This was where the serious runners trained, and I was the old man of the group. We would run track workouts with timed intervals to increase the speed of the fast-twitch fibers in our legs. Those fibers are responsible for speed repetition. Slow-twitch fibers are for the long endurance that gets you to 26.2 miles, but the fast-twitch fibers qualify you for Boston. So, we trained for weeks to get the fibers right, and it was difficult but also motivating as there was competition in our group. We also ran hills repetitively.

Running hills reminded me of football in high school and rugby in college. Run from here to there and back as quickly as you can, then do it again about fifty more times, then do it all again. I was in great shape. I can only dream about it now, but it was very satisfying; however, looking back, I could have done better. In our running group, I buddied up with a guy about my age and about three inches taller than me and we both had the same goal of qualifying for Boston. I wanted to beat him, and I'm sure he wanted to run me into the dirt. We were good for each other in training, and we helped each other out when we both signed up for the Tulsa Marathon in Oklahoma. It was run on November 17, 1995, my actual fortieth birthday, so I could not get much younger in my new age group. We went to Tulsa because it was an out-and-back qualifier for Boston and one of the flattest courses to be found. It ran along the Arkansas River, which was fun to look at if you were strolling, but running at a 7:49 per mile pace gave you no time to enjoy the view.

Ed was my friend's name, and his wife and family were there to cheer him on. Sandee was my support team, as she had been in six previous marathons, all at White Rock Lake. Sandee hung with Ed's group while Ed and I stood next to each other on race morning. The horn sounded, and we were off. We ran on our watches to make sure we stayed on pace, knowing that we would inevitably slow down in the last few miles. It was important to hold pace until twenty miles. Through the first ten miles, we were cruising nicely and would occasionally say something to each other but not actual conversation; we were breathing and working hard. When we got to the turn-around at 13.1, we crossed the river, then turned around and reversed course. Then it happened. As we got to fifteen miles, I began to feel a problem in my right foot and it began to slow me down.

Ed was kind to back down about ten seconds a mile for me, but I soon realized that I would not be able to hold the pace and told Ed to keep going and that I would see him at the finish line. So, he took off and I began to favor my right foot. Sandee was on the course, waiting for me at about mile sixteen or seventeen, and she could see I was now limping. I told her to go to the finish line, that Ed was out in front, and I would be there soon.

I am not sure how I made it to the finish line, but I was not going to stop, even if my leg fell off. I was a seasoned marathon runner, and stopping was not in the plan. But I realized that qualifying for Boston was out of the question when I saw on my watch 3:25, and I was still about two and a half miles from the finish line, right in the grip of "the wall," when you don't have anything left and you are on fumes. It was hard. Little did I know that Ed entered the area where the finish line was and was still close to qualifying pace. By then, Sandee was at the finish line to witness the finishers and the heroic effort put out by Ed at the end of his race.

The finish line was in a park. The course took us past the finish line, where we could see the official clock, but we still had to run the circling perimeter, which was about the last tenth of a mile. Ed came around the corner, entered the park, saw his time, and dug deep to finish as hard as he could and finished 3:25:03. Just three seconds off the

Boston qualifying time. I entered the park soon after, saw the clock, all the pandemonium that takes place, with cheers, music, and fanfare while contestants drag themselves across the finish line. I will never forget it.

I saw the clock and knew I had lost my goal of Boston, but still needed to finish. I also dug deep and pushed past the pain in my foot and gave it all that I had left. To run 26.2 miles as fast as you can without stopping is not easy, and at forty years old, I could really feel the damage to myself and my foot. I crossed the finish line and saw my time of 3:43:00, which is very respectable, but I had failed to accomplish my goal after a solid year of training. **You win some and you lose some.**

We went back to the hotel, where I slept and rested while watching the Ironman Triathlon on television while Sandee went shopping. We had a nice birthday dinner out and headed home to Plano the next morning. What a trip. And what about Ed's three seconds over the qualifying time? He filed an appeal to the Boston Marathon board of directors and was granted a three-second credit, which allowed him to qualify and run Boston. I talked to him after Boston, and he said it was great and wished that I had run it with him. So did I.

Congratulations, Ed. You did it, man. I have not spoken to him since. I ended up having surgery on my right foot to remove a nerve aggravated by a tendon in my foot from so much running. I was in a walking boot for six weeks and limped for another eight weeks before I was normal. That was the last marathon I ran.

14

Life after marathoning, building a new house, Odyssey grows, Samantha Gasmire born at just twenty-four weeks, Odyssey in Times Square at IPO, Ty Gasmire, Jaden and Tessa Werley born, losing our close friend and pastor, Kim Hall.

LIFE AFTER MARATHONING ... THE RACE GOES ON

Back at home, Sandee had our home running like a fine Swiss watch. When I would come home on Fridays, and sometimes not until Saturday, I just merged into the fast-paced world of keeping up with Sandee, Natalie, and Charlie in our new home at 5504 Wilts Ct in Plano. It never occurred to me until a friend asked me one time if I was worried about starting a new business and building a new house at the same time. I really wasn't worried about it, but I was really focused on it.

For the first year, we worked to get our Indianapolis operation up to profitability, and once that was moving along with a growing census, Dick started going to Pittsburgh so that we could split up and get them both going before running out of money in year one. At the same time, we had to negotiate our way out of our noncompete contracts with Vitas. We got it done, but not without some brain damage along the way. Now we were free to lock and load and get on the map with Odyssey Healthcare.

By the time Indy was at breakeven and Pittsburgh was still losing about $150k per month, we needed to begin the search for round two, which is Series B of an investment. In the B round, we raised another $7 million and kept going. All this was from our original three venture firms. We began buying our first acquisitions, beginning with Dallas and other cities. By the time we needed the C round, we had an enormous backlog of acquisitions in our pipeline. Enter Mr. Robert Sarna. Bob came aboard to join Dick and me around year three at Odyssey. Bob did great mergers and acquisition work and is still working with us in our current hospice gig at Three Oaks Hospice. Bob has been our VP of Mergers and Acquisitions for more than twenty years. He has also become a good friend.

I am very thankful for Bob and his "magic letter," which he authored to get hospice owners interested in speaking with us. It was two sentences, and that was it. It worked. When it lost its luster from repeated mailings to the same target audience, he created "son of magic letter," which has endured for the past few years, with even more deals coming our way. Low tech, medium touch, high impact. Just how we like it.

Our first large footprint was a deal with Amerra, where we bought about seven locations, and the lead guy was named David. He was a good guy to deal with, but his boss was a jerk. It was hard to get the deal across the finish line, and when we did, we suddenly had more than twenty locations in six states, and we were outrunning our operational bandwidth. We needed managers, and we needed to build out the corporate office, which was in a two-room office on the twenty-seventh floor of the Maxus Energy Building in downtown Dallas.

Now that we were billing and collecting money, we needed a CFO. Our first CFO was quirky and took himself way too seriously. We were building a culture of accountability, but also one of *not* taking ourselves too seriously but taking the business seriously. Our CFO could not catch that bus and flamed out after a couple of years. In his place, we hired Doug Cannon. Doug reported to Dick at that time, and the three of us got along great for a while. We hired Brenda Belger to run

HR, Debbie Hoffpauir to run operations as a regional vice president, and Kathy Ventre (from my Vitas days in Dallas) to run clinical compliance. Patricia Gross led our sales and training department. Pat was a dear friend of our family, and she and her husband Glen were very close to us. But at Odyssey, it was all business, and Pat did a great job as VP of Sales.

Ms. Lisa Pekar has served as an assistant to our respective CEOs and me for the last twenty years. A special recognition to Lisa because she has been a significant force behind the scenes, supporting boards of directors and C-suite teams. I hope we continue to work together for years to come.

BALANCING BUSINESS AND FAMILY

While we began the company in 1995–96, our family activities continued to accelerate with the ambitions of our kids. From 1986–1990, we had both Natalie and Charlie and met such dear friends that they are close to us even today. Lifelong friends, including our next-door neighbors on Faringdon Drive, our second house in Plano, are Greg and Mary Tyler. We loved being neighbors and have stayed close to each other throughout the big events in life, having children and grandchildren, moving, and retirement. We have known each other for more than thirty years, and our families have become very close.

Always remember this, my dear reader: your friends are a glimpse into your own character and the moral priorities in your life. Surround yourself with and keep your best friends. One day, they will need you, and you will need them.

A life well-lived includes having friends with whom you have traveled the road of life together and shared common interests and experiences. There are errors and victories that come with being an honest friend. We all have that in common, life's ups and downs. Both Sandee and I are proud of the fact that our friends from long ago are our best friends today, and it has been a legacy example to our kids, who see our friends as their friends. When we all get together, we see the essence of family.

Devoted friends are protecting and rewarding. They have a charm and innocence, ready to land a graceful hand on the shoulder or give a hug as a faithful friend. So many deep relationships with our friends and such wonderful memories of the past with each of them, and many more memories in the making still today.

Friends are the dimension of life that requires an effort by both parties, and in return, the sound of laughter, the dampness of tears, and the reality that we are human in common, with faults and promises, all of us.

It is important and rewarding to love your friends.

While Odyssey was in the early and mid-stages of growth, Natalie and Charlie were becoming such fun kids and very close sister and brother. It was fun to return home to find out that the reality of life was alive and well in our home. Sandee and the kids were so busy with schoolwork, after-school activities, and church group events, that in no way did things slow down when I got home. They were glad to see me, and I was glad to be home, but hey, there were events to go to or people that were coming over. Natalie wanted to be a weather girl on TV, and Charlie was ordained the cameraman.

When a babysitter came to watch the kids while we went out with our friends, they would turn the house into a TV studio and use our big-box video camera to film the weather report. It was a hoot, and we have the tape to prove it.

On Sunday mornings we would get up and go to Hunters Glen Baptist Church, where many friends joined us for Sunday school and worship, followed by two hours of laughing loudly during lunch. Our dear pastor and friend Kim Hall baptized both Natalie and Charlie and was a huge part of our Christian contentment, faith, and hope. He was one of the funniest guys walking the planet and so steeped in the Word and the ability to teach by connecting to your soul every Sunday. But he was, like all of us, a man with the demands and challenges and temptations that afflict everyone. It culminated in one of the greatest losses for our family.

Kim took his own life in a hotel room in east Texas. He had an inappropriate relationship with a new church member, and it was so crushing to him that he couldn't face what would have been a supportive family and congregation if he had given everyone a chance to hear his plea of repentance and request for forgiveness. His family would have granted it to him, and so would all of us. No one is perfect, not even pastors. It was an incredibly sad day for all of us to lose a good friend at his own hand.

I think of Kim from time to time and remember the last time I spoke with him, just a couple of weeks before he died. Did I miss something there? No, I do not think so, but I do have mixed emotions about having such a lighthearted phone call with him. We laughed together about silly things, then hung up. That was the last time I spoke with Dr. Kim Hall.

ODYSSEY FINALLY BIG ENOUGH TO SURVIVE

In 1998, Odyssey became profitable on a monthly cash flow basis, and I felt it safe to make a family purchase that changed, in a good way, our family memories for decades to come. We felt the need to return to the Gasmire roots of boating and recreate the fun of our youthful past. We bought a forty-foot Sea Ray Sedan Bridge cabin cruiser on Lake Dallas/Lewisville, then moved it to Cedar Mills Resort on Lake Texoma, just like Dad did when we moved our little seventeen-foot Mississippi family boat to Texoma in 1969. We named our new cruiser on Texoma *Lakebrain*, a suggestion offered up by Mary Tyler as she described how she felt after a cruise drinking margaritas. It was a perfect name, and our family stories of fun and many injuries during our ten-year ownership of her are irreplaceable.

During a family trip to Lake of the Ozarks in the mid-nineties, we bought a twenty-four-foot ski/family cruiser built by Celebrity. We had a dock at Texoma, and when we added *Lakebrain* to the fleet, we had two docks and all the fun trimmings. We also had a Sea Doo and just had a blast being the rednecks on the lake and surviving on the boat and on the dock. We had such a good time, and our close friends usually stepped up to make the craziness even more zany.

One time, we were anchored and tied up in a favorite cove we called Duck Cove, after all the ducks that Dad, Jay, Mark, and I had shot during many duck seasons over the years. We had settled into our anchor spot late in the day to enjoy cooking on the boat with the Brown family. We had the young'uns tie us up to trees on the close shoreline at the bow and the stern. We were locked down tight, ensign. We couldn't be pulled off those moorings with a Mississippi barge. Until we were.

We had the TV on in the cabin as a nasty storm began to blow in. We thought it would just be some fun rain that we could enjoy from under our Sunbrella canvas and the boat's cabin. We couldn't wait for it to roll in. Box wine will do that to you. The weather report on the TV gave us a different expectation, including hail the size of golf balls, heavy rain, and winds that were uprooting trees. I was kind of okay until they said the storm was ripping out trees by their roots. After all, more than half the boat was tied to trees.

I pictured an eight-ton ball of roots attached to a seventy-five-year-old hackberry tree being towed into the water as the wind blew. What could go wrong? There was nothing we could do about the wind but hold on, but we did prepare for the hail by covering all exposed windows and whatever surfaces we could with beach towels and duct tape. Box wine will do that to you too. There is something about putting yourself out there in the elements to be a man of destiny, protecting your family like a caveman, keeping your hairy wife and kids with long arms and bare knuckles free from bad beetle grubs.

When the storm hit, Ginger offered words of encouragement to her husband, Allan, and children, Andrew and Emily. As the hail bounced off the boat with the sound of a ball peen hammer at a Mississippi bridge repair party, she calmly said, “Wouldn’t it be terrible if we got hit by lightning and sank?” We all looked at each other. Then she said, “Wouldn’t it be terrible if the trees uprooted and landed on the boat, and we drifted out to sea into the full fury of the storm?” We all looked at each other. Then we got out another box of wine. It was a blast.

I could write the next book on Lake Stories: Injuries and Revelations. All of us got hurt at one time or another on one of our boats. I almost drowned Sandee and nearly broke her leg pulling her behind the Celebrity. Natalie took twelve stitches to the chin because of lake “turbulence.” Charlie ripped his back up falling into an open ski well. I smashed a big tow from a dropped wooden seat frame, cracked my sternum swinging from the Celebrity to *Lakebrain* … and the stories go on endlessly.

One last boating story had to do with a church event with our high school and middle school youth groups. Several boats and jet skis were brought to the lake for a day of skiing and fellowship. We offered up *Lakebrain* to be the mothership so that we had a place to stage all the other floating craft. It was never the intent to have all forty-five people on the boat. Until they were. Another tree-uprooting storm rolled in without warning. By the time it was in full force, we had forty-five campers aboard *Lakebrain,* with all associated watercraft tied in a conga line, drifting behind the boat for at least a hundred feet.

In a lightning storm, getting into a shelter can save your life. And there we were with the weight of forty-five people throughout the vessel, submerging the swim platform below the water by a few inches. Inside the cabin, everyone was doing all they could to keep from touching one another in the event of a lightning strike. *Lakebrain* was awesome, and she saved all of us without breaking. Thank you, Lord. Those kids had a blast, and we were glad to have another Duck Cove story for the ages.

The stories go on further, but no one died. That was our lake motto for parents trusting us with their kids for the day: "They won't die." Such good Parrot-Head times that our kids today have the same vision for their families one day. We hope Sandee and I will also be invited!

THE NEW MILLENIUM

By the year 2000, Odyssey was growing ahead of plan. In 1998, when we hit profitability, we still needed working and operating capital, and we secured our Series C financing, consisting of $17 million from our founding investors, and added $3 million in mezzanine debt financing from Sandy McGrath at Resource Capital Partners. We also brought in Wyc Grousbeck, the majority owner of the Boston Celtics and a partner at Highland Healthcare Partners. Now we had enough to get us to the financial exit and had a world-class board of directors and outstanding investment firms backing us. All we had to do was deliver results.

It was getting more challenging keeping up with the infrastructure necessary to support the growth without taking a hit to our operating margins. We were learning about the stair step to scale the business and the cash burn and margin growth positions on that stairway. We were able to begin setting strategic targets on growth and geography. In those days, with the hospice business so underdeveloped and the need so great, we had to decide in what part of the country we really had the best chance of success. As things turned out and in retrospect, we later developed other hospice companies that omitted parts of the country too difficult and expensive to operate in. That list now includes the West Coast and the Pacific Northwest, the northeast down to Pennsylvania, and all of Florida. At Odyssey, we were nearly everywhere but Florida, but we had plans to get there too.

As we got bigger, Dick and I had to divide/separate and conquer. We could no longer go to every Christmas party as we had in the early days. We could no longer travel to locations together, save for special circumstances, but mostly we were managing a company that was going way beyond what we thought we could do when we wrote the business plan. We stayed true to our culture-driven thesis. One of those key elements was the Odyssey Service Standards that we wrote on day one of the company. I had learned at UDC, and it was expected by Jim Kingston, to write our customer commitment and build the day-to-day culture of the company to comply with that customer commitment. It worked at UDC, and it was working at Odyssey.

We even expanded that general concept to include the acronym YCCOM, which meant "You Can Count On Me." I came up with the idea at CiCi's Pizza in Plano when Sandee and I took the kids out for pizza. We were ordering and paying at the cashier when I noticed the letters on her CiCi's uniform, something to the effect of WMTWBP, "We Make The World's Best Pizza." I asked her what it meant, and she didn't know. That made a point with me, to the embarrassment of our kids.

I asked to see the manager. He was able to tell me what the letters on everyone's shirt meant. I told him that his employee, at least one, didn't know what it meant. I made a commitment right there that we would not let the mission at Odyssey go forgotten by our teammates providing care to our terminally ill patients. We built a legacy around YCCOM that stands even today. I wore a small round pin that simply said "YCCOM" each day I was at an Odyssey office. Lead from the front, show what you want, and live it yourself so you can claim the expectations of everyone on your team. If you don't do it, they won't either. I loved it, and it worked.

Probably the most significant cultural development was the creation of the Odyssey logo and the story surrounding it. I had never fully considered the significance of the stories that come with a company's legacy of culture until we were faced with doing it ourselves. As it turned out, the 747 flight to Chicago with Mark Wan began what became a very emotional and heartfelt development for our company. In 1996, after our first round of $3 million hit the bank, we were faced with having to develop collateral materials for staff recruitment and marketing. We needed a full line of printed materials because websites weren't in existence until a few years later, but first, we needed a logo.

I had a contact in Dallas for materials we used for Vitas, and I called to ask for her help on developing our logo—and we needed it fast. We were in Indianapolis interviewing people, and we needed material and message legitimacy. A name is fine, but without at least a logo, you don't really exist. I called Bobbi Linkemer. She is a writer today, and very well published and accomplished. She has written at least twenty-four books, and at the time was my resource to find someone to develop our logo. Bobbi went to work right away on it and had a contracted associate who took the first stab at a variety of logos that Dick and I considered over a couple of weeks.

We finally landed on the logo that we liked, based upon the house element and the colors and front door opening or closing, depending on how you looked at it and what was important to the viewer. I got home from Indianapolis on a Friday night and called Bobbi to tell her of our decision and that we needed the camera-ready final artwork by Monday, only three days later. She said she would do what she could and would let me know.

On Sunday, just two days later, she called me with upsetting news. News that became a cornerstone message and emotional connection to the Odyssey mission of Serving All People During the End of Life's Journey. It became the story and reason many people devoted themselves to the work at Odyssey Healthcare. I told the story hundreds of times to hundreds of teammates over the years and every time I was overcome with emotion.

Bobbi told me that after I spoke with her that Friday night, she reached out to her contact that had developed the prototype and asked her to finish it and prepare to send it to us on that next Monday. The person she worked with was quadriplegic, and through her own will and determination, had built a life working with a computer and mouth wand to create these work-of-art logos. That Friday night, after she completed the final Odyssey logo, she made her way in her high-tech wheelchair to the therapeutic water of her indoor spa. She had ambulated this way for many years and was experienced using the equipment to take her where she wanted to go. However, this time, this night, was different, and something went wrong.

The next morning, her family found her in her spa, having drowned during the night. No one was there to know what went wrong, but she was gone. The last logo she ever designed, with her own heartfelt determination through a mouth wand, was the Odyssey Healthcare logo. When Bobbi told me this, I was just overwhelmed and stunned with grief, and I didn't even know this person. I asked Bobbi her name because I wanted to send the family a letter. She said, "Her name was Faith." In silence, I realized that Faith, the person, the emotion, the belief, had created a beautiful logo of meaning for the ages.

The story of Faith has stood as a reason we do this work in hospice. Regardless of a person's belief system and experiences, without faith, hope, and love, nothing else matters. And according to Jesus, the greatest is love. Our company now had new meaning. A revitalized purpose and message we needed others to hear. The story of Faith will always endure, and I only wish I had met her so my own life would have been blessed by her love and her spirit. God rest your soul, Ms. Faith.

During the 1990s, the entire Gasmire family was growing with children. We had Natalie and Charlie in 1986 and 1990 respectively, followed by my brother Jay and his wife Denise having Samantha and Ty in 1989 and 1990, and batting family clean-up were my sister Sue and her husband Troy, having Jaden and Tessa in 1997 and 2000. Over the span of fourteen years, we had a gaggle of fun-loving kids that have become very close cousins, and at our annual family vacations they would find fun things to do together. The most challenging and significant events came with Samantha first, then with Ty.

Denise carried Samantha to just twenty-four weeks when she went into labor and barely made it to Baylor Hospital in downtown Dallas before Samantha was born. She was so premature that she clung to life for the first few minutes in the ER, with the nurses and doctors unsure if she was developed enough to sustain life, particularly her lungs. As Denise tells it, when Samantha was born, they put her tiny 1.6-pound body to the side to tend to Denise. After a short time, Samantha was moving and responding slowly to her new world outside the womb, which was supposed to be her home for another eleven weeks or more. Struggling to breathe, she showed the strength and determination of a person who wanted to count in this life. She wanted to be Samantha Leigh Gasmire, and with the grace and plans God had for her, she slowly built strength in the Baylor Neonatal Intensive Care Unit (NICU).

The night Samantha was born unexpectedly, Jay was at a business dinner in Houston and couldn't be reached because cell phones were not yet in the pocket of every person in the free world. Denise left messages at his hotel and called Jay's work associates and left messages for them too. Finally, around 11:00 p.m., Jay got the message and called Denise at Baylor. It was advised by the medical team at Baylor that Jay hurry to the hospital, as it was not yet certain that Samantha would survive, which was stunning to all of us. Could this really be happening?

It was too late for any flights that Jay could catch, so I got in my truck and drove to Houston to get him. He didn't have his car there, but he had a friend who agreed to begin driving toward Dallas on I-45, and I would meet him halfway. We met in Huntsville. Jay jumped out of his friend's car and into my truck, where we wasted no time. Jay had been drinking at his business event but was becoming sober quickly. There wasn't much to say, so that left time for about three hours of quiet and prayerful meditation, racing up I-45. It was a reality that Jay's first baby girl might not be alive by the time we got to the hospital.

We pulled into the Baylor parking lot around 5:00 a.m., and Jay raced to the NICU. Sandee and I stayed in a lobby of the hospital, just staying out of the way, fearfully hopeful that Jay had made it in time to see his breathing baby girl. And breathe she did. Samantha's saving efforts and exertion were possible due to the advanced development of her lungs, which gave her the fighting chance she needed. Just a little more time is what she needed.

A while later, Sandee and I were in the lobby, just pacing back and forth, when unexpectedly, Jay pushed Denise in a wheelchair to come get us. Denise was doing well, but Samantha was not; she was barely hanging on. Denise asked if we wanted to go to the NICU to see her, and Jay, with tears in his eyes, decided to stay in the lobby and make calls to family.

I pushed Denise, with Sandee by my side, into the NICU, where baby girl Gasmire was resting with the full attention of a medical army. She looked so small and helpless and not yet ready for life outside of the protective cocoon she had known for only six months. She looked like she really wanted back in that womb; it wasn't time for her to be here yet, but God wanted her to get started a little earlier than planned. She was so small that her diaper was a cotton ball stuck to her among all the wires and tubes that were helping her to simply exist until she could get strong enough on her own.

I completely lost it when I looked up and saw a framed needlepoint picture and message over her fully glass-enclosed basinnet. It read, "Please be patient with me; God isn't finished with me yet." I came apart and had to leave the NICU. That little champion of a girl grabbed life stroke by stroke, breath by breath, millimeter by millimeter. By noon she was still alive. By 6:00 p.m. that day, she was still alive. A day or two later, she was still alive. Her weight went from 1.6 pounds down to 1.4 pounds. It was a real battle, and if she had any other complications, it was unthinkable.

Samantha was in the NICU for thirteen weeks, where she gained grams of weight at a time while her lungs grew stronger. By the time she went home, she weighed a whopping four pounds! Hailed as a miracle baby by the Baylor medical staff and the *Dallas Morning News*, Samantha Leigh Gasmire was on her way to a full life, which God had promised her. We were all very patient but prayerful that God would be finished with His work of healing her body.

Today, Samantha is in nursing school and is doing great. We all love her so much and wish we had just a morsel of Samantha's courage and determination. She taught us that even a small, weak, and totally dependent newborn infant can grow to make a difference in the lives of family and friends. She is a true champion, a hero in every respect, and we are so proud of her and love her so. She has shown that she is tougher than any of us. She has taught us a lot, and we can't wait to see how her life unfolds in the many years ahead.

Samantha's brother, Ty, was born in 1990 and nearly went full term, but experienced complications that have been life-changing in so many ways. Just a couple of days after his birth, he had a brain bleed that was undiagnosed as it happened. There was no reason to suspect anything was wrong with his development the first few days and weeks, but it became clear that this little boy had some struggles of his own. Ty was diagnosed with cerebral palsy, complicated by mental health challenges. This began a life for Ty that would require an enormous amount of help both physically and psychologically. No one could be prepared for this kind of news and the lifelong reality that this little boy wouldn't have a normal physical life and would be challenged with other mental issues at the same time.

Our family has rallied around Ty Alexander Gasmire. He has brought us together as a family, and his cousins include him when and where they can in their exploits and social fun. Ty is also the founder of Champion Services, which was created by Jay and Denise for the purpose of serving the long-term needs of Ty and other people like him who struggle with activities of daily living. It is a wonderful company, and Ty is very happy living with his friends in his group home in Tarrant County.

Over the years, Jay and Denise have been true heroes to Ty and Samantha. Ty has had multiple surgeries for his back and has gone through experimental treatments that required the tireless efforts of both Jay and Denise as well as his grandparents, Fred and Judy Scudder, and all of us as his aunts, uncles, and cousins. He is a joy in our lives and has been on a different path than the rest of us but equally rewarding in every regard. He has shown us what is most important in life: love. Samantha showed us that too. It has been a challenge of champions, and that is what they are. Champions.

A GROWING FAMILY WITH VARIED INTERESTS AND LOYALTIES

Phew. Our families have always been busy, and that trend continued with Troy and my sister Sue Ellen. The Werleys finally moved from Pennsylvania, where Yankees grow on trees, to the more desirable southern lifestyle in Texas. A devoted Philadelphia Eagles fan, Troy brought that disease with him to the land of the Dallas Cowboys. But they made it to Texas to be closer to family, and I do think Sue always wanted to get back to Dallas. Sue is a die-hard Cowboys fan, but that is a tough duty around Troy.

When Jaden Paul Werley was born on November 4, 1997, a good-looking red-headed boy became part of our inventory of champions. Tessa Ellen Werley, another redhead, came into the game of life on June 26, 2000. We now had a full complement of nieces, nephews, and cousins. It was time to race into the twenty-first century.

Sandee and I had been married for nineteen years when the calendar flipped to 2000. For our twentieth wedding anniversary, there were to be a lot of big events. It was time to update Sandee's wedding ring, so I conspired with her best friend Julie to have one made by Odom Jewelers in Plano, but I didn't want Sandee to know about it. It is a dangerous thing to surprise Mrs. Gasmire, but I was going to do it anyway. Which is always the first misstep to gaining valuable experience for the next time I consider surprising her. It's no fun if she knows everything in advance!

We planned—no, Sandee planned—a trip for us to Paris and the French countryside for the spring of 2001. We planned to celebrate our twentieth anniversary at the Eiffel Tower and enjoy French cuisine and wine and the cobblestone streets covered with people who talk funny. Sandee speaks a tiny bit of French, which helped us from time to time, but I only knew "adios, Pepe," which I do not think is French.

Once the jeweler finished the ring, and I paid for it in cash, I had it packed in my jacket pocket the night before we were leaving on our trip. I did not want it to get lost if a dirtbag thief opened our luggage, so I planned to carry it through security. I also thought I would experiment with taking half of an Ambien the night before so I would know if I really wanted to take one for the overnight flight to Paris. Being a pilot, I do not sleep on planes; I stare out the window, wondering what is next.

I had taken the Ambien and was softly slumbering my way to sleep when, in the background of my consciousness, I could hear Sandee talking to herself. I heard her say, "What is this receipt for?" She had found the receipt for the ring and was digging through the pockets of my jacket. But before she could get her paws on the ring that I had worked on for six months, I sprang to life and jumped up and grabbed the receipt and the jacket from her. That was a narrow escape. I wanted to give it to her under the Eiffel Tower, not at our home in Texas. I did not have the romantic ring thing when I asked her to marry me in 1981, and I wanted to square up on that memorable opportunity for good. We headed to Paris.

On June 20, 2001, just three months before the 9/11 attacks, and four months before the Odyssey IPO, Sandee and I could see the Eiffel Tower in the distance from our hotel window. During the summer it stays light quite late in the northern hemisphere of western Europe, so we did not head to the tower until about 11:00 p.m. She did not know I was going to give her a new ring, so I was trying to be cool and find a good place to sit where we could see the lights, which were still flashing and dazzling the crowds every night since the millennium celebration six months earlier.

I found a nice spot on the grass smack dab directly in front of the tower. I also had a bottle of champagne tucked under my arm. All we needed to do was to sit down before the lights went out at midnight. Sandee did not like the spot I picked. So, I gathered our "stuff" and followed Sandee around while she looked for a place for us to roost for a while. A couple of minutes before midnight, the bewitching hour in my schedule of events, she saw a park bench to the right of the Eiffel Tower, and we headed toward it. I suggested a brisk pace as I was running out of time to give her the ring before all the razzle-dazzle lights dimmed to a normal all-nighter display.

When we finally got to the bench and sat down, I reached into my pocket just as the lights went out. Sandee said, "Well, that was pretty." Now I had another hundred years to wait for the next millennial celebration. So instead of giving her the new ring, we opened the bottle of champagne and shared anniversary cards with each other, under a very dim light, I might add. When I finally presented her new ring, it was a bit anticlimactic in my view, at least for me, but she loved it. She deserved it. We enjoyed the ring on her finger the entire time we were in France.

9/11 AND AN INITIAL PUBLIC OFFERING

When we got home, things were really beginning to get into full gear with the Odyssey initial public offering. At the time, we were not all that big and we wondered if there would be widespread interest. The decision to take the company public was part of the exit strategy for our investors and ourselves. An IPO is simply a financing that shifts the margin growth risk from the private equity and venture capital investors to willing public investors.

With an IPO, the key element for deciding when to pull the trigger and make it happen is a matter of timing.

Timing in every regard, including how the company is performing, is having the books ready for public and legal scrutiny, ensuring the growth and margin story is a solid basis for the offering. Even if a company is solid on every front, if the stock market is in the tank and if other IPO attempts by others are not supported, then it is unlikely an IPO will be successful. Success in an IPO is defined as achieving a strong valuation for the company, but also how much demand there is for the stock shares being offered.

Our financial performance was impressive; our growth trends were strong, and we had a solid merger and acquisition growth pipeline for which we needed the capital from the offering. So, we moved ahead with planning our initial public offering for late in 2001. None of us had done an IPO before.

THINKING OF AN EXIT TOO EARLY

Several years before we prepared to go public, Dick and I were sailing in the Caribbean on a bareboat basis. We were the only crew, and Dick was the only sailor. We were alone on the seas, which is an intimidating thought. Before Dick invited me on the trip, he had received a call from Glen Cavallo, the chairman and CEO at Beverly Enterprises. He asked Dick if we would consider taking $2 per share as a preemptive bid for the company and just buy all of it from us. On our sailing trip, we discussed this offer.

One night Dick and I had the sailboat moored in a quiet cove at Marina Cay along with other sailing vessels, and we took our dinghy to shore to go to the only restaurant around. They had barbecue, and after a day of sailing and drinking rum all day, it was delicious. When we drove our tender back to the sailboat that was home for a week, we lit up a couple of Cuban cigars, poured a scotch, and sat on the deck talking about the offer from Beverly. By the end of the cigars, we decided it all boiled down to the open window of the market. Was it still opening, or was it closing? If we waited, were we risking getting nothing and having to wait another ten years for the market and the appetite for hospice to return? Or did we go now and sell too soon?

There were no other public hospice companies, so there was a big chance that a publicly owned hospice would not be well received by the public. Should the management of a company that serves terminally ill patients have economic gain by being a public company? That was a particularly good and real question. Dick and I and our investor board of directors agreed with us that our company was so solid in purpose and performance that we should swing for the fences. That meant finding an investment banker that had the scale and reputation to represent us in a public offering and not just take a lowball offer from Cavallo. Let the competition for our great company determine our value.

I was in my office one morning when Dick burst in and closed my door with some news. He had just had a call from Jim Jackson, the investment banker with Merrill Lynch. Dick said, "Merrill Lynch, can you believe it?"

I said, "Wow. This may be getting big time."

And it was. We had six investment banking firms come make their pitches to Dick, me, Doug, and our board about their capabilities to take us public. They were not Goldman Sachs, but the list was very respectable, including Merrill Lynch, SG Cowen, and CIBC. After the dust settled from all their presentations, we decided to engage with Merrill Lynch but also include SG Cowen and CIBC on the "cover" of the offering. The purpose in doing so was to access their sales force so that we would get strong sales exposure to get all shares sold, and if they really did their jobs right, we would be oversubscribed for more shares than we were offering. Merrill was the most balanced on valuation expectations and did not blow smoke in our faces, inflating the valuation to unreal expectations.

For the next three months we did nothing but get ready for the IPO, which was planned for an early September 2001 launch. It was a tight time frame, but Jackson said they could pull it off. Now Dick and I and Doug were in unknown territory and were being guided and directed by bankers, lawyers, and accountants.

The writing of the prospectus is one of the most underestimated heavy lifts in business. It is all about protecting the public investor. The Securities and Exchange Commission is in existence to make sure that the requirements, including disclosures, operating facts, risks to the business, management discussion, analysis, and on and on, are written in the prospectus so that every public investor has ALL facts available when making the decision whether to invest. It is all about protecting the investor, and it comes at the expense of the CEO and board of directors.

Our working writing sessions, which would frequently go to midnight and beyond, were excruciatingly detailed. About twenty people, made up of attorneys and accountants, lined both sides of a conference table that was about thirty feet long. On one side we had our legal team, consisting of Jeff Chapman, Greg Hidalgo, Brad Bickham, and Chris Miller (who was killed in a Christmas Eve auto accident in Dallas fifteen years later) from Vinson and Elkins, a very prestigious transaction legal group with offices worldwide. We later hired Brad away from V&E to become our general counsel at Odyssey.

On the other side of the table was Ken Bernstein and his accounting team from KPMG. The group would go word by word and discuss the meaning of such arcane issues that it made me want to scream "enough already!" They asked about FASB[7] impact and application on every accounting approach we used and stacked it up against accounting tests that were deemed credible by most reasonable and self-bloating accountants and attorneys. They are both rather self-serving groups, highly paid by the company to advise on matters that only they understand. It is a good business model. Talk about stuff that no one understands, convince them they need it, and then send them the bill and tell them, but wait, there is more. Then start the cycle again. It is not hard to become cynical when you get into these processes, which you are paying for, and see how the sausage is made. Until they began discussing what kind of jet we would use for the road show. Did someone say "jet"?

The prospectus was finished around the first of August 2001. We pressed the "send" button to the SEC with the required documents from our publishing company, Bowne. When we hit send, we celebrated with drinks and a load of silly string on all the team members that worked day and night to get the document complete. Now we would prepare for comments from the SEC in about thirty days to clear the final hurdles to go on the road show. We began working with Jim Jackson on the sales pitch for the road show. Our target date to start was September 14, 2001.

The importance of selecting the right investment banker and firm cannot be overstated. Their job is to sell stock in the company at the IPO. Jackson was a master at the stock market sales pitch process and a lot of fun to work with. The Merrill Lynch sales force was responsi-

---

7 Established in 1973, the Financial Accounting Standards Board (FASB) is the independent, private-sector, not-for-profit organization based in Connecticut that establishes financial accounting and reporting standards for public and private companies and not-for-profit organizations that follow Generally Accepted Accounting Principles (GAAP).

ble for creating demand for our stock and for setting up the dozens of face-to-face meetings we would have with interested brokerage firms around the country in a short amount of time. It was determined that we had enough demand that we did not need to include a road show in Europe. But we did need to hit about thirty cities in less than two weeks to get the offering completed. That is where the jet came in.

Merrill arranged for a Gulfstream 200, along with a crew of two and a flight attendant, to be with us throughout the trip, from start to finish. The participants on the road show would be Dick, me, Doug, and the Merrill Lynch road show team that included a team of support staff who would make sure we stayed on time and made changes to our presentation between cities if we were getting vibes from post-call discussions that we needed to change it or tweak it or otherwise make very subtle messaging improvements.

At the end of August 2001, we received approval from the SEC and began to schedule our meetings, which would begin on September 14 in Baltimore, MD.

Back in June 2001, when Sandee and I were boarding the Boeing 777 aircraft at Charles de Gaulle Airport in Paris to return to Dallas, I was able to take pictures of the mammoth airplane and ground operations as we walked on the ramp to the stairway up to the giant plane. It is one of the last photos of its kind on the ramp there, given what was to come on September 11, 2001.

As we made final preparations for the road show, we learned that we would be following another health care company making an IPO effort. Cross Country Nurses is a staffing company with an impressive record but did not compete with hospice. Jim Jackson told us that the Merrill Lynch team would try to not let their road show interfere with ours as we bopped in and out of many of the same brokers for our IPO pitch sessions.

Sandee and the kids were excited that I was going on the road show because they knew what it meant to me and our family. Leading up to September 11, I attended all of Natalie's basketball games, watching her dominate at point guard as she tried out for the high school team at Plano West High School. Charlie was playing football at Renner Middle School and was involved with his friends with many other things.

We were ready to get the Odyssey show started. The ticker symbol for Odyssey was an interesting discussion, with suggestions such as BYBY, but for a hospice company, that wouldn't work. We thought of CULTR (see you later, or culture), and that would not work. We landed on simply ODSY, and we prepared for launch starting in Baltimore, then on to New York City.

GOD HAD DIFFERENT PLANS FOR US

The morning of September 11, 2001, was a beautiful day. I was getting dressed for work, and the kids were off to school by 8:00 a.m. I was shaving in our bathroom around that time, waiting for Fox News to interview Jack Welch, the chairman/CEO of General Electric from 1981 to 2002. At the time, our company had GE debt, so we were a customer of theirs. I wanted to hear what Jack had to say about the economy and was hoping he would say something indicating he was bullish on the public markets.

When Fox came out of the commercial break, they showed Jack waiting to be interviewed, then the screen cut to a smoking World Trade Center with a big hole in it shaped like a raptor or something. The commentators were baffled, obviously, and they never returned to Jack Welch. Sandee and I stood in our bedroom watching the TV when the second plane hit the second tower. She saw it. I did not see it live as I had looked away for a moment. It was now obvious that we were under attack. It took several minutes to get our heads right and decide what to do. Sandee went to the kids' school to get them, and I jumped in the car to head to our Odyssey headquarters in downtown Dallas.

I wanted to be at our command center to monitor what was going on as we had dozens of offices in a couple dozen states and thousands of employees who would all be reacting to whatever this was that was happening. I called Dick, and he answered from his car and told me he was listening to Eric Clapton or someone that was really rocking out on his radio. I had to be the buzz killer.

I told him to turn on the news and that I would meet him downtown. When we got there, we stared at the TV from the health club across the street in order to get our bearings of what was going on before walking into our offices on three floors across the street. By the time we got to our offices, the World Trade Center was about to come down, and we all stood in our conference room, where we watched the buildings fall to the ground in what looked like slow motion as they crumbled on live TV. Not a word was spoken, just some gasps and a few expletives. Staff members were crying, as I recall. We decided to call every office, particularly those in downtown areas, and send everyone home. We also needed to care for our patients, so we put our emergency plan procedures into action. Our clinical management teams oversaw this effort.

We had seventy-five reps at a sales meeting in Las Vegas being led by Pat Gross, and now, with all airports closed, they were all stuck there. I told anyone at the support center, which was the corporate headquarters we were in, that they could go home if they wanted to. Some folks went home, but many stayed. There was nothing to do but watch and react. Any thought of starting the IPO in seventy-two hours was completely gone, and I did not even think about it for several days.

Everyone remembers where they were on September 11, 2001. Dick's youngest daughter and her family lived in New York City on that day, and Dick finally got in touch with Krista and Jason and their kids and they were all okay.

There is nothing I can add here that has not been said or felt by everyone on that horrible day. The loss of life, the broken families, the injured bodies, and the uncertainty of what might be in store for us was a never-experienced-before mental state and emotion. Everyone tried to continue and keep life moving ahead. In New York City, the fires and rescue efforts continued for weeks. And as unbelievable as this is, with New York still smoldering under millions of tons of debris, which included personal possessions and body parts, the will of the human spirit began to emerge.

The workaround to get back on our feet as a nation and New York as a city was an incredible and inspiring effort. Stories of leadership, strength, resolve, and determination emerged in the headlines. As electricity was being restored for the US economy to operate once again, there were signs that things would be back online sooner, much sooner, than expected. The Merrill Lynch offices in NY were just a couple of blocks from the epicenter of the destruction, and they had been totally abandoned on that day. Just a couple of weeks later, the Merrill Lynch team had relocated to offices across the Hudson River in New Jersey to attempt the enormous heavy lift of resuming operations, which included the protection of Merrill's client information at the cyber level. This included hundreds of people relocating to NJ overnight.

Just over a month since the attack, Merrill Lynch, with Jim Jackson and all the rest, was in position to begin the ODSY road show on October 15, 2001, still following Cross Country Nurses. Unbelievable.

We arrived in Baltimore for our first meeting with T. Rowe Price and met with one lady, who looked to be about sixteen years old, who listened to our pitch as we thumbed through the deck. She took notes on her phone, then left the room when we were done with our pitch. Just like that, lickety-split, we were whisked away to the limo and airport to fly to Teterboro, NJ, for our first run at the full Merrill Lynch sales force.

New York City was still smoking and smoldering. And very eerily quiet. For a city of nine million people, you could hear an occasional dog barking in the distance. You would expect that in the middle of Montana, but not in New York City. People were out and about, but they did so quietly among and near the rubble. It is indescribable simply because of the enormity of the disaster from an intentional human attack.

We did not know we would get to NYC, but we did, but not until after our pitch to the Merrill Lynch sales force. It took place in a hastily organized and crowded office building that had held a small Merrill Lynch workforce. And overnight they expanded it to include the team from the Manhattan office that had taken a hit from the attack just a few weeks earlier, just a stone's throw away across the Hudson River.

Ground Zero was visible from the windows of the New Jersey offices where we were about to begin our pitch. A couple of the Merrill executives told us what they saw from their windows the day of the attack. It seemed very odd that we would be here to transact an initial public offering of a hospice company when so many lives had been lost and bodies were still unrecovered. Yet the American spirit, including the economic sense of survival, continued in nearly full swing. We could see the smoke from the conference room where everyone was gathered to hear the Odyssey Healthcare road show presentation.

We stood at the end of a very long table; it was standing room only on all sides, and there was a live feed from the London offices so that we had full coverage from Merrill Lynch. This was friendly fire. These people were on our side. They believed our pitch, our story, and the value of our company to their investors. This proved to be a great start for us, as we had to learn the rhythm of this kind of audience, and with only twenty minutes for each pitch, we needed to be efficient with our words and also with how we answered routine questions. Once we were done with this initial give-us-the-goods pitch, we loaded back into the limo and headed to downtown New York City.

Although we did not have another pitch for the day, Jackson had arranged to give us a tour of the NYC Merrill Lynch offices, which were only one block away from Ground Zero. We were dropped off by the limo about six blocks away and made the silent walk among the New Yorkers shuffling in shock to wherever they were going. It was surreal. How were we here? Why were we here?

The corrugated matrix frame of the Towers had been canted forty-five degrees one way for weeks on the television, and now we were walking near it and still seeing the smoke, smelling very odd New York City smells, and trying to be nonchalant that we were dressed in business suits and trying to stay out of the way. I took pictures from the offices looking down into the rubble, and I felt like I was trespassing on a great calamity. We were ready to leave downtown and get back to the business at hand, selling stock in our hospice company. We took off in the Gulfstream from Teterboro, NJ, and began the road show with all intensity and purpose.

LEVITY AND IPO ROAD SHOW ENDURANCE

Road shows are legendary, and ours was no different. We worked seven days a week, either flying, pitching, amending the pitching, or rehearsing the pitching. You do not get much sleep on one of these little saunters in and about the country. We would hit an average of three different cities a day, then fly to the next city or fly late at night to be in position for a 7:00 a.m. meeting the next day. When Jackson and his staff were not ripping our presentation to shreds because of intel they received from the ground force following up on our presentations that suggested a different message or tone, we tried to enjoy the Gulfstream.

While we adjusted to this now routine and luxurious travel style designed for speed and efficiency, we had the chance on our first few flights from city to city to relax and enjoy the ride. So, I had Dick film me interviewing our flight attendant. She had been the flight attendant for an international celebrity for a number of years and described herself as "pensive." I was not sure what that meant, but once we got to know her, we had a better understanding of what pensive means. When Dick was filming, I was asking her to show us around the jet. As she did so, in the background you could see the Merrill Lynch team ripping out pages of our presentation while I cheerfully continued to interview the flight attendant with a big smile on my face.

Up until this point, we really had no idea of what we were doing. We were traveling like rock stars and enjoying the attention and that Gulfstream ride. I sat in the jump seat up front every chance I could. I sat there on one short flight from Detroit to Milwaukee in the middle of the afternoon during a driving rainstorm. Our full-time cockpit crew of two were pro pilots. They had their fly-boy chops on that day. We flew through some heavy weather, but they got us there on time. I had wanted to be doing what they were doing, but instead, we were selling hospice stock.[8]

One night during the road show, we arrived in Colorado Springs very late and we also had a very early first meeting the next morning, which meant about a five-hour timeout. We stayed at the Broadmoor, which is a fantastic hotel. We had a 5:00 a.m. wake-up call for a 6:00 a.m. ride to our first meeting.

I got to my room around 1:00 a.m. and took half of an Ambien to try to get at least three or four hours of sleep. I turned the light out and closed my eyes. A few seconds later, the phone on the nightstand was

---

8 The stock-selling process and strategies on an initial public offering are very interesting and based on the investment thesis of the brokers who will be placing it in investment portfolios. A new offering from a new, not-yet-marketed company in public securities gets an appropriate amount of close scrutiny during the road show. Of particular interest are the growth projections of the company. The growth investors, those investors who are looking for a relatively quick hit early and continuing for several quarters thereafter, are the typical "momentum" investors. They will stay in the stock until the growth momentum slows in a signal that the true growth is no longer accelerating, which is viewed as a risk to the investment. Once there is a signal that the growth is slowing, or worse, a full correction takes place, the momentum investors and their shares are gone in an instant. I learned this the hard way three years later when the guidance we were giving "The Street" (Wall Street) was not keeping up with the research that was being provided by the research side of the house.

ringing off the hook. It was Dick. He said that Jackson wanted to see us for a meeting to rework a couple slides in the presentation. I told Dick I was not coming, that I had just taken a sleeping pill and it was not a good idea for me to go to the meeting. About a minute later, the phone rang again, and Dick demanded that I get to his room ASAP. I said, "Okay, but I am coming in my jammies!" And that is what I did. I was trying to stay awake while they reworked our spiel. Okay, rework it, but I am going back to bed.

Four hours later, we climbed into the limo at 6:00 a.m. without any breakfast. Jackson and his team wanted to flip through the new pages that had been reworked, reprinted, and rebound during the four hours we slept. They were incredible. Two hours later, we were done with the meeting and winging our way to our next city. It went on like that for two weeks. Good thing we did not have to go to Europe!

The work of the Merrill Lynch team was superb. The reason the selection process to choose a banker is so important is because of the detail that goes into the work on their end. The best banks are the strongest at knowing who they should sell the securities to, what their appetites are for the new issues, how they invest, and over what period of time. Even more valuable is having the inside intelligence about the personalities and tendencies for each group we called on. It got down to the "say this, don't say that, because this guy did XYZ deal that had a similar profile, and he swears he would never invest in a similar deal again." That kind of stuff.

So, we stayed true to the Merrill Lynch sales guidance. Another *huge* reason to choose the right banker to lead your deal is the research analyst(s) that come with the firm.

The sales side of the firm gets you out and in the market, creating a currency with the stock. The analysts provide the research for investors to decide to buy, keep, or sell the stock. Once the stock is public, the analyst holds all the cards.

The research side of the house learns the business inside and out and attempts to provide objective "guidance" to public investors, down to the point of modeling their own expectations, which will be viewed by The Street as gospel. However, at times, they do not know everything going on in a company, nor could they, so they simply get it wrong. They do not take the public beating; the company and the CEO take the beating. So, the strategy about willingly giving guidance to the analyst(s) is a very slippery slope.

In the early 2000s when we completed the Odyssey IPO, it was a market expectation that we provide guidance expressed as a firm earnings per share amount, and only a very few and very large companies refused to provide guidance and forecasts. For example, a guidance statement could be as bold as confirming a specific profitability at a specific time. Or it could be stating that things are looking good, and we are optimistic about the future of the business. Both are quite different references to forecast. One gives a number the company is committed to meeting or beating, and the other just says we like where the company is heading without giving a specific number. Either way, it is guidance, and rarely works to the favor of the company and the executive team running it.

Today, in 2022, providing guidance is far less common. There is an inherent risk in becoming a publicly held company CEO, and most say that after the experience, they would avoid the opportunity in the future. The average tenure for a public CEO is quite short, less than a year, and there is a reason for that turnover. The CEOs running public companies loathe the demands of guidance because it is restrictive and forces the executive team to concentrate on that guidance instead of the attention to building the company that it needs.

As of this writing, publicly traded companies are not obligated to provide earnings guided statements; however, many of them do provide guidance one way or another. By teaching the research analysts the dynamic drivers of the business, they can piece together what they model for future performance. In my view, you have to decide if you want to take the risk that they understand the business correctly enough to be accurate in their projections or take the mystery out of it and provide an earnings forecast for them. In either case, guiding expectations to conservative results is always the correct protection for the stock, as long as the company is performing its growth plan accordingly.

Either way, if the company misses that projection, the market cap of the stock (market price X number of shares) can be significantly affected. If you provide guidance that your stock will achieve a certain EPS (earnings per share) and you miss it by a penny, the stock price will take a very unsympathetic hit. When the stock goes down in a big way, enter the attorneys to begin suing everyone and the chain of economic and legal disaster is fully underway. Guidance is Russian roulette.

At the end of one week of the road show, we laid over in Dallas, so I had the limo take me home to pick up Sandee and the kids and go to an ice cream parlor as a surprise visit. We had a great time together, albeit short, as the limo then took me back to the hotel near downtown, where we would depart for Houston early the next morning. We navigated to most of the hot investment spots, including, as I remember, Dallas, Houston, Denver, San Francisco, Los Angeles, Salt Lake City, Milwaukee, Minneapolis, Detroit, Chicago, NY, Boston, and several others. The pre-scheduled twenty-minute meetings used a small twelve-inch leather-bound flip deck that could be moved on a table to pass to the next guy during the presentation. One guy we were pitching to kept interrupting Dick's story by asking questions. Dick would answer, then attempt to begin again, and the guy would stop him again by asking another question. This went on for about six or seven minutes, and Dick was still on page one.

Dick is not a very patient person, and when he had given the guy enough tries to shut up and listen, he gave up, flipped half the pages in the deck, then slid it over to me. Then the guy did the same thing to me, so I just flipped to the last page and slid it over to Doug, who stared at the guy and said, "And that is the end of the presentation. Got any questions?"

The guy said, "No, I don't think so."

Doug said, "Good." And we left. He never really saw the presentation.

At one point, the three of us hit the wall and had a meltdown in Boston. Doug was going to go visit his girlfriend in NYC, and Dick and I were planning on flying in the jet back to Dallas to regroup for the road show, which would continue after a day off. It was the last presentation of the day, and we were spent, silly, cranky, and just a little bit worn out from it all. So, we decided to make a game of it. I would do Dick's presentation; Doug would do mine; and Dick would do Doug's.

We got off on the wrong foot, and I started to laugh a little bit from the humor and the seriousness of it all. I could not quit giggling, then went to a full laugh. Dick and Doug caught the same sense of compression release and started to laugh their asses off. None of us were talking. The investor group of three people just stared at us like Roy D. Mercer letting a caller get it "out of their system." But we never stopped. Finally, they just said, "Well, I guess that is all the time we have today. Thanks for coming."

We were still laughing when we got into the limo. Not sure how that turned out. We had to come up with something else to change things up, so we decided to enact the "word rule" for each presentation. We would give each other a word that we had to work into the presentation without the investors realizing that word had been used. It's an age-old rule of road shows. Word Rule was hilarious and a time-tested road show shenanigan, and we were certainly not going to ruin the tradition of previous IPO road show warriors.

We were at Fidelity Investments when we gave Doug the word "aardvark." Deep in his presentation of the financial modeling and forecast, these special words rolled off his tongue like a Nashville singer-songwriter. In describing the financials, Doug said, "And these financial projections have been as stable as an aardvark on a telephone line." Silence. They all looked at each other, and Doug had this damn-I-did-it look on his face and he was about to completely lose it. We would have, too, if he had not pulled it back in and kept it together.

Some of our shenanigans on the road show were unforgettable. Like the time I pulled out an Elvis wig, and we took turns wearing it on a long late-night flight while we were drinking scotch and beer. We got a picture of Jackson yucking it up as Elvis, and we threatened to send it the Merrill Lynch CEO. There is a time and place for everything, and to destress the road show, we introduced some zaniness to it that our bankers were not initially in favor of. But by the time we learned to unload the intensity of all the meetings, we began to have so much fun that the next thing we knew, the road show was over, and the charter company asked for the jet back.

I was quite certain that I was going to buy an airplane once I got my head above water after the offering. The travel turmoil following 9/11 all but cemented that in my plans, and flying around on the private jet finalized those intentions for me. But now it was time for our pricing call with Merrill Lynch, our attorneys, and our board of directors.

We were outside of Philadelphia when we gathered at a ridiculously small Merrill Lynch office. The purpose of that last stop before heading into NYC and the Plaza Hotel was to have Jackson report the total number of shares sold and if there was demand for more than what was available, thus creating an oversubscription. Achieving an oversubscription is proof positive of a successful road show. When Jackson gave us his report, we learned that not only had we come in at the top of the pricing range of $13 to $15 per share and sold the 3.6 million shares at $15 per share, for a total of $54 million raised, but we had demand for ten times more shares than we offered. We were oversubscribed on the deal, a badge of honor for Jim Jackson and his team at Merrill Lynch.

It was unbelievable. We could have sold the entire company if we wanted to. It was a walk-off home run. We now had the cash we needed to accelerate the growth of the company with acquisitions and building out our infrastructure. At the time of the pricing call, we had the Merrill group with us, the board of directors on the conference line, attorneys on another conference line, and Jim Jackson had a phone in each ear as he directed the sales force on what to expect.

After the board officially approved the pricing and authorized Merrill to proceed with trading our stock the next day, Dick and I left the room for a moment. Among the cubicles outside the meeting room, Dick and I hugged each other and danced in a circle like two elementary school kids playing ring around the rosy! We were both elated and stunned at the same time. Then we all packed into the limousine and headed to the city of New York to prepare for the opening bell the following morning.

I got a call from Sandee when we pulled up to the Park Plaza Hotel. She told me that our room number was 921. The same room number as the Marriott Residence Inn in Indianapolis that served as our first Odyssey office while we got the company started. What a fun coincidence. Scary, really. That night, Sandee and I joined Dick and Sally and their family, along with Jim Jackson and his group, for dinner at a very swank Manhattan restaurant. We proceeded to get "over-poured," and it was a wonderful dinner. Sally said she had never had a martini before, so we all joined her.

We had trouble getting down the stairs back out to the limo just one more time. It had been a long road, and now we were twelve hours from being a public company with all the fanfare that comes with an accomplishment of that magnitude. It was surreal.

CROSSING THE FINISH LINE TO BEGIN THE NEW RACE AS A PUBLIC COMPANY

The morning of October 30, 2001, was a cool and cloudy day in New York City. It was also the day before my dad's birthday. We were about to be listed on the NASDAQ exchange with the ticker symbol ODSY, and the launch was to begin at 9:30 a.m. when shares would begin trading. I decided not to wear a tie that morning and had to borrow a jacket of Dick's to the opening. We arrived at the NASDAQ exchange about 9:00 a.m. and had to wait a few minutes while security put us through their newly reinvigorated screening process after 9/11.

We were in a state of suspended animation as we waited. Then my phone rang and brought me back to reality. It was Natalie calling. I was excited to tell her where we were right then and what we were about to do. Then it hit me. The reason she called had nothing to do with the IPO. She had called to tell me and Sandee that she had just learned that she had made the Plano West Senior High basketball team as a point guard. She had been playing basketball since she could dribble a basketball, and this was a lifetime achievement for her, and we were so proud of her.

When she graduated from Baylor with her undergraduate degree, we rented a suite at the American Airlines Center in Dallas for a Dallas Mavericks basketball game. Several weeks earlier, I had been invited to play in a charity basketball game there with the likes of Mavericks owner Mark Cuban, Roger Staubach, radio personalities, a few rich people, and me. After taking pictures with Cuban in our charity game player jerseys, complete with our names on the back, I picked up Cuban's contact information. Later, when I booked the suite for the game, I reached out to Mark and asked him if Avery Johnson, the Mavericks' head coach at the time, might have a few minutes to drop by the suite to say hi to Natalie and get his autograph.

Cuban sent me an email late in the afternoon on game day and said, "Coach Johnson will be busy with pre-game preparation and will not be able to visit your daughter's suite. Congratulations to her on her graduation." But if I remember correctly, we did receive an autograph of Avery Johnson's in the mail the following week.

God has a way of keeping what is important, well, important. We were so happy for Natalie and congratulated her as they opened the door for us to go into the presentation room at NASDAQ. We told her we loved her and that we would be calling her shortly. Thank you, Lord. I will never forget being re-balanced in my family priorities.

While we were getting our pictures taken, the NASDAQ team served us champagne to toast the success of the IPO shortly before trading started. The ceremony was being filmed for marketing purposes, and Dick and I were able to say a few brief words. After a toast, a sip, and high fives, the photographer had us follow him out of the building to Times Square for more pictures. The picture that summed up the entire journey to that point was us in front of the Jumbotron in Times Square, for on that giant screen, high above the street, was the glorious four-color Odyssey logo, which Faith had created more than five years earlier. The story of Faith was now cemented in Odyssey lore, and we pray and trust that God smiled on her at those very moments. There was not a dry eye among us.

The rest of the morning we just roamed around finding coffee and watching the ticker ODSY scroll with updated pricing every time it moved. We were now in a new world as leaders of this company. Now we needed to post continued quarter over quarter revenue and earnings growth in a business that had never been a public company. Now the work really started, along with the risk of failure, lawsuits, and stock value turmoil. The focus and goal for a public company leadership team comes down to one very basic premise: to grow and feed the business to produce quarter-to-quarter earnings growth, year after year, without letting the research analysts get too far in front of you with expectations that aren't in line with your conservative reality. Simple to say, and very challenging to accomplish.

Consistent performance over long periods of time is difficult, and sometimes you're up and sometimes you are down. It is true in life and very true in business. We found this out the hard way in 2004, after we had been a public company for three years. But before then we accomplished what could be done, and the personal side of our lives resumed in full force.

15

Life as a public company, losing Si Winkler, Sandee's banners, the kids and their antics, mission trips, my secret weapon

LIFE AS A PUBLIC COMPANY

After the IPO, we went about our normal business efforts and adjusted to the demands of high public scrutiny and the changes in the balance of where Dick, Doug, and I spent our time. There were also life events that continued, regardless of our stock price or how hard we worked to fend off life's difficulties. Two weeks to the day after the 9/11 attacks, Silas Winkler died of dementia Alzheimer's at a nursing home in Plano. I had my hand on his chest and felt his last heartbeat. Ruth and I were by his side.

When I first met Si, I never imagined I would be in this most intimate of moments at the end of his life. He had never even asked me to play golf with him and kept a bit of arm's distance from me, although he did give me a two-week summer bridge construction job in college. But after having also lost Sandee's biological father in November 1991, there was a great sense that Ruth had raised Sandee on her own shoulders.

Ruth clung to her friends and family for support and life's joy. She also loved Natalie and Charlie, as Tena Kolb would say, "up to the sky and down to the ground." Ruth devoted herself to being "Grannie," and she was a delightful success at being so. Our kids, their cousins, and the rest of the family all supported Ruth. She was one of a kind and still had many years left to look forward to after losing Si. She was just beginning to enjoy the kids becoming teenagers, and they were more able to relate to her regarding life's issues. Their relationship with one another had been a character-building success from every angle. They honored and cherished their grannie, and she was going to be big in their lives for years to come.

"Ma" continued to lead our family as our matriarch, and we learned more about her love of family and ambition to live life to the fullest, with only the one kidney that she had been born with. She always said, "If a man cain't dance, what good is he?" She would cuss with something like "hells bells," then cover it up with "excuse my French." One time she asked us during Easter lunch at her house in Fredericksburg if we knew who her new prayer partner at church was. We offered up the name of a dear friend, to which Ruth replied, "Hell no!" She could always be counted on to speak her mind, and she didn't particularly care who to, when, or where! We loved her and still miss her dearly.

FINDING A TIME AND A WAY BACK INTO THE LEFT SEAT OF AN AIRPLANE

I had taken off ten years from flying simply due to time and economic reasons. The contract I signed for Sandee had long expired by the time of the IPO in 2001, and the shutdown of air travel after 9/11 was the catalyst to get me back in the cockpit. I enrolled in flight school so I could get current again and get my stick and rudder skills back. I had an instructor, Lance Lujon, who got me checked out in a 172 at Addison Airport. I remember flying solo again, and I loved it.

With the resources to continue flying, it was time to order a new Bonanza A36 from Beechcraft. I became obsessed with flying again, and we used the Bonanza to fly just about anywhere we went unless the airlines made more sense. I also began to add more ratings to my private pilot ticket. I went to ATP in Arlington to get my multi-engine rating, followed by training at American Flyers at Addison to earn my Commercial Multi-Engine Instrument rating. Years later, I went to Alaska to train and earn my Seaplane rating. And finally, during the COVID pandemic in 2020, I went to Flight Safety in Wichita, Kansas, to earn a single pilot type rating in a Citation 525 twin-engine jet.

From 2001 through present day, as of this writing in late 2022, we have always owned an airplane. As of today, we have owned twelve airplanes and I have racked up, one hour at a time, four thousand hours in total so far. That equates to one hundred and sixty-six days in the air, twenty-four-seven. That equals nearly six months nonstop in the air. Not exactly career commercial airline numbers, but having had to pay for every hour with no tax advantages or economic relief or gain from it, it is a lot of self-earned and paid-for flight hours. The airplanes allowed us to explore new adventures, which is one reason we landed in the Texas Hill Country.

From late 2001 through late 2004, our family was busy. Natalie and Charlie were busy at school, at church, and with their friends. They were so fun, but they had their normal issues as sister and brother. Natalie was developing sometimes obnoxious leadership skills, as all teenagers do. Charlie was playing sports, but when he was little, he developed a tick that drove us crazy. And he had a temper. He wanted his shoes tied so tight my fingers were bleeding, and I just knew it was cutting off the circulation to his feet. His tick went away; he began enjoying comfortable shoes that Sandee bought for him, and he was a joy to have as my sidekick.

It was fun to make both kids' events—basketball games, soccer games, football games, choir events, mission trips, birthday parties, sleepovers, lock-ins; whatever they were doing, Sandee and I were there. I can tell you what we attended, but I cannot tell you what I missed at work by doing so. And that is a BIG life lesson.

You will never remember what you missed at work, but you will remember enjoying being with your family.

And more importantly, your kids will never forget and will always appreciate the parental involvement and support for their activities. It is love, and they feel it and will live up to that responsibility in their own lives as they get more friends, become more social, go to college, and move on to the rest of life itself.

Our existence at Hunters Glen Baptist Church in Plano was a huge influencer. We met some of our closest friends while attending Hunters Glen, and our kids were involved in all the activities for them. One family favorite was participating in the Easter production of "Living Pictures." Living Pictures portrayed the life of Christ and the full Easter story of Christ's death and resurrection. The choir director asked if I would take a role as the innkeeper where Jesus was born. I accepted and then found out it had the first solo in the production, complete with orchestra and choir as a backup. I was scared to death. I had to sing "Everything Was Going Crazy," and once I got over the numbing fear, it was a lot of fun. I had never sung a solo in anything, so it was a big step for me.

I started a running club at church, and some friends and I would meet there on weekdays at 5:30 a.m. to run four to five miles together. On the morning of one of the shows, I decided to run in my innkeeper costume and hand out tickets to Living Pictures. I surprised a middle-aged woman when I caught up to her, in my fake beard, head dressing, and dressy-looking smock, so stylish back in the day. She looked at me, and I looked at her and said, "I have some free tickets for you here to come see Living Pictures, which is the portrayal of the life of Jesus, right over here at Hunters Glen Baptist Church. Would you like a couple of tickets?"

And she said, "No thanks, I'm a Methodist." Oh well.

It was an awesome and moving production, and Natalie wanted to play the dead girl healed by Jesus. So, Danny Roberts, the choir director, gave her the part. She would have killed to portray the dead girl, she wanted it so badly. Sandee was the sobbing, grieving mother in black, and I, having changed clothes from my earlier role as innkeeper, carried a "dead" Natalie in my arms to Jesus. Natalie's long hair hung, shining like it was in a commercial, combed and brushed to perfection; and as much as the audience could see, she looked dead! Until Jesus healed her. The crowd gasped, and Natalie sat up in my arms and jumped to her feet, hugging me. Sandee's grieving sobs then turned to joy, and we ran back up the aisle of the church. Natalie was Natalie once again. How fun and funny was that!

MISSION TRIPS

For about ten years, our family was involved with several mission trips to areas of the country that needed the youthful help the high school choir could provide as a swarm of workers. Natalie and Charlie made all the trips, which usually involved very long drives to the far reaches of south Texas, Louisiana, and Arizona. On one trip back from New Mexico, Sandee drove off the road in the middle of the night from being so tired from the week of manual outdoor summer labor, sleeping on the church floor, sharing one bathroom for fifty people, no air conditioning, and virtually no sleep. On the way back to Texas, she dozed off and left the roadway in a construction zone. She woke up before it got worse, and we decided then to find an easier path of transportation for this physical donation of suffering for the Lord.

TAKING THE GOSPEL OF CHRIST ON THE ROAD INTERNATIONALLY

When Pastor Kim Hall was alive, he asked me to become a trustee in the Center for Global Ministries (CGM), his vision along with Steve Thompson. Together, they created this ministry to teach the gospel in far reaches of the world, where it can be difficult to reach people primarily because of politics, social mores, and persecution. Over a couple of decades, a variety of home group churches was established in Israel, India, and Russia, with an eye for expansion into the Baltic states.

Our board of trustees met in London, England, to meet with the pastors charged with running the home churches in Russia and Israel. Funding and support for these missions came entirely from donations, and no one involved with the CGM was paid for the work because we were all volunteers. On that trip to England, and when our meeting was over, Steve and I continued to Helsinki, Finland. It was February and felt like the coldest place on the planet. We went there to scout out the possibility of placing a home church group there. After a couple of days of dealing with five feet of snow, eating reindeer, and not making any progress, we flew home.

The next year, Steve and I took a trip together that I will not soon forget. We first flew from Dallas to Shanghai, China, stayed the night, then continued to Luoyang, China, in the western interior of the country. I could author a book about that trip simply from the perspective of being in a communist country with such tight reins on the people that you hoped they would let you out when you needed to leave.

We stayed in Luoyang for three days, where we took the risk of teaching about American culture in a class for students learning English. We had arranged for the teacher to stand outside the room to warn us if we needed to change the subject quickly. Those kids were amazed that two guys from America were in their classroom. I placed a cell call back home to Sandee, so they could hear someone speaking from the United States. They loved listening to her on the cell phone speaker. It was morning in Luoyang but about 10pm back in Plano, where Sandee took our call.

After our day at the University of Luoyang, we made our way to a nearby hospital to pray with dying patients. The hospital rooms were dark and very cold. The patients' belongings were stuffed under their beds, and they wore their street coats and parkas, including toboggans and knit hats on their heads, while covered with sheets in the bed. A translator showed up to translate the prayers we were giving at the bedside. We never knew the people's names, but we prayed with them just the same.

The next day, we went to the basement of an underground Christian church where at least a hundred people, nearly all women, were waiting to greet us. They wanted us to sing. They had a piano player, but we were the only people who spoke English. The piano began playing, and somehow, despite the language barriers, the whole room sang "Amazing Grace." Not a dry eye in the house. After the song, Steve gave a message of hope and encouragement to the crowd.

It was cold. When Steve was finished, a frail little old man walked slowly up to me and told me something, but I didn't understand. The translator took us to a back room, where we could meet with the gentleman in private. There, with tears in his eyes and a runny nose, he began to speak. Through the interpreter, he told me that he had given his life to Christ, and per the laws in China, in doing so, he forfeited his right to work, to have a home, and to have money. He was unable to provide for his family; he had nothing. With trembling hands, he bowed, then offered me a gift.

He gave me his personal Bible. I began to give it back to him, but the translator stopped me and reminded me of saving face. I accepted the Bible and again prayed with him, then he left the room as quietly as when we had entered it. I still have this solemn gift of love from a man I will never meet again. It was heart shaking.

FROM CHINA TO INDIA

Once we left China, we flew to India and landed in Chennai on the eastern coast of the country. We went to visit our good friend and pastor Dr. Chris Kola, who was leading an orphanage of fifty children ages six to eighteen, both boys and girls. It was there I realized I didn't have the body language customs down. Folded arms in front of you is a sign of respect. A wobbly head, neither a yes nor a no, is a form of a non-no. And standing when elders walk in the room is expected.

These fifty kids, most of whom were left on the door step of the orphanage before some parents committed dual suicide (not an uncommon occurrence), or were left because the family couldn't care for them anymore, were in school and trying to be children. They ate together, they studied together, they slept together. It was unbelievable. There are so many people in India. As of 2022, the population of India was 1.326 billion, 3.7 times more people than the United States. There are people EVERYWHERE. Poverty is as common there as affluence is here. In my experience, there's complete chaos everywhere, including no marked lines on roads for people to drive, families living in boxes at the entrance to stores, a family of four seen riding on one motorcycle at the same time, with the driving father wearing the only helmet. Billboards of people who are full figured/slightly overweight as a social sign of affluence and stature are contrasted with our billboards of skinny models with sharp elbows and pointy shoulders. The contrast to how we live here in the US could not, in my experience, be more striking.

On the day we got there, we had a three-hour drive to a small town called Nellore, with a population of just under one million people. Four people escorted me and Steve to the orphanage. Two were handlers and two were bodyguards, all arranged by Dr. Kola. We checked into our hotel, which was not much better than a bad college dormitory, although the shoeless room-keeping staff seemed proud of their work as they showed us to our rooms. That night, we were greeted by over one thousand screaming and cheering lovely Indian people as we were driven through the gates behind the orphanage. I could not believe it. Families of old and young were lined up from fence to fence and side to side. It was amazing. Then we were asked to say a few words. To a thousand people? We did it with two or three different interpreters to speak the different dialects of Telugu, the primary language in those Indian states.

When Steve was finished with his lesson, he offered a prayer to the masses, and I mean masses, of people. He told them we were available to pray with anyone who wanted or needed prayer. I was thinking that I would pray with a family or two over in the corner; instead, we were mobbed! Steve and I started out about five feet apart from one another, but more than two hours later, we were at least fifty feet apart and still praying with no end in sight. I had to tell myself, *I am not trained or qualified for this, so maybe I should just tap out*. But they kept coming.

Two families of note were a small teenage husband and wife standing about five feet tall, each carrying a very small baby with dysentery. They wanted prayers for a miracle that their precious babies would survive. And if that wasn't enough for my exhausting imitation of knowing what I was doing, a group of people, all tangled up together, fought their way through the line in front of me to bring me, what else? A devil-possessed woman! They told me it was a problem that she was possessed (ya think?), and I needed to pray that Satan would be bound and rid her of the evil.

Lord, help me here. How … do … I … do … this? I trusted that It Can Be Done. So, I prayed for her the best I could. Over the several minutes we continued to pray, everyone was saying something. She calmed down, and when we were done with her prayer, I was nearly unable to stand. It was a hot Indian night, and I'm no Billy Graham in a revival tent, that's true. But what I was, was a guy just doing what God wanted. I saw Steve already sitting down among his throng of people, so I pleaded the fifth and took a seat. I was drenched in sweat, but that did not stop them from continuing to come.

It is amazing when throngs of people, young and old, complete strangers in a land far away, hold you in such high regard to the point they bring their sick family members, including babies and possessed people, wanting the healing blessing from a stranger who professes Christ as the healer.

They were so excited that these two real-life "American missionaries" had come to see them, and they saw me and Steve as an answer to prayer. By the time we were done, it was after midnight. Dr Chris prayed for me and Steve as we drank some water and just tried to get ahold of ourselves emotionally. It was one of the most significant and consequential experiences of my life. A thousand people, young and old, excited to see someone they never knew and would never see again, just to hear the Word of God. It wears me out all over again, just reliving it as I type here.

Steve and I thought of starting a shoe company in India because no one in India wears shoes. We decided it was a bad idea because in India, no one wears shoes. Go figure. It's like thinking of starting a trash company in Israel so everyone can throw away their trash instead of letting it blow all over the roads, city streets, and countryside. The problem with that idea is that no one throws away their trash. They don't, they won't, and that's it. And our trip wasn't over after visiting India. We still needed to go to Singapore.

As we left the orphanage, we said a teary goodbye to the children. I had taught one of the young boys how to throw a ball. No one had ever taught him, and he didn't have a mom or dad around to show him. So, I did. He would try and try and try, and finally before I left, he threw me the ball before I got in the car to leave the compound to head to the airport. I pray that little guy has grown into a healthy young man with Christ in his heart. I had a big tear in my eye as I waved goodbye to the little boy through the dirty window of the car, never to see him again. There were five of us packed in that hot car, heading through the chaos of people surrounding us as we pulled down the street on our way to the airport. God bless you, my little man.

RESPITE IN SINGAPORE

Steve and I arrived in Singapore after a very long flight. By the way, Singapore Airlines is the real deal, and I would gladly fly them again. We left at midnight and landed in Singapore during the morning hours. This trip had no missionary purpose other than to relax for a few days before starting home. Singapore is incredible, with hundreds of people groups with their bright colors displaying many heritages, along with very organized social behavior and cleanliness on every front. Not a speck on the ground and not a stone out of place.

I asked the bell desk at the very nice hotel we were staying in if there was a safe part of downtown where I could go run. Everywhere is safe in Singapore. They don't tolerate spitting, so they sure won't tolerate a cash-paying tourist getting mugged downtown. It was great. Steve and I hired a guide for half of a day, and he took us to some of the hot spots, including the Buddhist temple and the Muslim mosque.

Steve had been learning to speak Arabic, so he confidently led me into a mosque and asked for the imam. Freaked me out. He gave us a very short tour as he walked us back to the front door. Then we headed to our favorite restaurant on the beach alongside the Indian Ocean. Peppered crab served steaming hot, and so messy it required us to wear plastic bibs. We went there two days in a row, and the waitstaff recognized the Americans coming back for more. Singapore was great.

We flew home a few days later, flying from Singapore to Brussels in Belgium, a long delay there, then nonstop to Chicago, then to Dallas. By the time we got home, we had literally flown around the globe, stopped in three very different countries, and were only gone twelve days. What a trip. Thank you, Steve Thompson; those are memories that I will never forget, and I am a better man for having made that exploration with you.

It is a wonderful experience to travel with another person to distant lands that are so different from home. Steve and I trusted each other to care for one another as we made our way to areas of the world that may be, shall I say, unpredictable. I wouldn't trade that trip for anything. This world and its cultures and politics is simply awe-inspiring. At the human level, we are the same. The gentleman in China needs and wants friends as I do. The little boy in India wants and needs family and the hope of a future, just like we all do. I hope I touched their lives in the way they made my life better. Love is the common language among all of us, and I collided with and embraced it without any words spoken.

MY SECRET WEAPON

Sandee has always been a tireless lifemate. She has the determination, organizational focus, and commitment to make a household run like a fine Swiss watch. She is also, although she might not call herself this, an adventurer and curious achiever of things not of her own interests. She is a trooper, as they say, but that description is inadequate. She is an example of hard work and determination. I have always told her that if I weren't married to her, I would hire her for every company I started. She can be counted on. She has an enormous sense of responsibility, and if she says she is going to do something, it … will … be … done. Period.

In the more than four decades we have been married, she has done so many things because she wanted to prove she could do it. She began distance running in support of my interest in the sport. She learned to slalom water ski, has done so since I have known her, and just a couple of years ago, established the family age record for slalom skiing at sixty-five years old! She has pursued road biking and ridden in the Hotter'N Hell bike ride in Wichita Falls, Texas, the twenty-five-mile route. She took up golf just a couple of years ago, and we golf together and plan some of our travel to include golf.

She had been my spectator for years, but now she is a golfer herself. She has camped with me in a tent at Lake Texoma; she goes fishing with me, sits in the deer blind with me (only on opening day), and tells me where the deer are and when to go shoot one for the dinner table. She has cared for her horse, Casey, and has competed on him and won various ribbons, including second place. She has won ribbons at the Gillespie County Fair for her Flying G Ranch Salsa. She cans okra and makes pickles. She cares for our dogs and watches over each and every health care need of every animal, including me. She has been a lifelong walker with Julie Reach and other friends. She can sew, and made her own maternity clothes when we lived in Oklahoma. She has made beautiful pillows for us and for friends, either on the sewing machine or by needlepoint and cross stitching. She has made quilts. She made beautiful, God-honoring banners for Hunters Glen Baptist Church in Plano, inspired by dreams that she had, then followed through by occupying our entire dining room for weeks while she lovingly planned every single stitch, color, and perfect placement for a humanly perfect banner to celebrate Jesus Christ.

She led Mission Friends and Acteens at Hunters Glen for years. She will tell you that she is not a public speaker, but guess what? Yes, she is. She may be nervous, but what she says has been planned out. Every word she speaks is honoring the people and to the event that she is speaking about. She is an incredible fundraiser for nonprofit work. She will not let go of a potential donor and will find ways to get the donation and reduce costs, so the donation goes farther than the face value. Sandee is also very cost conscious and knows a bargain when she sees it; it bothers her if she overpays for something. She is balanced in her expectations of her lifestyle. Sure, she loves nice things, but not at the expense of more important priorities.

Sandee is also smart. Very smart. She is thoughtful and asks questions to understand things. If you tell her something, you had better be prepared to back it up. She was a straight A student in school and graduated from Baylor Cum Laude, with all the honors that go with that. She is also a good listener and feels things deep down in her heart. She tends to stress over details that get her blood pressure up. She's very much a perfectionist simply because she has joy in things that range from calculating donation projections to putting a good paint job on the raised beds of her vegetable garden. She takes great joy in doing things right.

In her sixties, she decided to take up golf! So, we joined Boot Ranch and she went hard at it and today is a solid golfer who is great fun to play with. If my dad were alive, he would be so pleased to be Sandee's cart mate for a round of golf. She took lessons, bought new clubs, and has played in the annual women's golf clinic for the past two years. If she puts her mind to it, she can accomplish anything.

Sandee is a wonderful person, a beautiful lady, a class act, and a trusted friend to all who know her. I am extremely fortunate that I am married to her. She has always supported me, even when—no, especially when—I have not deserved it. She is fiercely loyal to her husband and family and friends, and I could not be more honored to be her husband.

Marriage is not for sissies, and it is not a fun social look-at-us game. It is serious, life-altering stuff that many couples do not survive but could if they tried and simply did not give up. When things do not go as planned, you must be there for one another. Sandee has always been there for me, and I can never repay her enough for her devotion.

16

When a big public company acts like a big public company, investment gains and losses, taking the heat as CEO, being fired from a company I cofounded

Over the three years Odyssey Healthcare had been a public company, we continued to meet our growth targets on census, revenue, and margin. Things changed late in 2004 when two things happened that dropped our stock price by 47 percent in one day. Read that again. Almost half of our market capitalization went kaput in a few hours. Nearly $275 million of investor money was wiped out. When investors leave a stock, they do not stick around for formal goodbyes. My super-mentor, Tom Erickson, had told me two years earlier this would happen. He advised me to resign, take my stock, and get out. He had seen it repeatedly with his peers and told me each of their stories. I did not believe him, but I do now. That is the problem: you get the experience first, then the lesson second. I should have listened to Tom.

Our market cap was $600 million (market cap is the stock price multiplied by the number of shares outstanding), and we were on our way to $1 billion in market cap. Dick had announced his retirement at the end of 2003, and I was promoted from president/COO to CEO. It was bad timing.

During 2002 and 2003, a new financial dynamic began to take place in the hospice industry. It was called the "Medicare Cap." At the time, no one had ever heard of it although it was deep in the fine print of the Medicare hospice regulations. The "cap" was an average maximum annual payment per patient (beneficiary) that was calculated by taking total revenues divided by total number of patients served for an average per patient. Each year, the cap was established as the benchmark, and if your hospice was over that benchmark, the monies would be recouped from Medicare on a self-reporting basis. Because patients had different lengths of stay on service and different payment rates, it was impossible to know where you stood against the cap. But with the accelerated growth and lengthening days of care, the fine print cap rule began to be relevant. Very relevant.

Doug Cannon and I had gone to San Francisco for the annual JP Morgan Healthcare Conference, which most of the health care world attended every year. He and I were to speak to analysts and investors during the five days we were there. One night after dinner, Doug called my room and said to meet him in the lobby to talk. That is where I first heard about the cap and how the potential repayment of who knows how much would affect the guidance we were giving to the analysts. I told Doug that I wanted us to finish the conference, then get back to Dallas to do a fine analysis to see what we were really looking at and figure out how we were going to deal with it.

We continued to have meetings at the conference, and without any hard facts yet about a potential cap hit to the financials, we stayed the course with our message. When we got back to Dallas, we learned that Doug was right. If we did not grow admissions, we would likely be in a negative cap situation. The increase in admissions would add a credit of approximately $30k for each admission, applied to the aggregate of all patients. We knew our patients were appropriate, but we needed to increase the admissions.

I made a mistake at that point. I saw a pathway out of the potential cap but did not make it a big deal with our board of directors just yet.

Anytime there is a revelation that the fundamental understanding of how a company performance will likely change, that is the time to put it up for transparent discussion.

I did not do that as I saw it as something to deal with but that was ultimately not yet a game changer. I was too optimistic, as I believed we would fix it and move on. I spoke with Dick about it, and as I recall, he agreed that we needed a renewed effort on the sales/admissions side, and we did not need to make it a big deal with the board. Doug continued to work the numbers, and when we knew the cap hit was a legitimate fiscal impact to be reported, we braced for the Wall Street reaction to missing our guidance for the first time ever.

FRYING PAN TO THE FIRE

To make matters worse, another storm was developing. I received a letter from the OIG, the Office of the Inspector General. It was from a staffer, a form letter, and it said the OIG was preparing to requisition information from our branch in Milwaukee and that they would be in contact with us soon. I called Dick as soon as I received it, as he was still chairman of the board. He was working on the head/toilet of his sailboat when he took my call. In hindsight, that was the perfect metaphor for what was going to happen.

I read the letter to him, and we agreed that since we didn't know what we were up against yet, or what we were being accused of, we shouldn't make it a big deal until we had more information. Simultaneously to this, we released our third-quarter numbers, which now included a huge hit to earnings because of the revenue reduction due to the cap calculation. It was the perfect storm, and I got swallowed up in it like a cosmic black hole.

In the late 1990s and early 2000s, there was a high degree of scrutiny in Congress and the Securities and Exchange Commission. The Sarbanes-Oxley Act of 2002 was a law that was designed to protect investors by mandating certain practices in financial record-keeping and reporting for corporations, including disclosures made pursuant to securities laws. What this new law required was full disclosure of any potential financial circumstance that might affect the value of the stock. To make it worse, corporate boards were terrified of being made an example of by the new "Sars/Ox" law, so these issues fell in my lap.

A new law, a new financial dynamic not yet seen in the hospice industry, and a Qui Tam lawsuit filed by an employee in Wisconsin, fueled by an attorney who wanted ODSY to pay a big price, and we came under intense pressure to do something about all of it. All in one tight, uncontrollable time frame. In hindsight, the cap issue did not completely develop overnight. The cap was part of the rules, and we had run so strong on growth that the balance of payment calculation should not have been a surprise, but it was, and that was on me and my team. But being a public company, you cannot just "work the problem, people," land the spacecraft, and go out to lunch.

And that is where my inexperience as a public company CEO really showed up. I did not know any better, and I wasn't getting advice that I trusted. Furthermore, other outside attorneys piled on for a class-action lawsuit against ODSY and a derivatives lawsuit, which essentially provided attorneys a way for the company to sue itself. Crazy. Attorneys feed on this stuff, and it got way out of hand.

The OIG did step in to conduct a three-year investigation, which produced no wrongdoing, no civil or criminal charges, and no damages. Under the terms of the settlement agreement, ODSY agreed to pay $13.0 without acknowledging any wrongdoing. So, it was a tough time all around.

When all of this hit the fan inside a thirty-six-hour time frame, I spoke with David Steffy on the board and we agreed that we needed to have an immediate conference call of the full board, right then, that evening. I had planned on going to Charlie's football game, and I still committed to being there and told Sandee that I'd get there as soon as I could and that something had come up, to put it lightly.

On the board call, we had the full board, our general counsel Brad Bickham, our investor relations VP, Jenny Haines, Doug Cannon, Brenda Belger, and me. I outlined all that was going on and my plan to deal with it all. In the age of public companies under Sars-Ox, my plan to handle it was deemed not aggressive enough. The board felt that we needed to have a Wall Street conference call within twenty-four hours to announce the lawsuit and the OIG investigation and that we needed to have a crisis communication team from NYC come help us script how we were going to fall on the proverbial sword to all our public investors, which included large funds but also every ten-share owning farmer in the wither and dither of America. So, you want to be a public company?

I told the board that I refused to do so. I justified my position by saying that until we knew all the facts of the lawsuit and until we knew what the OIG was looking for, I did not want to upset our employees and freak them out. This position was unacceptable to the board. It was not enough risk-averting leadership in their view. And in hindsight, they were right. If I had understood how overreactive a public CEO needs to be, and that guiding down is more important than bragging about what you can do and will do, I would have taken an entirely different approach to the whole thing. But I did not have that experience, and I was not getting a lot of board help other than pushing from behind and that doesn't work with me.

I paid the political price for my position and for my inexperience as a public CEO in this highly sensitive and complicated situation. I knew the board was going to ask for my resignation. Brad Bickham told me that he thought any change in my CEO position would be an "overreaction." And in my view, I agreed.

I left the office, and it was dark outside. I raced up Central Expressway to make it to Charlie's game. But I was mesmerized by what was taking place and drove five miles past the exit I should have taken for the stadium he was playing in. I turned around, got to the game, and sat in the bleachers next to Sandee. Go Charlie!!!!

BRACING FOR GOD'S CHANGE IN PLANS

When we got home that night, I told Sandee about the board call and that I expected a change of some kind the next morning. At eight the following morning, I got a call from Dick, asking me to meet him and John Carlisle, our audit chair, at the Sheraton Hotel in downtown Dallas. They told me not to go to the office. I walked into the lobby. Dick and John were there, and we sat in a corner of the lobby. I was told that I was not taking enough action to protect the company and the board and that they felt a change was needed to go a different direction. I told them I did not agree with the decision, but they must do what they thought they should and we should get together for a beer sometime.

Carlisle told me he was having trouble making the change because I was such a good and nice guy, but those were his instructions. They told me not to go back to the office, that they would ship all my stuff to me. It was brutal and a serious overaction. I complied, but I called my team on my way home and told them what was happening. When I got home, I walked in the kitchen at 10:15 a.m. on a weekday morning to the loving arms of Sandee, who was waiting for me. I took off my YCCOM pin and tossed it on the kitchen counter, told Sandee that I was done, held her, and wept. Fired from my own company. So, you want to be a public CEO? Think about that real hard, mister.

The news got out quickly. I mean in an instant. My phone began ringing from all over the country. The press, employees, and friends. Friends called me expressing sympathies, and I thought, *I'm not dead! I'm just winged. I'll get on my feet again.* Then Bob Reach heard about it, not sure how, but he called me at home and told me to go dark for a few days. And that is what we did.

It just so happened that we were taking delivery on another new airplane over the next few days. We had a fractional ownership in a jet (Citation Excel) at that time, and we flew on it up to Wichita to take delivery on a new Beechcraft Baron 58. On the private jet, once we were in our seats, I opened the *Wall Street Journal* and got to read about my demise on the front page. Not only did it describe the event of my departure, but it also published my without-cause release and the financial impact on the company. It is an out-of-body experience to read about yourself on the front page of the *Wall Street Journal.*

To notify shareholders that might be reading, they published my exit package, which included two full years of fully loaded salary and a total of $0.02 per share hit to the stock price, which equated to a lot of money. What do they say about there being no such thing as bad press? Well, it depends if you are pitching or catching. It did not seem good press at the time, but in hindsight, it was the best business experience I have ever had. It was also sinking in that I had two years of free time coming, "on the beach" as they say. Then my cell phone rang, and it was my mom.

"Dave, I'm reading in the paper here in Jupiter, Florida, that you are no longer at Odyssey!" she said.

Holy cow, even Florida knew. We left town, picked up the new Baron, flew Chris Potter, the Beechcraft salesperson, to Love Field in Dallas, then flew to Fredericksburg and went underground for a while. But not before I received a call from Richard Laughlin, our ranch builder and one of our best friends. He called and immediately said, "Congratulations!"

I thought he meant because I was no longer employed. I said, "Gee, thanks."

He said, "Your guest barn home just received a building award at the STAR awards in Ft. Worth!"

Oh, okay, great! At least the sun shines every day.

Things died down over time, and I had a good long think about what I had learned from ODSY. Some of the more influential and consequential lessons I learned include having a disciplined analysis of the business and its drivers of growth, establishing and maintaining solid financial modeling and compliance, providing very conservative and understated guidance expectations to shareholders, and driving a culture of service and respect for all coworkers who are the essence of the organization. I also learned that patience is required to run high-growth companies, and knowing what to be patient about comes with experience. When considering an IPO, a recapitalization of the business should be considered to keep the company private and still create a liquidity event for investors without the burden and risk of a public offering. And lastly, I learned how to communicate up to the board of directors.

It was time to consider what was next for me. And what I was going to do with those lessons. I was not done and wanted to do it again, only better, with what I had learned. But for those days, I would just try to enjoy the much-needed time off to regroup, have some fun, then get back in the game.

17

Life's valuable lessons, the best worst thing, ranching in the Texas Hill Country, more flying, new friends in the Hill Country, more airplanes and hundreds of commuting hours, Phil Mickelson, Davis Love III, starting "The Flying GT's," Leavin' Tracks

THE UPSIDE VALUE OF MAJOR SETBACKS IN LIFE

It doesn't always seem likely or even possible that when you get knocked on your keister it can turn out to be one of the best things that has ever happened to you. When we first went public in 2001, Sandee and I finally had the abundance of resources so we could begin planning our long-term future and retirement. In 2002, Sandee found an advertisement in the *Wall Street Journal* for Land/Water/Sky. It was a land broker who had rural properties for sale. He also was a professional pilot, including flying a helicopter he used to show prospective clients Texas Hill Country properties. It is a fun and efficient way to look at multiple properties in a day. Land/Water/Sky was owned by Michael Luigs.

We became very good friends with Mike as we learned more about the Texas Hill Country, and we also learned about his big, intense, and sometimes explosive personality. In a war, I want him in my foxhole. He is a no-holds-barred kind of guy. A very accomplished pilot from a wealthy family. His dad, Russ Luigs, also became a very good friend. Russ was in the offshore oil business and had an oil tanker named after him. I've put names on forty-foot boats but *his* name was on an eleven-hundred-foot tanker that honored him and his life's work. He was a great guy.

About a year before Russ died, Steve Allen and I bought a 1942 Boeing Stearman from him. It was his pride and joy, the Yellow Rose of Texas. It won awards at Sun n' Fun and was flown to Oshkosh Wisconsin for Airventure. That is a long, long flight in a hundred-mile-per-hour open cockpit Stearman. Steve flew the airplane quite a bit, but I never really took to it because I found it difficult to land, and I was never begging to solo the airplane. Steve bought my half of the airplane back from me shortly before Russ's death. The Luigs were very special to us, and they secured our interest in finding a place in the Hill Country.

Mike had flown us in his helicopter several times to look at interesting land that he had control of and was trying to sell to new owners, then help the owners to improve the land to increase the investment. A couple of times he sent a Challenger 350 midsize jet or a King Air 200 to pick us up in Dallas and bring us to either Fredericksburg or Kerrville. It made it easy to look at a lot of properties.

Each ranch property, usually raw land, took at least one half of a day to see it. Two ranches in one day were all we could muster. At some point in late 2002, and two years before I left ODSY, we began to look at properties other than Mike's. The sister of a broker friend of Mike's had something she wanted us to look at in a vanished community called Grapetown. We had already searched the Kerrville area high and low, had looked in Blanco, Stonewall, Medina, Sisterdale, even made a run and several flights by Luckenbach, but hadn't found anything that checked all our (read: Sandee's) required boxes.

But on November 17, 2002, Sissy DuPier took us to Grapetown. The before-the-rebuild-pictures show a wreck of a homestead, which had not had any material improvements since it was built in 1891. To quote a good friend of ours, Greg Tyler, as he stood staring at this home that came with one hundred and two years of unmaintained history and all the trimmings, "I don't know, Dave. I just don't know." Coming from Greg, that rang my bell and we both stood there in contemplative silence, assessing the life-changing work that would have to go into such a fixer-upper. This was more than a DIY project. And it would be expensive.

Things began to get interesting about the prospect of buying it when I heard Sandee ask herself while staring at the dilapidated milking barn, "I wonder if that could be a guest house?" I knew at once that Sandee had her creative eye working, along with an expensive dose of dreamy home in the Texas Hill Country. We told Sissy we were interested and wanted to make an offer on the historic Grapetown property.

When we asked Mike what he thought about this property and the one hundred and forty-eight acres with live creeks, rolling terrain rife with fields and woods, only nine miles from Fredericksburg, he told us that if we didn't buy it, he would. He saw the gem that we couldn't see. Yet. Mike offered to be our buyer's broker along with Sissy and take no fee for doing so. His interest was in getting to know us better for larger investment deals that he was planning in the future. He also knew the property could be a great investment for him if we backed out. And he had an idle crew of about thirty people that he had to put to work fixing properties while he waited to fix his own next investment property. He wanted to deploy his land crew. He is only the dirt guy to clean and trim all one hundred and forty-eight acres.

With the trusted assurance of Mike's commitment to a successful deal for all parties, we stormed ahead with the purchase and closed on it on January 17, 2003. After the close, Sandee and I were sitting on the front porch, taking it all in while consuming an expensive bottle of champagne, when Mike's clean-up crew began bringing in heavy tractors, trailers, and a D5 dozer. We had not owned the property six hours, and Luigs was getting started. I would not leave ODSY for another two and a half years, so this was going to be a big project while also running a public company. But I had a secret weapon. Sandee.

BUILDING THE FLYING G RANCH

In the summer of 2002, six months before we bought the epicenter of Grapetown, there were floods that are still talked about. Over fifteen inches of rain fell in less than forty-eight hours, and every river, creek, and tributary overflowed to five-hundred-year levels. People had to be rescued by helicopter, and goods and drugs and other life-sustaining deliveries had to be made to stranded landowners. Mike Luigs later received an award for his helicopter work during the flooding and his efforts in the aftermath.

We weren't landowners when that happened, but we were faced with the challenge of the cleanup on one hundred and forty-eight acres. The water rose so high that there were dead trees deposited at the tops of live trees. Debris of every kind littered the spans of the high-water lines in every direction. We found washers and dryers, refrigerators, deer feeders, culver pipe, goat and hog wire, trash, beer cans, whiskey bottles, and deer cadavers. No telling how far these items were washed down the flooded waters to conveniently land in our backyard.

Welcome to the Texas Hill Country. Now we understood what it meant to "mend fences." Yep, we got it.

The clean-up started as phase 1 (the phases never end on ranches) to deploy the Luigs team to move all this debris out and begin cutting and trimming trees. The effort was so significant that Mike's team, led by a supervisor nicknamed "Gaby," brought in a single-wide trailer and deposited it in our field just below the milking barn so the Hispanic crew had a place to live while they worked for the next six months. They lived on the ranch twenty-four-seven while we were flying back and forth in our Bonanza as often as two times a week.

Charlie was about twelve years old when we began construction on the ranch. He would play outside because we had no inside place to stay there yet. He came running up from the creek to our east, South Grape Creek (which flows downstream about five miles to the center of

Luckenbach), quietly animated, telling us there were men taking baths in the creek! The crew was living in the trailer together and living off the land. They worked hard, and twenty years later, those trees are still looking trimmed!

MORE LAND, MORE INJURIES

We were at home one night when Mike called us and told us there had been an accident at the ranch. Gulp. He said the crew was cutting down large dead trees, and Gaby had been hit by one as it fell. A big tree had landed on him near the creek and pinned him to the ground. His leg was shattered in multiple places, and he was badly injured. His crew lifted the tree off him using equipment they had, and an ambulance had navigated the rough terrain, including crossing a fast-moving South Grape Creek, and had stabilized him at the accident site, but they weren't ready to move him in the ambulance just yet.

The cell coverage was still terrible at the ranch, so it was hard to reach and be reached there. We got Mike's call in real time. He told us that we needed to get to Fredericksburg now and sent a King Air 200 to pick us up at Addison Airport in Dallas to fly us to Fredericksburg, where Gaby would then be loaded up in the King Air and be flown to a trauma center in San Antonio. We got to the airport at the same time they were ready to load us up and go. On the taxi out, the crew turned the airplane around and went back to the ramp. In their haste, the first officer had forgotten to load more fuel. We needed gas. So, we were delayed another thirty minutes.

We landed in the dark about an hour later and the ambulance was there with Mike and Gaby ready to take our place aboard the King Air. We got off, they got on, and they were off to San Antonio.

We saw Gaby again three months later as the crew was wrapping up their work at the Flying G. He had pictures of his X-rays that were hard to look at. How he did not lose that leg, or wasn't killed, is amazing. He had no hard feelings and accepted it as a hazard of felling multiple trees at the same time and place with a large crew. Mike took great care of Gaby, and it said a lot about Mike and his commitment to do the right thing with his worker colleagues. Man, we had not even gotten started and someone was nearly killed on our new "ranch." Welcome to the country. Oh, and watch for the water moccasins in the creeks.

FLYING G RANCH CONSTRUCTION PHASE TWO

Richard Laughlin and his crew began work on phase 2 of our construction by converting the cow barn to a guest barn. It took just six months to complete the renovation of twenty-five hundred square feet into a very cozy four-bedroom guest house. Sandee was just getting started. Once we got everything done with the barn, we enjoyed staying there and inviting friends and family to enjoy it with us. For about three years we forgot about the larger house that needed more than a facelift. We just enjoyed the simplicity of staying in "the barn." Rainy and nasty cold weather were the best getaway times on record! We just had a ball and created so many memories with our family and friends.

So many good times, but I was still working at Odyssey, and we were fortunate to have the barn built prior to my departure from there late in 2004. We continued to commute back and forth, back and forth, and back and forth. In one two-year stretch, my pilot logbook shows a hundred and seventy-five round trips between Dallas and Fredericksburg, which was a total of three hundred and fifty flights and averaged one leg every two days for two years.

It was a lot of work living and working in two places, and we had not even started the "big house" yet. We could not have done it without the airplane. The jet was nice for certain special purposes, but our workhorse was the Bonanza N620DG. That was followed by Baron

N621DG, Bonanza N721DG, Skylane N6218B, Cirrus N681SG, TBM N930VM, Citation N681GG, Skylane N741CH and today we have Kodiak N324KD to be changed to N681GG. The 1970 Super Cub came at the same time the guest barn was completed late in 2003.

N8524Y is still in our rolling stock in one of our hangars. We purchased the Cub from Mr. Robert Snowden. One of our dearest friends, Bob and Karen Snowden, are a big reason we decided to land in Fredericksburg and to build there and call it home. Mike Luigs flew with me and Sandee in our Bonanza in late 2002 to Fredericksburg from the Luigs ranch while we were looking for property. Mike introduced us to Bob and Karen, and we have been great friends now for more than twenty years!

Mike introduced us so that we might rent a hangar from Bob, as he owned several rows of T-hangars. The airport was not yet booming like it is today, but it was coming, and getting hangar space is a major land grab for any aircraft owner operator. Securing a hangar from Bob and Karen helped seal our commitment to establish a home in Fredericksburg. There was a day when T82 was a sleepy local airport, but today, the world has found this little gem in the Texas Hill Country.

BOMBAY SAPPHIRE SQUADRON

With such a tight aviation community with a fabulous uncontrolled airport, it was inevitable that our flying community would find an occasional and interesting and edgy technical flying to pursue. Bob Snowden led about ten of us in seven airplanes to the back country in Idaho. Flying in loose formation in two groups, we made it to McCall, Idaho, in two days. We flew over the spectacular deserts of New Mexico and Colorado to the glorious fourteen-thousand-foot peaks around Salt Lake City, over the squelched and scorched desert in southern Idaho, and back over the mountains and the Snake River into McCall. It was an amazing journey just getting there. I rode with Charlie in his iconic red Skylane, and we took turns in the left seat.

By the time Bob organized us on the ground in McCall, we had our formation flying chops well in hand, ready to fly the valleys and steep canyons east of McCall. We flew into some technically demanding mountain strips that are not for rookie pilots. To organize our radio communications and to keep our "flight" to a manageable number of airplanes, we split up into two groups, Bombay and Sapphire. The sequence where you were in the formation determined your specific call sign. If you were in the Bombay group and were the second "ship" following the "one ship," your designation was "Bombay 2". The lead ship is always "one."

The challenge is flying in formation without hitting each other. That is accomplished by not taking your eye off your wingman. There is a lot more to it, but you get the idea that our two flights of airplanes went into these canyons following one another with rising terrain on all sides, and no airplane had the ability to outclimb the terrain.

We had to be smart, well planned, and disciplined in our flying and communication. So, all day long on the common frequency that mountain fliers use, you could hear our various flight callouts. After the first couple of days of flying, which included landing in iconic mountain destinations, including Johnson Creek (more on that in a minute) and Sulphur Creek and others, many other pilots heard our constant radio callouts while we all stayed together.

That night, at the hotel where other pilots were also staying, someone asked us at our every-evening-post-flying-happy-hour, "You guys sounded cool! Where did you get the name Bombay Sapphire for your two groups?"

Bob Snowden responded, while pouring gin into a glass, "It's because we like gin and tonics." We all busted a gut, thinking the guy asking thought we were an official FAA- designated flight group. Nope. Just some fly-boy cowboys from Texas!

At the end of the week, we flew home from different directions, and Charlie and I headed home in formation with Tom McKnight and his lifelong friend, his Cessna 182. We made it home from McCall, Idaho, in one exceptionally long and sweltering day. When we made it to Santa Fe, the outside temperature was in the nineties and the density altitude was reported as greater than 110 degrees Fahrenheit. That is pilot lingo for the airplane will not want to fly very well because it won't be able to generate enough power to climb sufficiently.

I suggested to Tom and Charlie that we wait until the next morning and leave when it was cooler, but no, they were ready to go, so I switched to Tom's airplane to ride with him, and Charlie followed us out. We got in the air and went to eleven thousand five hundred feet eastbound. Charlie went to thirteen thousand five hundred feet above sea level for a while, trying to find cool and stable air, but we never found it and bounced our way to Midland, Texas, where Tom was stopping there at one of his many homes for the night.

Charlie and I refueled and flew the rest of the way to Fredericksburg with the sun setting behind us. We landed an hour after dark and in time to make it to our favorite Mexican restaurant to meet Sandee and have a very cold and well-deserved beer. The rest of Bombay Sapphire flew the north route out of Idaho and made it home the next day. It was quite the trip.

One quick, head-turning story about Johnson Creek. On our first full day of flying the mountains after arriving in McCall, we ventured out east to Sulphur Creek to land there for a hearty mountain breakfast. To this day, Charlie says it was the best breakfast he has ever had. I agree with that assessment. Although it was late June, with summer in full swing, it was cold in the mornings. The cold was a welcome change from the Texas summer heat, but it added the possibility of carburetor ice in our airplanes, even in the summer. Ice can shut down the carburetor by freezing it because of the humidity and venturi effect of the air speeding by and through it during flight.

Charlie and I kept the carburetor heat applied to prevent this, and it was working fine by redirecting engine heat directly to the carburetor, keeping it above freezing. But doing so robs the engine of some of its performance. In the mountains, you need every inch of manifold power and the resulting increase in RPMs you can get in order to climb out of the terrain.

After breakfast, we did some light hiking as a group, checking out some of the local attractions, such as the nearby river that was flowing the direction of the runway for departure, and we noticed the wind for our takeoff would be a tailwind, so we waited a while to see if the wind would die down. Taking off with a tailwind is also one of those physics lessons that you do not want to fail. Whenever possible, you always take off facing into the wind so that the airspeed above and below the wings is more than sufficient to create lift.

Johnson Creek is complicated from several aspects. First, at an altitude of nearly five thousand feet, unless you have a turbocharged engine or are a turbo prop, the engine starts out at a performance deficit, and the higher it climbs, the more that performance deficit grows. It is very tricky. Johnson Creek has a grass runway thirty-four hundred feet long and is also one way in and one way out. The mountain valley climbs dramatically on the south end, and there is a house in the way of a south departure, so you typically have to take off to the north, which for us that day would be a tailwind departure and not on the list of fun things to do.

Another complication is that once off the ground, you enter a big mountain bowl that requires a left or right turn and a climb to get back on top of the peaks towering over nine thousand feet. With seven airplanes preparing to depart, our two "flights" briefed the procedure and the sequence of departures for each group so that everyone would know where to be once in the air.

Another complication was emerging: the cloud deck was lowering, and the visibility was beginning to drop. We needed to get going, and it was now getting late in the day. It was my leg to fly, as Charlie had flown our arrival into Johnson Creek and now I was in the left seat, with Charlie's approval, since it was his airplane. We prepared to depart as Bombay 3, following John Klaerner, a rather newly minted eighteen-year-old private pilot in his Cherokee, and Tom McKnight in his high-performance Cessna 182. Following Bombay was the Sapphire flight of Steve and Scott Allen, Jake Akin and our leader Bob Snowden, who was keeping an eye on everyone from the last position.

The grass at Johnson Creek is cut probably a good four to five inches long, so it is sticky and draggy, which is great for landing but is more drag during the takeoff. We were warmed up and in line for our series of departures. I watched John go by us in his Cherokee, thinking, *I hope he has enough power to get out of here*. Then Tom began his takeoff roll a few seconds behind John. We counted to about six, then started our roll down the runway, all the while conscious of our ten-to-fifteen-knot tailwind. This was going to be tricky, and we needed everything to go right.

As we got about halfway down the runway, we were getting light on the tires and left the ground ever so modestly. We had performed a soft field takeoff maneuver, which gets the airplane out of the drag of the grass but not yet enough airspeed to begin an aggressive climb. We were in the air, but not by much. We slowly climbed to about fifty feet off the runway with the stall warning chirping, reminding us that we were at or just above minimum-controllable airspeed. Important not to make any aileron movements here, because the stall speed of the wing goes up during a bank and we were critically close to stall speed as it was, which was made more marginal with the tailwind.

Charlie and I called out the trees at the end of the runway, which were higher on the right side but not by much. We were headed straight for the tops of the trees. I applied just enough back pressure to create another twenty feet or so of lift, and the trees passed below us. It was helpful for me and Charlie, both being Super Cub pilots, to fly close to terrain, trees, and other obstacles without freaking out. An inch is a mile, and we kept going.

Later, when we were back on the ground, Charlie told me, "I thought those trees were in play." I agreed. After we passed the trees, we put in a little right rudder to move right toward the wall of the rising terrain to catch the lift from the updrafts, and it helped us get our vertical speed climbing to a paltry, if I remember correctly, three hundred feet per minute.

In under thirty seconds, it was time to lock in on Tom ahead of us, who was following John, and begin a climbing left turn out of the canyon. It was beginning to lightly rain, with sprinkles on the windscreen. We cleared the first set of ridges as we turned one hundred and eighty degrees and could see Johnson Creek down below on our left. We kept climbing.

From the number one position, John made a tactical decision and told the rest of the flight on the radio, "We can't get out going this direction; the visibility is down and so is the ceiling. We have to turn left and go back over Johnson Creek to find another way west out of here."

He made the call of our lives. If he had continued the original flight plan, we would have ended up in the clouds as a group in rising terrain. We followed John. From the rear of the flight, Bob was talking to John about the plan to get headed west, perpendicular to mountain ridges and about four hundred feet below the lowering cloud deck. We had Tom in front of us and John, in his speedy Cherokee, was pulling away from us. We held our position and kept going.

I remember seeing how the mountain wave of wind would pick John up a couple of hundred feet, followed by Tom, then me and Charlie. Then we would go back down a couple of hundred feet. Flying mountain wave is tricky, but it can be a lot of fun if it isn't turbulent.

We didn't have very far to go to get to McCall, but it seemed like an eternity with it sprinkling, getting late in the day, and not much room between the clouds and the mountaintops. We began to relax, focused on staying in position as Bombay 3, following Tom. We flew over ridge after ridge and canyon after canyon until we broke out over the McCall valley, where it was flat, lush, and green. We began our descent, following Tom, with a renewed interest in enjoying the remainder of the flight.

We left traffic into McCall, landed as a flight, taxied in as a flight, and parked wing to wing as a flight. We felt like the Blue Angels, and when Charlie and I got out of the airplane, what a relief it was. We parked next to John, who jumped off the wing of his airplane, and we gave each other serious manly bear hugs, screaming what an excellent job he had done leading us home from Johnson Creek. When everyone's bacon is on the line, you need an awesome leader that others have confidence in to remain as wingmen in order to successfully get out of a tight spot. I will never forget that for as long as I live.

Charlie went back with a smaller group a couple of years later. I thought about him all the time he was there, knowing how unforgiving the mountains can be. He did great, but it is a long way to Idaho. I think Arkansas is a blast, flying the hills and grass strips there, and it is only about a five-hour flight in the Super Cub from Fredericksburg, so it is way more convenient and every bit as much fun, at least to me.

BACK AT THE RANCH

One of the unexpected pleasures of restoring an 1888 barn into a place where guests stay was the conversations about their visit. They would say, "We never thought we would go on vacation and stay in a barn!" Over the next three years we simply enjoyed staying in the barn and did not think a lot about the big old house. I was still working full time in downtown Dallas, and we still had our home in Plano. There was no way to devote all our time split between two full lives in two different towns.

In 2003 and 2004, I was busy with Odyssey, leading up to my departure in October 2004. In the spring of 2003, I was given the chance to play golf in a Bank of America Private Bank golf tournament at Colonial Country Club in Ft. Worth. With my handicap, I tied with another person to earn the opportunity to play in the Colonial Golf Tournament on the Pro-Am day, which is the day before the official tournament begins. The tournament paired me with Phil Mickelson in 2003, and in 2004 I was paired with Davis Love III. My brother Jay was my caddy when I played with Phil, and my brother-in-law Troy was my caddy when I played with Davis. It was so much fun.

More importantly, my dad and Peggy came to the Pro Am when I played with Phil. My dad was so proud as he walked outside the ropes while I walked up the fairways with Phil inside the ropes. For the record, when I played with Phil, he and I both sunk birdie putts on hole number one and were tied at one under par. His caddy, Bones, gave me knuckles walking off the green as he said, "You're tied with Phil Mickelson." I will never forget that.

Sandee and I had gone to a Bank of America private bank party the night before at Billy Bob's, which featured Willie Nelson and Pat Green. It was also a blast, but we did not stay late as our tee time was 7:00 a.m. and I did not want the burden of a late night in my golf bag. But what was in my golf bag was a new Callaway three-wood that I had bought a couple of days before at our home club at the time, Stonebriar Country Club.

I had never swung the club until Phil followed me to my ball in the rough after my tee shot on number eleven. The ball landed in the second cut and was not buried in the deep grass, but was not on the more desirable flat fairway. Bones continued to walk down the fairway to Phil's ball, about three hundred and twenty-five yards down range. Jay and I realized Phil was going to our ball with us.

When we got to the ball and saw the lie, Phil walked over to my golf bag, pointed at the new three-wood, and said, "Hit that three-wood and aim it straight at Bones."

Jay handed me the club. It still had the price tag on it. Sandee had her camera rolling while she stood behind the ropes behind a tree nearby. I was so nervous. Then I crushed it right at Bones. We started walking as if it was just another shot when Phil said, "Nice shot, Dave."

I handed Jay the club and said, "Thanks, Phil." I will never forget that for as long as I live. And we have it on video. I was not an imposter. I was playing golf with a world-ranked champion golfer. My dad was thrilled, and it checked a box for him. And for me too. I am glad Dad got to see his boys on such a wonderful golf stage.

A year later, at the same Pro Am at Colonial, I was paired with Davis Love III. Troy caddied for me, and I was more comfortable playing with Davis since I had played with Phil the year before. They are two vastly different people. Both genuinely nice and super professional. Phil is expressive, vocal, and interested when he doesn't really need to be. Davis is more of an introvert but also interested. On the front page of the *Dallas Morning News* Sports Day section, the cover picture was of me and Davis lining up my putt on number eighteen, with Troy in close, looking over Davis's shoulder. It was quite the experience.

To this day, I really cannot believe it. Let us see the replay again. "Nice shot, Dave," says Phil. "Thanks, Phil," says Dave. Too much.

There was another big lifetime event leading into 2003. Dick and I were featured in *Forbes* magazine as the founders of a hospice company, and the article's focus was on "the end game," which is an uncomfortable way of referring to the industry and the potential successful opportunity for an exit. To make it even a little more macabre, they took a picture of me and Dick together in our conference room against the floor-to- ceiling windows, which produced a soft, whited-out chromatic of us in a ghostly kind of effect.

Sandee and I went to Barnes and Noble a couple of days after the article was released. We were looking through the magazine while others were flipping through various magazines of their choosing. But we were looking at *Forbes*. And we were in it. We were on the map. Big time. It was time to look beyond ODSY and begin building the big house at the ranch.

THE KIDS GROW UP

In 2004, during all the mayhem at work and with the ranch, we were also watching our little girl Natalie, Nigh, Shug, prepare to graduate from high school, and Charlie was just entering the same high school, so there was a lot of transitioning going on at home. There was a lot going on for Natalie and our family as she prepared to go to Baylor University in the fall of 2004, and Charlie was looking forward to doubling his footprint upstairs by also taking over Natalie's room.

In the spring of that year, Natalie also graduated from the teen activities at Hunters Glen Baptist Church. A ceremony honoring the high school seniors was always an emotional rite of passage for the church's young people. Natalie had grown up through Mission Friends and Acteens, and many of her close friends were with her along the way. Also along the way was Sandee, who had instructed the young girls and ladies in these groups and was an especially important part of the girls' lives from young girls to full-grown adult ladies ready to take on the world.

I remember trying to keep my emotions together as we helped robe Natalie in the recognition service of church graduation. She looked so grown up. And she was. Charlie was four years behind her, and I remember thinking, *Oh boy, we get to go through this with Charlie when he graduates high school in 2008.*

When we took Natalie to Baylor to help set up her room with her best friend Lacy Kolb, we all said a prayer, cried, and said our goodbyes before getting on the highway back to Dallas. About twenty minutes into the drive, we decided to call Natalie as an excuse to see if we had forgotten anything. She answered her cell phone with all her friends in Walmart, already shopping for stuff they needed. They didn't miss a beat. They were on their own, and away they went. And away we went, back to Dallas to pick up where we left off with Charlie, Sandee, me, and Honey, our dog. Now Charlie had the entire upstairs to himself, guitars and all.

It did not take long for things to return to our normal and hectic pace. Charlie was playing high school football, playing guitar in the praise band at church, and found himself in a couple of different bands between middle school and high school. He and his friends would come home from football practice at Plano West High School on summer mornings and jump in our pool to cool off. Life was flying by, and we were getting acquainted with the transition that was coming.

We always attended the kids' sports games. We have since commented that we don't remember our parents going to any of our sports or social participation events. Different times, I guess. While sitting in the stands at one of Charlie's football games, we were sitting with the parents of one of Charlie's high school friends, who was also on the football team. His name was Jesse Thompson. Not only was Jesse playing on the football team, but he was an outstanding budding musician. He and Charlie would get together and play with another guy on drums, and they called themselves Absolute Zero. They got a couple of local gigs and played their own stuff and a few covers.

At the football game, Jesse's father, Randy, and I were talking, and he told me about his days playing drums in California in a Christian rock band. I had never been in a real band, although I'd done some hacking it up stuff with Bill Merten in St. Louis, but that wasn't a real band. So talking to others who were pro musicians was always interesting to me. I asked Randy if he was still playing drums and he said, "No, they are up in my attic, and I haven't played them for a while."

I looked at him, grinned, and commented, "Maybe we should get together and jam someday."

Randy laughed and agreed as if it would never happen but was fun to think about.

A few weeks later, while Sandee and I were at a neighborhood Christmas party, the subject of a summer block party came up. There was some interest, but no one stepped up to give the idea wings. So I said, "If someone organizes the block party, I will start a band from scratch, and we will play at the party." Someone took the bait, and now I had to start a band.

I called Randy and asked if he, Jesse, Charlie, and I should get together at their house, since he had the drums in the attic, and see if we could make a sound or two. We did, and we did. It was a blast. I'll never forget the smile on my face, playing with drums and a bass back-beat while Charlie and I pieced together "Pride 'n Joy" by Stevie Ray Vaughan. I couldn't believe I was playing in a band.

Charlie and I would haul our gear in our car to Randy and Jesse's house usually two to three times a month. By the time the party came around, we had a sound; it was rough, but it would do for the party. I rented a four-foot-tall stage that was thirty by thirty, complete with a covered awning and a sound board out front. I bought all the equipment we would need for sound—mics, cables, towers, bass cabinets, PA, soundboard, the whole enchilada. I figured we would never do this again, so let us do something we would never forget.

The party was on Memorial Day in 2006. We honored vets and read the names of all the neighbors' family members who had served in the armed services. We had a talent show for a couple of hours before our band got up to play. Adults sang to soundtracks, kids performed dance routines, there was poetry, and it became a very American Memorial Day event. Our good friends Greg Tyler and his son Marcus got on stage and sang a couple of songs together.

The stage was HUGE! The hold-down lines stretched a couple of houses up the street and were put in the ground with three-foot stakes. It was so big it looked like a legitimate outdoor concert venue featuring somebody. People brought their grills out to the street, and we had a keg of beer. Everyone was having a grand old time, and we blocked off the street with police barriers, so it was a safe place to celebrate. We had stage lights and streetlights and danced in the cul-de-sac.

The sound system was fabulous, and the lights were on when our band took the stage. We called ourselves Geezer. We had T-shirts made with our first logo on the front, and on the back, it read, "Supporting our Troops since 2006." We sold the T-shirts before we had played a single note. We did a vocal rehearsal in our house before going on. Randy was really our leader since he had been a pro and knew what to focus on.

One of our neighbors, Bud Hebert, a former Oklahoma defensive back who was co-MVP in the Orange Bowl and a close personal boyhood friend of Toby Keith, was wearing a cap with a pretend ponytail, drinking a beer, when he introduced Geezer to the crowd. And off we went, playing about six songs. I was so nervous I almost passed out.

We pulled it off. We had so much fun, our band, later renamed The Flying GT's, kept playing for another fifteen years and recorded one album. We played all over Texas and got better as the years went on.

We had, and still have, a band trailer with all our gear in it, ready at a moment's notice. We played restaurants and bars, private parties, big galas, balls, weddings, and fraternity and sorority parties. And we practiced a lot before each gig. Our gear got better, and we got better. One gig at a pizza place paid us $28 and all the pizza and beer we wanted. The next day we had a band meeting and decided no more. No more shitty gigs that did not pay us anything.

From that day on, we made no less than $2000 per gig. Things got better but also more complicated. As a band, our tastes overlapped in some areas and did not in other areas. Sometimes we all got along, sometimes we did not. Band life is hard, and the general public has no clue what goes on behind the scenes. When we recorded our album Leavin' Tracks, we believed we were done as a band. Randy wrote the lyrics to the title track, and the boys and I came up with the music while on break at our album recording session. We recorded it in just two takes on the same day. I heard it on the radio while driving one day. A friend of mine dropped our CD off at the local radio station in Kerrville, TX, and suggested he give Leavin' Tracks a spin. And I heard it in my truck. It is pretty satisfying to hear your original band work played on the radio. Fun and memorable stuff. What is cool to me today is that the lyrics that Randy wrote are so true.[9]

The boys graduated high school; we made the album, then played for thirteen more years until Randy drummed himself into drum retirement! We had so many memorable gigs, including on the famed Sixth Street in Austin. We played in San Antonio, in west Texas, in Dallas, and in several venues in the Hill Country. At one time, we gathered at the ranch and worked on a second album in our studio. We wanted to produce new and original songs, so we tried to mix up the teamwork on writing songs.

---

9 The lyrics to Leavin' Tracks, recorded in two takes in 2008 at Bass Performance Labs, Dallas, Texas:

They know me by the me they see,
Deep inside, a mystery,
The who I am, they'll never know,
I'm so much more than just the show.

I'm leavin' tracks, they mark my way,
And lead me back to yesterday,
And all that I am, and all that I'll be,
Are in the steps that follow me.

No words, no songs, no dance and few wrongs,
I look behind, to see beyond,
The setting sun, the breaking dawn,
Holding onto the light.

I'm leavin' tracks, they mark my way,
And lead me back to yesterday,
All that I am, and all that I'll be,
Are in the steps that follow me.

For a while I would work with Jesse to see if we could produce something and Charlie would work with Randy, then we would all switch up again. What we came up with was about six original songs we wrote and wanted to try to record, but life got in the way; gigs and the rehearsals got in the way; and so did everyone's careers. I still have the songs, so who knows. If Randy heals his drumming joints, maybe he'll be back … I sure hope we play again one day. Our website is still up, so check it out if it is still around. It is www.theflyinggts.com.

18

Charlie graduates from high school, moving to Fredericksburg full time, picking up board of director gigs, starting the next investor-backed hospice company, losing a private equity friend to suicide, selling New Century Hospice, grabbing a place in Colorado, flying with my Top Gun instructor, getting arrested and going to jail in San Antonio, getting detained by Mexican soldiers in the desert town of Hermosillo

It seemed like five minutes passed when we were at Charlie's robing ceremony at church as we had been with Natalie four years earlier. We were in the final finishing touches of the big house buildout at the ranch and looking forward to one day moving there full time. During 2006 and 2007, a couple of years before Charlie graduated high school, I offered him the Super Cub as a gift for agreeing to leave Plano West in his sophomore/junior year to move to Fredericksburg so we could live there, and he would go to school there as a Fredericksburg High School Battlin' Billie. Billie, as in billy goat.

He would have none of it. I understood. He had a girlfriend who lived not far away. There was no way to talk him into leaving high school in Plano before he went to Baylor University. I'm glad he didn't take me up on the offer. The Cub will be his one day anyway. When Charlie graduated and moved to Baylor, he and his friends grew into an army of college men. They were all great friends, and we loved each and every one of them. Charlie pledged Kappa Sig, and Natalie pledged Chi Omega. They were both frat kids. Natalie loved it and one day claimed to us, "I'm going to stay at Baylor and just be a Chi Omega."

Charlie had a different view. He more or less said, "You can have it. I hate it."

I think Natalie loved the society she was in with her "sisters." Charlie liked his friends but didn't like someone else being in charge and telling him what to do twenty-four hours a day for weeks on end. Such are each of their personalities. We have been so blessed to have kids whose friends we also consider family. They all still visit us today from time to time. They are all grown up and have stayed in touch.

I am so proud of Natalie and Charlie. They are solid people with healthy amounts of self-respect and self-confidence. They are fiercely driven and determined to pursue their dreams in a relationship-based moral code. They are so fun to be around and are still very different from one another.

WE LEAVE PLANO FOR THE TEXAS HILL COUNTRY

Ruth was the first of our family to move full time to Fredericksburg. She beat us by several months as we tied up loose ends to get Charlie to college and sell our house. She never batted an eye about having to sell the house that she had been in for forty-five years and moving to the Texas Hill Country. What she really didn't want was to be left in Dallas with none of her family there. Ruth was not going to spend one single hour living in Dallas with all of us gone. And she wasn't going to lose track of her grandkids at Baylor and beyond. Natalie had graduated with her undergrad in education and was now in grad school for her master's degree in educational psychology. Smart kid, that Natalie.

BUSINESS LIFE AFTER ODSY

Not long after I left ODSY, I was recruited by a couple of investor groups in Boston to join the board of a pure-play hospice company. My noncompete and financial consideration had expired, and I was free to come "off the beach." I was not crazy about the company business model but believed I could help with the strategic and operating plan. The CEO was a guy named Dan Kane. He was a hardened northeasterner with a rough demeanor and an inflexible personality. The board and investors were comprised of a couple people that I knew and liked. Chris Grant, who I had met working for Kingston, was a principal in Salix Ventures. Darren Black, at SV-Life Sciences, was a budding dynamic private equity player. He flew to Dallas to meet with me before I went to Boston to meet Dan and the others. Darren's father was a health care icon named Chester Black, and Darren was picking up with his legacy. Darren could smell money from a thousand miles away. He was very gracious in asking me onto the board, and he and I got along great.

I visited his home and family one time for dinner with other board members. He was a very social guy and very well-connected. One of his partners at SV was Eugene Hill, who also sat on the board of Allegiance. Gene and Darren and I always got along, although Darren later left to join Summit Partners in Boston. He was at Summit when he and I hooked up again later in another deal.

Mr. Alan Solomont was also on the board and in 2011 was the chairman of regional fundraising for the campaign of then Presidential candidate Barack Obama. The last rite of passage for me joining the board was a breakfast meeting in Boston with Alan. He held court there most days, one at a time, almost in single file as he had the hostess bring donors to his table for thirty-minute meetings. I was packed into one of these slots for his interview of me for the board position at Allegiance. Alan and I got along fine; boards have their own personality dynamics, and this was no different.

But I was back in the game and knew a lot more after the nine-year ODSY experience. Those experiences made me the operating expert in the room. That is why I was recruited to the Allegiance board of directors. How I left ODSY no longer mattered. Wall Street and private equity folks have very short memories largely due to there being so much money out there; they don't have time to squabble about this or that. They need people who have done it before and want to do it again. I did not see that angle of it until I started getting calls to go back to work helping others make a lot of money.

When the company was sold to a company familiar to me, I made a nice little bundle that I set aside to start my next company. Once you experience the taste of business success and realize what you learned from the experience, you want to get back in the game to prove that you can play even better.

MEANWHILE, BACK AT THE RANCH

We sold our house in Plano in less than a week to the first people who looked at it, conveniently just one week before the market crashed in 2008. When we drove away from Plano, I genuinely believed we would not be back to live in the Dallas area again. But that was before twenty years of ranch living and two grandkids being born. With Ruth in Fredericksburg (she was eighty-one when she packed up and moved there before we did) and already involved in the community, we had some catching up to do. I had the not-so-good idea to buy forty-four acres of land to turn into a housing subdivision. Always a bad economic idea to invest and back yourself in something you know nothing about.

"Seems like a good idea" is not a good business plan. The first version of anything is usually a disaster. Real estate is no different.

After the collapse of the market in 2008, I had invested over $1 million into the development property we called "The Orchard" on a street we built and named Harvest Hills Lane. It was an innovative idea, a convenient location, but the timing was terrible. I did not want to sit on the investment, and at the strong suggestion from my sage soothsayer in business, Tom Erickson, I shut it down and sold it.

When significant market factors arise that make the financial risk of a speculative investment unacceptable, the smart move is to shut it down quickly. Get it done, shut it down, live for another day. This is where Pollyanna and over-optimism in the face of reality can cost a lot of money. The other option is to exercise an enormous amount of patience and wait for the industry or business to come back. Unfortunately, most private equity investors have a three-to five-year, and at a maximum, seven-year time horizon, so waiting out an industry to come back to earn five times the initial investment can be a painful ordeal. Take the hit now, enjoy the tax write-off, and don't look back. I personally lost $1 million on the lesson but was now free to do what I did know how to do. Healthcare services.

During the ranch-building process and the search for furniture at Robb and Stuckey in Plano, we ran across an interesting piece of furniture made by a company called Century. I needed a name for my next hospice venture and that was it. Century Hospice. I founded the company using my own money in 2006. By 2008, we needed more private equity capital to grow into new markets. At the beginning, I made a few calls to people I knew, looking for the right source of capital for Century. We needed somewhere between $10 and $20 million to pull off what I wanted to do.

A close contact at Bank of America on the corporate banking side referred me to David Fitzgerald at Petra Capital Partners. I called him, and we met a week later in Frisco for a quick glass of wine before he and his founding partner, Mike Blackburn, went into a board dinner. Bob Sarna went with me, and we met with these guys for less than thirty minutes. They were interested in knowing more about Century Hospice. David then introduced me to a syndicate partner at Scale Ventures in Menlo Park, California. Mr. Mark Brooks invited me to pitch my company deck to the partners at Scale at the same time another group at SV Life Sciences invited me to make the same pitch to their partnership.

Oddly enough, both firms I would pitch to on the same day were in the same building. I asked Tom Blake and Bill Ward to be on my board of directors during this fundraising process. I needed trusted eyes and ears to help me make the right decisions on this particularly important financial growth strategy.

I flew to San Francisco the night before my presentations and had dinner with Mark. He asked me what happened at ODSY. I told him. And we moved on. He wanted to get to know me, and I wanted to know him and his firm, Scale Venture Partners. Mark is very, very smart, a very likeable guy, and great fun to be around. We became and still are exceptionally good friends.

The next day I made pitches to both firms, then flew back to San Antonio. When I landed in Dallas about 9:00 p.m. that night, Mark Brooks called me and wanted to hammer out a deal to bring in Scale alongside Petra to be our equity package. SV wanted to do the deal on their own. I spoke with Mark during my drive back to the ranch and told him that if I lost signal, I would call him from my ranch office. That is exactly what happened.

Around midnight, I got to my office and called him in California. He was on vacation with his family and was talking quietly on his phone in the bathroom of his hotel room. We talked until shortly before 5:00 a.m., hammering out a deal.

At 6:00 a.m., after pulling an all-nighter and having flown back from California, I reached Bill and Tom. We voted to accept the offer from Mark Brooks and Scale Ventures. I now had to notify SV that we had gone a different direction. They were disappointed that they did not get the deal. Yes, I understand, but business is business and we had made our decision. The guys at SV are good guys, but it's business too.

It is funny how a deal is a deal, but the look forward in the private equity world is always the next deal. I have run into many investment firms and bankers over the past couple of decades, and they are always interested in the next deal, forgetting about any unsuccessful deals in the past. Just bring the next deal.

THE NEXT CAPER

I had run the idea of another company by Tom Erickson before I started Century. I met with him again when I decided to recapitalize the company with money from Petra and Scale. We had done the right thing, in his view, and I was applying all that he had taught me over the years and all that I experienced, which he had foretold through the years. He is an amazing guy. Kind of a soothsayer, and business nobility to all that know him. I still could not get him on one of my boards simply because we were too small for his interest. But we still get together for lunch and talk about the next caper, as he describes every next deal. He is an incredible and legendary guy. I just love the man.

We closed on the financing of Century Hospice in September 2010 and renamed the company New Century Hospice. I hired my former boss from ACC, Jerry Lyden, to be our president and COO. With our new investment partners, we were able to close on the deals we had in the pipeline, which were the basis for the $20 million in cash that we raised. We were able to purchase five more locations in two companies to give us six locations in Texas.

Over the next six years, we amassed a total of eight offices in multiple states, serving fifteen hundred patients each day. We had substantial new patient growth that created enough cash flow to only need one small equity round of financing during our first year of operations as New Century Hospice. When it became time to consider a banker to run our sale process, we reviewed five different investment bankers and decided to work with Cain Brothers out of Boston, MA. After a process that took about four months, we agreed on a purchase agreement to sell the company to Curo Health Services for $120 million, which was more than a five-time return on the capital invested.

What was amazing was that when we got down to the final offer from Curo, they were the only bidder left from an initial batch of twenty, then fifteen, then ten, then three, then just Curo. But they didn't know it, as Cain did a spectacular job of keeping the intensity of a competitive process because we were such a quality asset in the hospice space. It allowed us one more ask, which got us another $5 million on the purchase price. They cannot say no unless you ask.

I stayed on the board of directors at Curo, backed by TH Lee, until the company transacted again a couple of years later. However, the CEO and I had a bit of a contentious relationship. He was a hard-driving CEO, less culture and spirit and more shave the penny and keep all meetings and phone calls as short as possible. He is not a conversational guy. One time at a board dinner at President Donald Trump's country club in Charlotte, the CEO asked me if he was the only bidder at the end of the process. I did not answer him and just smiled and told him that he had won the deal. Smoke 'em if ya got 'em.

I can say the process of a private sale versus an IPO is dramatically different. In today's investment climate, there is so much cash sitting on the sidelines that the private markets are matching or surpassing valuations usually only seen in initial public offerings. Consequently, most companies are electing to pursue private sales or recapitalization rather than endure the brain damage of an IPO. I agree with this and have only done private deals since.

TELL IT TO THE COLLEGE KIDS

In 2010, I was asked by the business school at Baylor University to become a guest speaker/teacher for a day each semester. I met with the faculty in the entrepreneur school to discuss this volunteer opportunity and decided I had a message I wanted to share with these seniors and graduate young adults. Specifically, the school wanted me to teach how an IPO works, but over the five years I spoke to these classes, I realized that they needed to know more than just the harvest of a business. I began to expand my message to be more real world and not just one topic out of a textbook.

Some students were interested in the nuts and bolts and the nitty and the gritty, and I could see their enthusiasm for their ideas taking shape. The funny thing, at least to me, was that I never went to Baylor but have a wife that did; we paid to put our two children through undergrad degrees and master's degrees, and a few short years later, they were asking me to speak to their students.

I traveled to and from Waco from Fredericksburg on my speaking days. Sometimes I drove the three hours each way or flew the one hour each way, but I was always on time and went out of my way to be professional with the school. I was prepared for my talks and provided PowerPoint presentations and handouts that would be helpful to the class. When my speaking engagement ended, I never even got a letter of thanks. I did get a phone call, asking if I would invest in their angel fund. How about that? Get me to volunteer, then ask for an angel donation.

A good life lesson here: always thank people when they help you, and don't take advantage of them. I guess that is why they are still in academia. There are those who do and those who only talk about doing. Always remember that.

PUT THAT DEAL ON PAUSE AND GO TELL IT TO THE JUDGE

Since New Century was based in Dallas and I was the executive chairman, Sandee and I rented a small house in University Park. A cute little twelve-hundred square foot house that was convenient to downtown and close to where the kids were living at the time. We rented it for about five years until we sold the company and no longer needed it. For five years, I commuted to Dallas, leaving Sandee, the dogs, and the horses at the ranch to fend for themselves. It wasn't until I was back home full time, after selling New Century, that I realized how hard that was for Sandee. Living in the middle of nowhere is great, but you are on your own for protection and security, and Sandee was there with a shotgun by the bed. I was so caught up in the next gig that I had no handle on the realities of what she was living with and having to do to keep things running at the ranch.

In February 2014, the morning after the Super Bowl, I was catching a flight from San Antonio to connect through Dallas to meet up with Jerry Lyden to fly to Richmond, Virginia, to close on a company we were purchasing. I had originally planned to fly our plane to Dallas the afternoon of the Super Bowl so I would be in Dallas to catch the flight to Richmond the next morning, but the weather got bad, and I decided to go commercially. When I got to the airport and went through security, I had forgotten to take my handgun out of my briefcase/bag, since I packed it thinking I would leave it in Dallas.

I stood at the end of security, waiting for my bags, when a cop came over and asked me if that was my bag they had detained, and I told him it was. They brought the bag over and pulled out my handgun and asked me if it was mine. As I was getting out my concealed handgun license, they handcuffed me. I went blank after that. The next thing I knew, I was in the back seat of a San Antonio police car with a cop in my face, giving me my Miranda rights. Just like in the movies. You have the right to remain silent … the whole nine yards.

When the police officer asked me if I understood my rights, I just stared at him and said, "Really?" The police officer in the squad car said he was doing me a favor, doing the paperwork on the curb at the airport rather than downtown because, he said, "You are not going to like where you are going."

Gulp. I felt like I was going to vomit. My nose was running. I had tears in my eyes and thought I was going to Richmond. Nope, I was going downtown.

When we got there, it was about 5:30 a.m. This police officer's name was Michael. I told him that he would have no problem with me, and he said he knew that and believed me. He held his cell phone to my ear so I could make a call or two. That is a good reason to memorize a few numbers, just in case you do not have your own phone for autodial. I called Sandee, who had to wake up and grab the phone, seeing an unknown number from the police officer's phone. When she answered, I told her I loved her and told her what had happened and to begin finding me an attorney and get me out of jail ASAP. She said, "What?" I repeated myself, and the police officer hung up.

He took me into the San Antonio magistrate and booked me. I was thrown into a cell by myself, then a few minutes later moved into the cell with the general population of the Mexican gangs, drunks, drug addicts, and various other social malcontents, who now included me. A few hours later, I was cuffed and made to walk the line to the judge, chained to three other people. I had to answer three questions for the judge. They asked did I know what I was arrested for, did I have an attorney, and did I have a job? No, no, and yes, five of them. Meanwhile, Sandee saved the day. She connected with an attorney, his assistant, who she took to lunch, and eight hours and fifteen minutes later, Sandee had me in her car.

The first time I was released, I walked out of the building and couldn't find Sandee. I had nothing on me at all. They had taken everything. I was trying to place a collect call to Sandee's cell phone to try to find her, but I couldn't get the call to go through. So, I went back out of the building, walked around to the back door where I was released the first time, grabbed the door from closing when an inmate left, and walked in to ask the cop at the release desk if I could use his phone. When I told him who I was looking for, he said, "Why yes, she was here a few hours ago."

He let me use his phone, and I reached Sandee, who had just parked in front of the door that I reentered the jail through. When I finally got out of the building and into Sandee's car, I was sobbing with relief.

It is worth it for Sandee to tell the story of what she had to do on her end to get my bail posted and get me out of jail, beginning with the call that woke her up at 5:30 a.m. In her own words:

When the phone rang at 5:30 a.m. and I looked at it, I almost didn't answer it because I didn't recognize the caller ID. Thank goodness I did answer, because it was Dave's voice, and I could tell he was scared. He told me that he was in a police car on the way to jail in San Antonio because he forgot that his gun was in his briefcase, going through security.

What??? I could not believe it, but he kept saying, "You've got to get me out of here!!!!!" I thought, Well, I've never had to bail someone out of jail, and I don't have any idea where to start. *Dave told me to start with an attorney in Austin who we used to fight a Bikinis Breastaurant from opening in our community!*

Well, most offices do not open at 6:00 a.m., but I found the attorney's phone number and email in our files, so I quickly left messages for him. In the meantime, I got dressed and called our friend Mark Thompson for more advice. I thought he might be working in San Antonio that day and might provide some help, but no luck. He was back in Dallas, but was kind to provide moral support to me, the nervous wife!

I must have answered three collect phone calls that morning from the San Antonio detention center, and Dave would always begin with, "You've got to get me out of here!" Of course, I was trying my best, but still hadn't been able to contact a lawyer that early in the morning!

Finally, by 8:00 a.m., I called again and got the name of a criminal defense lawyer in downtown San Antonio. I had to leave a message with his assistant, Carmen, since Mark Stevens was on his way to court. So, I decided to start driving to San Antonio with my checkbook to get Dave out of jail! On the way, I talked with Mark Stevens. He suggested that I pick up his assistant at the office downtown, and she would help me navigate the system.

Carmen was very sweet and calm, so that helped me as well, but we had to find a Bank of America to get a cashier's check to take to the jail. The county jail was our next stop, but Dave was not being held there, so we had to find the detention center, which is a holding place until the sentence is set by the judge. It looked just like a jail to me, and Carmen and I quickly went to the front desk, with my check in hand, hoping we would be out of there as soon as I paid the bail!

Well, that didn't happen! I was in tears by then when the officer said it would take several hours before Dave would be released, partly because the computer system was down! I thought, What did they do BEFORE they had computers??? *However, I did not say it, and asked the officer to please call my cell phone when he was out.*

By that time, it was close to noon, and Carmen asked me if I wanted to go to lunch! I also had the silly thought that I might be able to get some food to go and bring it back to Dave! It would not have been a good idea for him to have lunch delivered, as I later found out.

After lunch at a local Mexican restaurant, I took Carmen back to her office, since there was nothing else to do but wait for Dave to get out. I parked where I could see the door and started calling my good friends to pray for Dave. When Dave was finally released later that afternoon, the police officer forgot to let Dave use his phone to call me, and Dave did not see my car. When I finally saw him and drove up to the door, I was relieved he did not have to spend the night there, and he was overwhelmed with emotion. We hugged, and I told him that I loved him; however, we still had to go to another facility to collect his personal items, coat, and briefcase!!! Then we drove to the airport to get his truck and make the long journey home. What a roller coaster ride for both of us! I hope it never happens again!

They had taken everything from me and sent it to the police evidence complex, where I got all my stuff back, but not my gun. A week later, I was catching another flight somewhere, when I decided to check my bag again, just in case. When I dumped my bag out in the back of my truck in the parking lot at the airport, the five bullets that were in my revolver when I was arrested must have been put back in my bag, and they now fell out on the back seat of my truck. They took my gun but forgot the bullets. Freaked me out! I almost went through security again, but this time with ammo and no gun! What an almost-idiot again!

The process to get through the legal system is daunting. I had letters written by prominent people I knew, including board members, business professionals, and the county sheriff, and had them packaged and sent to the DA. My attorney, who Sandee found the morning of my arrest, suggested I might need to go before the grand jury to state my case. I had written a summary of the events that led up to forgetting about my gun, and he did something with the summary statement.

Just a few weeks after my arrest, Texas changed the law about handguns at the airport because so many people had the same thing happen to them. Now, if they find your weapon, they give it back so you can go put it in your vehicle.

I can tell one lesson here among dozens of lessons that stood out to me. The biggest lesson I learned is how much I cherish *freedom*. For the time I was in jail, I could not believe I had no ability to do anything normal. For a brief time, everything was taken away, and the only hope

I had was that Sandee would pay the price for me and would show me the love to save me from my mistake. Such a Christlike response from the love of my life.

I prayed in that cell that no one would try to kill me. I prayed that I would get out soon. I prayed that I wouldn't get sent to prison. I prayed for my family. I prayed for all my immediate wants in those moments, but then it hit me—I needed to thank Jesus. This was a serious wake-up call for me to see what was important. To His will and His control was what I needed to surrender to.

I began to pray to Jesus that I was thankful that He loved me to protect me. I prayed for forgiveness for not always putting my family first and only pursuing the life of run and run hard to be increasingly more successful. I had eight hours and fifteen minutes to think about it all. There was zero else to do. I could not go anywhere, and I learned quickly you did not talk to anyone, you did not look anyone in the eye, and you remained hopeful and prayerful.

It was so cold in the jail. I asked a jailer who had bar cuffed me to get me chained up to go "tell it to the judge" why it was so cold in there. He got about three inches from my face and said, "Because of the bacteria." All I could say was, "Really?" I began to pray for Sandee and her safety and asked for forgiveness for shocking her out of her sleep to immediately go rescue her husband from jail in San Antonio. That was an awful thing to put her through, and I am still very remorseful about it. Instead of thinking about myself, which I did for the first three hours, I began to think of others.

At one point, after they moved my group of inmates to another cell to spray and clean the cell, we were crammed into an even smaller cell. I had nowhere to sit, so I just stood in one place. For two and a half hours. I was wearing my good boots, but those wearing shoes had their laces confiscated so as not to be used as a weapon. They made them keep the tongues of their shoes hung out so the jailers could see there were no laces. Really.

I could see the clock on the clock-in for the employees, which gave me a sense of time. Five minutes seemed like an hour or more. It was a life-changing experience that I would suggest people get outside of jail. It is the worst. Do not go there. I cannot over emphasize how bad it is to experience it. It just is not worth it. My charge was dropped by the district attorney and three years later was expunged from my record. No history of it, and I would like to just forget it. Back to normal is a good thing.

SPRING THE JAILBIRD

One of my best friends, who I met in the early days of Hunters Glen Baptist Church, has always been an avid hunter. Fred Winter, who we now fondly, and for good reason, call Hunter Fred Winter, and his wife Allison are dear friends. The story of Hunter Fred is legendary among me and my hunting buddies. Hunter Fred has hunted all over the world, including the Northwest Territory, Alaska, Africa, Argentina, New Zealand, and Mexico. Hunter Fred finds dream hunts from the best outfitters and books the trips as far out as five years, but on average three years in advance.

I became a benefactor of Hunter Fred's obsession with hunting after he asked me to join him in attending a fundraising dinner for the Dallas Safari Club. At the dinner, Hunter Fred bought a predator hunt for two and took me on a seventy-two-hour adventure to south Texas with the president of the Dallas Safari Club and a former lineman for the Cleveland Browns. It was an exciting trip as we shot feral hogs and javelina, which I had never done before.

Fred had always been on deer leases in Texas and would invite me from time to time to join him as his guest. Eventually, Fred invited me to his lease in south Texas, where the trophy whitetail deer are in Texas. Hunter Fred was on this lease called Dos Rios, along with Leighton

Weir, Sully Woodland, Mike Jones, Gary Koehl, and the man, the myth, the legend, Morris Champion. These guys had been hunting together at Dos Rios for thirty years or more.

It was a tight group, and I was honored to be a guest several times before being invited to join the group as a full-fledged member when an opening became available. Those guys were a blast, and we became very good friends. Hunter Fred and Richard Laughlin had big plans for some big hunts in distant places that they wanted to include me in. I finally had the time and the resources to enjoy the company of my close friends. However, every hunting trip we took, I couldn't help but miss my family because I have traveled for business for so long that I'd hate to add up the days.

On every trip, there were times I was very much looking forward to getting back home. Particularly when things weren't going well on the hunt, or we had danger to consider. We have been on four huge lifetime hunts. We have hunted in Mexico, the Northwest Territory in northern Canada, Alaska, and northern New Mexico. A book could be written on those four hunts, so I can only give you a morsel from each here, including the life lessons I learned from each of them.

MEXICO AND THE SONORAN DESERT

Hunter Fred, Richard Laughlin, and I went to Mexico to hunt desert mule deer. Fred's favorite outfitter of all time had driven from his Alaskan operation all the way to Mexico. Along the way, he was fleeced by the Mexican federal officers on the side of the road for cold hard cash. He was on his way to pick the three of us up from the airport for our hunt, and we had no idea that had happened until he told us about it, while we were surrounded by the Mexican "police" in the parking lot of a Costco in Hermosillo two hundred and forty miles south of Tucson, Arizona.

Our guns were in hard travel cases in the bed of Stan's truck. The guns were seen by employees at Costco while they put four new tires on Stan's truck, so they called the Mexican cops. Hunter Fred, Richard, and I walked out to the garage to see if the truck was ready, when we were asked, at gunpoint, to wait in the parking lot.

I kept thinking that if these guys were with the cartel, we were in deep trouble, and we hadn't even gotten to our hunting camp yet. I began to wonder if this trip was worth the robbery, exertion, and physical danger we were putting ourselves in.

We had to show our credentials, take our guns out of the cases and prove they were ours, and a general big hassle took place. The thing that saved us was the fact that the landowner of the place we were trying to get to for our hunt was an attorney and knew everyone in town, including the police officers holding us at gunpoint. After some Spanish was thrown around among the people who mattered, we were on our way to Mexican deer camp.

By the time we left several days later, Richard had been robbed of $500, the local prison had a riot, and our outfitter fired Hunter Fred's guide, who we hoped wouldn't tell the cartel of our whereabouts. Not to mention the harshness of the Sonoran Desert and the cactus that was so thick, I still have needles buried in my skin. I shot a nice mule deer and a coues deer, but not before I wounded one first, and Hunter Fred and his guide tracked it and unbelievably found the bullet that had only wounded it.

Hunter Fred shot his deer from the truck with his guide Jesús by shooting from the shotgun seat in the front, pointing across Jesús the driver with his eyes closed and his fingers in his ears.

BAM! No big deal to a Mexican guide in Mexico! When we got back to Texas, Hunter Fred decided we were done with hunting in Mexico. As in business and life, we should always assess the real risks posed by our decisions to evaluate the likelihood of unintentional consequences, particularly the life-threatening kind. We got out of Mexico alive, only to put our necks on the line again in the Northwest Territory a couple years later.

THE NORTHWEST TERRITORY

Fred has been on so many hunts I can't keep track of all of his trophies, but I do know he wanted me to shoot a moose; he already had one. And he also wanted me to shoot a caribou, and he already had one of those, but he needed a new hide to replace the hide on the one he already had because something had happened to the hide before it was mounted on his trophy. He only wanted to replace the hide, so we went to Northwest Territory for a late summer hunt for moose and caribou. This is a great example of being smitten with a hobby and so committed and loyal to the activity that stories like this seem to be ridiculous and out of line with a normal, risk-averse lifestyle. And we didn't see what was coming. After all, it was supposed to be good late summer "seasonal" weather; instead, we were met with eight degrees, wind, and snow. Lots of snow.

We got stuck at moose camp, where we had been inserted by helicopter, for a couple of extra days after I shot a moose, and literally stayed in our tent and sleeping bags for thirty-six hours until the wind and snow died down.

At times like those, trapped in a snow-covered tent on a summer hunt, stuck in a snowstorm with nowhere to go, and a hundred miles away from the nearest anything, you get to thinking about what is really important to you. You think about your family and those important to you that you want to spend more time with. All the business success in the world doesn't give you any additional time on your life clock. We were in our sleeping bags for thirty-six hours, and for much of that time we traded stories. Hunter Fred and I had known each other for more than twenty years, and now we had a chance and the time to really learn more of each other's life stories.

We traded our stories of firsts. Who was your first date, what was your first bike, car, and baseball glove? Who were your favorite sports heroes and in which sports? First job? Best job? Worst job? And the longest conversations were about girls and best concerts. There is no better therapy than lying in a sleeping bag in eight-degree weather, laughing so hard the beef jerky falls out of your pocket. By the time the chopper came to get us the skies were clear and we were off to go find the caribou herd.

A quick stop at base camp for some wild sheep for lunch, and back in the chopper to go to caribou camp. We set up camp, and then it began to snow. Lots of snow. Good thing it was a summer hunt. We both got our caribou, flew out in a flurry, leaving our camp behind for the guides to pack it out, then got stuck for two more days at base camp because of the weather. The hunting season was over, and the outfitter was boarding up camp for the winter, then pulled out several half gallons of whiskey and rum and let the guides "unwind." They unwound so much they tattooed themselves with sewing needles and ink from a ballpoint pen on their thighs, with lifelong memories they will never forget, such as "F*** You." On their legs? Pretty low rent.

We flew out the next day when the weather cleared, spent a night in Whitehorse, and made it back to Texas a couple of days later. Hunter Fred likes to hunt. We saw the northern lights our first night there. I will always remember that hunt, but mostly I will remember missing Sandee and the kids and being hunkered down in a sleeping bag for a day and a half.

ALASKA

I decided before this hunt that it would be my last adventure hunt without my family. There are places to take my whole family fishing in Alaska and fun places in the lower forty-eight, for that matter. There are birds to hunt in Texas with my family, who all like to hunt quail.

Hunter Fred, Richard Laughlin, and I trekked to Alaska to hunt black bear. I was the big-time rookie on this hunt. Richard had a necklace with bear claws and teeth from several bears he had shot with his bow, which he called a stick and string, and Hunter Fred had shot brown bear before, but not yet a black bear. The travel on this hunting trip was an adventure, flying to Anchorage, spending the night, flying to Juneau, and catching a float plane to an eighty-foot hunting yacht where we lived for a week while we made daily excursions to hunt the mighty black Alaskan bear.

So many stories from that trip, but suffice it to say, we all had shots at bears in dramatic fashion, and I was the only one that brought one home. Richard was with me when I killed my bear, and he, our guide Carl, and I, took turns carrying the sixty-five-pound backpack containing the full hide and head nearly three miles in the dark as we hiked to our pick-up point for the skiff. It had dropped us off in high tide, but we were getting picked up at low tide, which in Alaska means a couple of miles of water disappeared.

So, we started packing out about thirty minutes before dark. By the time we got back to the ship, we were spent and really enjoyed a tall scotch and a home-cooked meal. I made this trip hard because I fell multiple times while fording the rivers in swift current, wearing boots that were two sizes too large while navigating rough and slippery rocks under water. The day before I shot my bear, I fell hard two times and landed on my left shoulder, with my gun in the water. That day I was hunting with the outfitter, who was a fellow pilot who built the Alaskan Harvest entirely for hunting and fishing. He was tall, strong, and knew how to hunt and fish in Alaska.

After I fell the second time, he cut down a walking stick for me. I was not only embarrassed, but I was hurt, having landed on rocks with my left forearm, which also jammed my shoulder up. Since that trip, I have now had my shoulder injected and examined by MRI to figure out what I needed to do to fix it.

On the way back home, we left the boat on a float plane that Richard paid for, which flew us over glaciers and tall peaks containing mountain goats and sheep we could see from the air. We spent the night in Juneau, where there isn't much to do, so we went to a bar at 3:00 p.m. for an early dinner and left at midnight, with the owner of the bar giving us a ride back to our B&B. It was one of the most fun bar nights we had had in a long time. Three great friends enjoying too many libations, sharing too many fun stories, and celebrating the end of a terrific journey together. I was honored to be on another trip with two of my best friends. It was unreal.

All three of those trips, and others, would never have happened had it not been for Hunter Fred. There have been so many influential people in my life's journey that, had I not known them, my story would have turned out very differently. I owe him a debt of gratitude for his hospitality and generosity for these magnificent hunts. As a token of his appreciation of being included in some of my business enterprises, he provided me with two custom rifles about five years apart that I would need for the type of game he was planning for us to hunt. My trusty .270 Weatherby Mag and my .300 Winchester Mag will forever be my two favorite rifles, which I will hand down to Charlie and Natalie one day. But not yet!!

I'm sure Hunter Fred has already scheduled our next exotic hunt. I just don't know when it is or where we are going, but next time, I'm taking my family. Life is short, and I want to be with them.

NEW MEXICO

Richard organized a magnificent hunt in northern New Mexico, about thirty miles of Clayton. Richard had organized hunts for antelope and elk several times and would invite his hunting friends from time to time. One time, he and his son Garrett, Charlie, and I flew in our Beechcraft

Baron to west Texas to hunt antelope. Charlie killed his first antelope there, and we had a great time with the hunting and flying and flew home after the hunt in some rainy weather. But on this trip, we were hunting northern New Mexico, not very far from the Colorado border, on about forty thousand acres of high desert/mountain wilderness. The land was owned by the family of a hunting acquaintance of Richard's, Sam, and was operated and tended by a caretaker who was married to the owner's daughter. His name was Jake, and he oversaw the operations of this sprawling piece of remote property.

Sam and Jake were brothers. Richard and Sam had permission to occupy a home on the ranch, where about six of us stayed for the three-day hunt. I told Richard that what the ranch needed was about three landing strips so you could get around the entire property. It was enormous. Richard and the caravan of others and the equipment and vehicles it would take for a hunt of this scale left early one morning.

Hunter Fred and I left in the afternoon and flew my turbocharged Cirrus SR22 up to Clayton. The caravan had reached the ranch before we got there, so Fred and I flew north of Clayton to find the ranch and guys. We found them and made a couple of low passes, signaling that we had arrived so they could send a truck to pick us up in Clayton. We had the easy travel and appreciated the work they did to get there. After sighting in our rifles to show Richard, Sam, and Jake that we could shoot, we got unpacked and settled into the rooms we were assigned to. We ate like royalty since Lew Savannah, master chef of August E's restaurant in Fredericksburg, prepared wonderful *Bon Appetit*-quality delights! My favorite was duck bacon. Yum. We all pitched in where we could on meals and provided a lot of clean-up teamwork.

The first day of hunting, I think we got a couple of antelope, but by day two, we needed at least five more to fill out all of the highly coveted tags. At dinner the second night, that's when the fireworks began to jeopardize the hunt. We had brought all the food and all the wine, whiskey, scotch, and beer, and word got out from Jake that we had all the makings of a party. Somehow, about twenty "neighbors," mostly drunk cowboys and gadfly drags looking to mooch some booze, showed up at our house just after the afternoon hunt. When it was time for the hunters to eat—after all, Lew had made a gourmet dinner—we began serving the hunters.

We were gathered in a small dining room; hats and caps were removed and Richard said, "Brother Dave, would you please bless the food?"

I said, "Sure, Richard, I'd be honored to say the blessing." So, I did. When the food was blessed, we dug in on some magnificent ribeye steaks and all the high-caloric trimmings that Lew had prepared. However, on the other side of the wall in the kitchen, were Jake and the gadfly cowboys, who had not made it into the dining room to participate in the blessing of the meal.

Jake was so pissed that he took issue with Richard about it, telling Richard that he was going to settle things with me and even things up. I think that was code for kick my ass. Richard did not tell me about it, as he was sure if Jake had approached me about it that things would have gotten ugly and violent. Given how drunk Jake was, that was entirely possible.

After dinner, I was clueless that Jake was trying to take it to me. Richard had ushered me, Hunter Fred, Ken Katner, and Jerry Lyden outside to the stock barn, where the grill was and where we were enjoying a beer after dinner. Ken started telling us about outer space and all that he knew about the heavens, and we were spellbound listening to him.

When you are that far from civilization and the heavens are on full display, it makes you feel oh-so-small. It also shows that there is an architect up there!

Inside the house, Richard and Lew were keeping Jake from coming outside to find us at the grill. We still had no idea. Finally, we decided that the guys at the grill were ready to turn in, so we headed to the house. Fred and I were sharing a room together and made no big deal with anyone and just turned in, having brought our own bedrolls. Richard came to our room and said good night but never told us what was going on with Jake until the next day.

We turned out our light at about 2:00 a.m. and set our alarms for 6:00 a.m. to get up and get the next hunt started. When I woke up, I walked out of our room to head to the kitchen to start the coffeepot and saw that Richard and Sam had never gone to bed. They were playing pool, Richard's bedroll still rolled up on the couch, having not been touched. I asked Richard if they had been up all night and he said yes, that he would explain later.

After another incredible breakfast, five of us piled into Sam's truck. Over the next few hours, Hunter Fred killed his antelope. I shot mine from a personal record five hundred and seventy-eight yards away with my trusty 270 Weatherby Mag. We used GPS measurements to get the yardage. I got lucky, but that 270 Mag with the Barnes bullet, even at that distance, about cut that goat in half.

After I shot mine, Sam started to field dress the animal while Richard pulled me off to the side to tell me what was going on. To de-escalate Jake and his foolish rage against me for not including him and his misfits in the blessing at dinner the evening before, Richard agreed that all of us hunters would be off the ranch by sundown today. We were being booted from the ranch, old-west style, but not before Richard was going to get each hunter their antelope.

We hooked up with our other hunting party of Lew and Ken, and Richard told them we needed to break camp and get gone after we got one more goat, then have lunch, break camp, and load out. Jerry was the only one without an antelope and was also the only one that didn't know we were on the clock to be gone by sundown, or Jake was coming to hunt me. Jerry had missed a couple of goats earlier; time wasn't an issue then, but now it was becoming relevant.

At one point, we stopped so Jerry could get out and take a long shot (all antelope shots are long, at least three hundred-plus yards) at a goat on the left side of the truck. I was sitting in the middle of the back seat and wanted to get out to see if Jerry was going to kill this goat so we could tell him what was going on and get the heck out of Dodge. While I was scooting to the left door to climb out, Jerry had moved his shooting angle from the right front corner of the truck to the back left corner of the truck. I was about to open the left door and get out of the truck, not knowing Jerry was aiming from there and I was potentially in the line of fire.

Richard, sitting in the front passenger seat, lunged with a long reach and grabbed me by my jacket and stopped me from getting out of the truck. Jerry did not shoot and got back in the truck. We kept driving, running out of time, until we peeked out on a road at the top of a ridge to find an antelope asleep in the middle of the road, not more than twenty yards in front of us in the truck. Jerry could not see it.

The wind was in our faces, so the goat could not hear us and had not woken up. We screamed with whispers to Jerry, "He's right there!"

"Where?" he asked.

"Right there in front of us!" we all screamed quietly.

He still did not see it. He got out of the truck and finally saw it asleep on the road. He took his time getting a gun rest on the right side-view mirror while we all just waited for him to get it done. WABOOM! That antelope never knew what hit him, and Sam was immediately on him, starting to get the gutting done while Richard told Jerry we were getting thrown off the ranch and he was the last to know.

Jerry said, with his signature toothpick in his mouth, "Get out! You gotta be shittin me?"

We hastily made lunch and began packing up. Between goat kills, Richard was in the background, making phone calls to find rooms for everyone in Clayton. We pulled out of the ranch about an hour before sundown, and we never saw Jake. I saw his truck, but never saw Jake.

We all gathered in the bar at the Eklund Hotel, had steak for dinner and enjoyed a nightcap, although I abstained as Hunter Fred and I were flying home in the morning while the others began the journey back to Fredericksburg. We had to dodge various weather events on our flight home but made it in about three hours, and the guys made the drive in about twelve hours. It was an incredible hunt, and Richard was an amazing host. We have since hunted ducks and geese in the Texas panhandle with the same group, including Woody Grossman.

Hunting with your friends is always an adventure, and I sincerely appreciate and thank these guys for their hunting generosity. We have had some great hunts, and I hope and pray we will enjoy more adventures as we all move through our sixties and into our seventies. Thanks, guys!

True success is not measured in things owned, captured, or controlled. It is measured in relationships that bond one another at the human love and respect level. Adventures make the reliance on those relationships a two-way street that requires all the fruits of the Spirit. They are love, joy, peace, patience, kindness, goodness, faithfulness, gentleness, and self-control. I am so grateful for my hunting buddies and for the meaning they bring to my family, other friends, and my life.

AMBITION ACCELERATES

By 2016 when we sold New Century, my business relationship and friendship with Woody Grossman was deepening. We were learning that our skill sets were a healthy combination of business development, financial management, and compliance oversight, critical components for any successful business. The twelve months after the sale of New Century to Curo were a nightmare with respect to closing the books on the deal, and our CFO at New Century, Andrea Bohannon, was already on her next gig and unavailable to help Woody, Tom Blake, and me wrestle with the post-close working capital adjustment and the hold back in the deal.

I had negotiated only a $5 million hold-back that would come to us as sellers once we reconciled all the financial accounts on the books for the company and solved for any missed reps and warranties. The Curo legal team put the screws to us. They had never intended to give us the $5 million, which, in retrospect, is why they did not argue the amount. They knew they would not pay it anyway, through legal filings, lawsuits, you name it. And Tom Blake, Woody, and I spent most of the rest of 2016 dealing with it, all while I was also on the Curo board of directors. It was an ugly thing.

I was on the board while also negotiating and fighting with that board to release the $5 million they owed us on the deal. At the same time, I was the operating safety valve for the company in the event they needed an industry operating leader to step in. I learned a lot about working capital adjustments and hold-back amount negotiations, as well as representations and warranties as a seller and as a buyer.

It is legal and accounting pieces that create much of the turmoil in negotiations, particularly in larger deals. It is not exactly fun reading material for your coffee table, but if you are a transactional investor or CEO, you need to understand these lessons. Working capital is an adjustment of the purchase price based on the working capital of the target company in an acquisition. What gets sticky and contentious is the accounting of the working capital amount and its impact on the purchase price. The other point of contention in acquisitions is the amount of the purchase price held back at closing for potential breaches of representations and warranties, which are spelled out in the purchase agreement.

Through the years, the lessons have been adding up as we get more sophisticated in our transactional knowledge. The most important element any solid leader or manager needs is knowing how to find the right person for the job so that these don't become problem issues.

Woody and I continued to work together after New Century Hospice and found our niche when we decided to form Grapetown Healthcare Partners, LLC

ROCKY MOUNTAIN HIGH

After we sold New Century, the kids purchased me and Sandee a couple of nights at the Ritz Carlton Hotel in Bachelor Gulch near Beaver Creek. It was a very generous gift, and we took a trip there in February 2016. While we were there, we decided, just for grins, to look at real estate, which was probably just what the kids had planned. By the time we left, we had scheduled a second trip to follow up with a local real estate agent. He was a great guy and a spectacular agent, and when he took us to Hummingbird Lodge and we walked into a unit for sale, we were so stunned by the view looking across the Gore Range and down the Vail Valley above Beaver Creek that we told him we would take it. On the spot. At the time, we thought we would spend an abundance of time there, including weeks and months during the summers, and multiple weeks during ski season.

The saying there is "Come in the winter, stay in the summer." The reality is that because of ranch responsibilities and our dogs of various names and species, we just would not be able to use it as much as we hoped. But for four years we had a ball staying in our own condo and sitting in front of the fire with a nice warm libation and enjoying the magnificent views. Spectacular views, which Peggy used as a model for a multimedia painting she painted as a gift to us. Our view captured in this warm, home-style painting, looking over the Vail Valley, hangs in our ranch home every winter with Peggy's signature on it.

More importantly, Peggy returned to her easel to pick up her paints and brushes and relearn how to paint, as she described it to us. After losing Dad in 2017, returning to her back bedroom art studio was just the thing to help her deal with losing him. We are so happy she started painting again. She is very talented, and we love her dearly.

I also took the Colorado condo ownership as a basis for mountain flight training. I trained two summers for one full week each time. Once in the turbo Cirrus and once in the TBM. I flew with a former Top Gun commander, Tom Trotter, "Trots." We flew some mighty mountain missions that were not for the timid, intentionally flying up and down box canyons to learn how to turn around without killing myself. We flew "mapping" missions, flying down low, near the terrain, climbing and descending with the forests and rivers and close to walls of spectacular red rock of copper and granite. These flights were intense and took a great deal of physical and intellectual energy.

We took breaks for lunch in fun places like Aspen, Steamboat Springs, Telluride, and Glenwood Springs. Thinking about flying up the Glenwood Canyon makes my heart race. One time we stopped in Steamboat for lunch with a Top Gun friend of Trot's. I just sat there listening to their real stories, not the Tom Cruise version of being a pretend Top Gun pilot, but the *real stuff*.

When we got back in the airplane, it was so hot that our performance numbers in the Pilot's Operating Handbook were off the charts, so we had to improvise. We got out of there, but the airplane did not like it as we struggled to climb in the heat and high mountainous terrain. What a blast. I will never forget it. It was very intimidating.

19

Losing our beloved parents, life as a reflection

WINDING UP AND WINDING DOWN

We all spend so much of our life's time winding up to meet the demands of life that when things begin winding down to the inevitable completed journey of life, it makes one wonder. I started noticing the phenomenon of more life behind me than in front of me. In aviation terms, the metaphor is less runway in front of you than there is behind. That past runway is used up; it cannot help you now, and you only have so much left in front of you, so you better figure out what this is all about. If this realization has not happened to you yet, I believe it will someday. My first experience with mortal life at its end was when my grandmother, Grandma Gasmire, died in Michigan in the early seventies. She was followed in the eighties by Granddad Gasmire, who is buried alongside my grandmother in Union Dale Cemetery outside of Pittsburgh.

You expect your grandparents to die one day, and if you are fortunate enough to have had a great relationship with each of them, their passing will leave a mark on your heart and steer your perspective of life to a deeper meaning. After grandparents have died, what sneaks up on you next are friends of your parents passing away. Acquaintances to you, really. Not family, but kind of like family, but still a good arm's length away from the emotional epicenter of you not yet in midlife. Then, unfortunately, your parents become "older" and things quit working on them, and they either die suddenly, or if you're lucky, you have some time to prepare for it.

My mother's mother died in a nursing home in South Bend, Indiana, in 1996, and Jay and I were there the night she passed away, although we were in a rental truck, driving back to Texas in the middle of the night with many of her willed personal effects in the back of the truck. We got a call from the nursing home that she had passed. Her husband, Russ, had died in the early seventies, so now, all our grandparents were gone. Sandee's too.

I am glad God gives us life in measured doses, but eventually everyone gets to experience their last. As Willie Nelson sings, "Live every day like it's your last, because one day, you're going to be right."

My mother, Grannie Ellie, lived a good full life, but she didn't take the best care of herself because of her smoking and drinking. She was a wonderful person, and deep down inside, she loved her family. In September 2012, while Sandee and I were in Salzburg, Austria, my mother passed away in Florida. My siblings were there with her. I had just seen her two weeks earlier and had brought her flowers and played music on my guitar to celebrate her birthday. When my sister told me while Sandee and I were huddled in a phone booth on the square where they filmed scenes for *The Sound of Music*, I began to cry quietly. We went to a coffee shop and sat outside upstairs and overlooked the square while I attempted to pull myself together.

We kept our schedule for the day, kept going, and went on a *Sound of Music* bicycle tour. I was deeply saddened while riding the bike as it sank in while I was trying to have fun. That is what my mom would have wanted. When the tour was over, I had a deep sense of guilt that I went for a bicycle tour at an hour when I was in shock that we had lost her. The rest of the day, we were active but quiet and contemplative until we began to tell stories about her. I deeply regretted not being with her when she died, but I have a picture in my mind of the last time I saw her for her birthday, with her holding her birthday roses.

We each only have one mother, and I loved mine very dearly. I just wish we had all lived closer geographically so she could have been in our lives in the last years. It is a message to us that we want to stay close to our family so we can enjoy them until it is our time to go.

The lasting difficult memory is that we don't know where Mom's ashes are. A few months after she died, her husband Tim died, and we didn't even know it until we tried to reach him. He didn't attend Mom's celebration of life, and before he died, and unknown to us, he had ordered his ashes be mixed with hers, then sent to England to his daughter, who we don't know, to be scattered.

We have no idea where Mom's ashes have been interred, spread, or buried. It is a very sad ending for a wonderful person. I try not to think about it. For me, it is unimaginable that with all my years in hospice, my mother's demise would play out that way. We all miss Grannie Ellie.

From 2001 until 2017, we lost all our family matriarchs and patriarchs except Peggy, who today is our senior matriarch and recently turned ninety years old! After Grannie Ellie died in 2012, our beloved Grannie Ruth, after a life of living with only one kidney, living life as large as a grannie can live one, died on September 8, 2016. A full book could and should be written about Ruth. She treated me like the son she did not have, although she had a stillborn boy a couple of years before Sandee was born.

Ruth and Sandee were very close all their lives, and Sandee was her loving guardian as she cared for her during her dialysis in the last few years of her life. She moved to Fredericksburg before we did, but she never left the side of her grandkids. Natalie and Charlie were the world to Ruth, and if she had lived long enough to go to Charlie and Corey's wedding and to see her great grandkids Caleb and Collins today, she would have been over the moon.

As we are also learning, grandkids will change everyone's life in a family. They are so beautiful and wonderful, and Sandee and I want to be around long enough to enjoy them growing up. Natalie was with Ruth when she passed away quietly at about 8:00 a.m. in Fredericksburg. We all knew it was coming but still could not fathom moving on without her, but she didn't want to live in poor health like that. We celebrated her life at her memorial and funeral, where she was buried next to Si in southeast Dallas at Grove Hill Cemetery.

The very next year, we lost my dad—Grandpops, as he preferred to be called. He had been ill off and on for a long time, having endured and survived dramatic surgeries. At eighty-two years old, he had quadruple bypass surgery, followed by repeated esophageal surgeries. He was a tough man and was old school about dealing with it on his own as long as Peggy was taking care of him. He told me a few times that he wanted to die first so that he would not have to die of a broken heart without Peggy. It was not like Dad to want to leave a party early or be the first one gone, but with life, he was ready. Sue was with him when he died.

Sandee and I were driving to the airport to fly ourselves to Florida when Sue called us. It was very sad, and a week doesn't go by today that I don't think of him and ask him questions out loud, as if he was sitting next to me. I miss him, and at the same time, I think I understand him better today, without the noise of my own biased thinking about how he should do things in real time.

I understand where his heart was in his final years, and as I grow older, I better understand his preferences of how he lived, what he did, what he said, and how he prepared to die. Things that I thought he should do, according to me, which were foolish and unrealistic to expect of him, he struggled with participating in. He looked realistically at the approaching end of his life, and I was looking at it like he had so much more to do.

It was very selfish of me until I changed my view on it and understood him better and dialed back my enthusiasm and energy to a listening state, hungry to understand who he was in his final days. He was his own man, and he taught me so much in my life. Everything I do today is because of him. I hope I can be the same influential father to our kids and grandkids and the great ones to follow. At my age now, I am beginning to run out of an overabundance of time, but I will make the most of the runway remaining there for my use in achieving a meaningful life, honoring God, family, and country. My father taught me great things.

WHAT'S THE MEANING?

During reflective time preparing to write this book, a question dawned on me. Who in my blood family lineage, going back thousands of years, or even further, were great people of their day? Those stories will never be known, but there had to be some direct relatives who were bigger than life in whatever time span they lived in. There are probably a few primitive cavemen or Roman slaves or soldiers along the way that figure into any birth lineage, but what were their stories? Where did they live? How long did they live? What did they do, what wars did they fight, who did they mate with to extend the family, and how did they die? No way to know, but that reality is out there. It happened. And here we are.

So, we have a choice to make. When the ages look back through recorded time, what heritage will we have left for our future Gasmires? Who will want to learn of us and to know how we lived, what we did, and what was important to us? Will people even care or have any curiosity about what happened to their ancestors before them? Can you imagine what the social experience was for our real ancestors during the days when Christ walked the Earth? Or how about during the Middle Ages or when fire and the wheel were invented and discovered? Technology in those days was simple inventions, uses and applications of tools used to survive. The explosion of new technology today was slow in coming over thousands and thousands of years. But each of those years had its people groups taking steps toward the future each of us lives today.

Who were these people? Who were the heroes? I find it fascinating to think about, really. No telling what life will look like in one hundred years, but you and I will have some legacy in all of it. We all have influence, and we get to decide what difference we want to make. We will be an example for our future relatives, but what example will each of us be? You get to decide and live that life that is worthy of future interest, curiosity, and example. It does matter. Choose wisely.

20

Keep trying to do it better with some balance, another hospice, the pandemic, the annual guys sailing trip in the Caribbean

NO RETIREMENT FOR THE UNRETIRED

At one point, during the first fifteen years of 2000, I thought about retiring, but not for long. There was nobody to play with. Sandee was busy with the Pioneer Museum, the kids were working in Dallas, my business friends were scattered across the country, and there are only so many hours to fly in a week, or play golf, or hunt, or do anything.

With several companies behind me that piled on enormous amounts of financial, operating, and compliance experiences, it was time to start another company. Woody and I and our investors at Petra Capital Partners and Granite Growth and Health Velocity all remained bullish on the hospice business. So, we started another one. This time, we recruited our former CFO at New Century Hospice and made her the CEO of our new company. Three Oaks Hospice was named by Bob Sarna while we were working on the business plan for the company in the home of Andrea Bohannon, our new CEO. We just happened to be drinking Silver Oak wine from Napa Valley, discussing what elements were important in the new name of our company. Somebody said the stability and majesty of oak trees, and Bob offered up, "How about Three Oaks Hospice?" And it stuck.

The launching of Three Oaks was important in several ways. First of all, we had enough experience in the industry to know how the operating model and its components needed to be set up and managed to avoid problems we had experienced in previous years. Second, we knew how the financial model needed to work, and the amount and type of capital we needed, from our past syndicate of financial partners. And last, and probably most importantly, Woody and I built a new model for our ownership in these new companies we were starting. With the help of David Fitzgerald at Petra Capital Partners, we developed an independent sponsor model of investing. Woody and I would find the deals under our new investment company, called Grapetown Healthcare Partners, LLC, and sign Letters of Intent (LOI) to buy health care companies we intended to invest in with our other private equity partners.

Grapetown doesn't operate companies directly but rather connects companies with our investor groups and builds new brands in various medical service companies that stand and operate on their own. For example, Three Oaks Hospice is a company founded by Grapetown but operates on its own with freestanding investment, financials, and management teams. We also put our own cash into each deal. We take success fees in stock for doing the heavy lift of finding, founding, and bringing the deal across the finish line. We also take a management fee for our board of directors' work and strategic and advisory work in the form of stock options, which grow in value as the company grows.

It has become an interesting model. I became the chairman of the board at Three Oaks Hospice, Inc, and was directly involved, and I must say, instrumental, along with Bob Sarna, Woody Grossman, and Andrea, in getting our first hospice platform snatched from the hands of a Private Equity firm in New York. We convinced the owner of Total Hospice and Palliative Care, Jimmy Martin, to sell to us. We purchased the company and raised $20 million in equity and debt among our partners, led by Granite Growth, Health Velocity, and Petra Capital Partners.

With an extremely experienced management team led by Andrea and supported by a great board of directors and investors, including my dear friend, Dick Burnham, Three Oaks Hospice is on its way to becoming another hospice success story. As of this writing, Three Oaks is serving more than one thousand patients every day, and we are just getting started. We started the company in May 2019, and shortly after, COVID-19 started rearing its ugly head. Grapetown Healthcare Partners continues to research active areas of health care services where we can put deals together as they operate under their own identity, though initially founded by Grapetown.

SURVIVING LIFE AND BUSINESS IN A PANDEMIC

When word of COVID-19 started being known, I was active on the boards of Etairos Health, ABS-Kids, and Three Oaks Hospice. Each was in various stages of development, but everyone took a hit as the full widespread impact of COVID-19 began its assault on the United States. Over the first two years, US society, fueled by the government and the mainstream media, became unrecognizable. It also became very political, as President Trump was reacting to the emergency and trying to do something about it, but the press resisted giving him credit for what he was trying to do. For us as Americans, we did not want blame; we just wanted the truth of what was going on and what we should expect. The government shut down the economy by restricting face-to-face businesses from serving customers. Society went into full shutdown, waiting for the pandemic to subside.

LET'S GO SAILING ANYWAY

The pandemic created a lot of opportunities to search for adventures that were still available. Not only was flying my jet a great example of occupying unused social space, but sailing was also still on the agenda. For several years, my friends Dick Burnham, Doug Cannon, Brad Bickham, and Mark Hollis had ventured into the Caribbean, sailing in January or February when the weather down there was perfect. Originally, Dick and I had gone by ourselves and bare boated a vessel for a week without dying. I am a pilot, but I am not a sailor, so I relied entirely on Dick to be in charge and tell me what to do.

The following few years, I was unable to go with the guys on the trip due to schedules, but Doug and Brad and Mark picked up the annual tradition and, for several years, had some incredible journeys. In 2018, I rejoined the swabbies on a hundred-foot fully crewed vessel that Dick chartered for us. We had a blast, and no one died.

The following year, Doug and Brad invited Dick and me, and we had another great sailing journey. We had a captain, a first mate, a chef, and a cabin mate who was also the bartender. It was her job to serve our first round of rum drinks by 9:30 a.m., ahead of the normal sailing departure time of around 10:00 a.m. We would sail all day to our next mooring, eat and drink all day, then eat and drink until it was time to stop for the day. No one ever got seasick, as I remember, though there were times when it was necessary to take a pill or put on a patch. But everyone did quite well, given the open-seas nature of this kind of adventure sailing. It is easy to put on about a pound a day or more with this kind of schedule.

In 2022, it was my turn to host the boat. I leased a ninety-foot transatlantic racing yacht that was owned by a guy in Italy. This boat was made for speed and less for the creature comforts, but everyone had a nice sleeping berth, and the crew was amazing. We had a crew of four, and this time, Woody Grossman joined us on our journey. We each had several turns at steering from the appropriate cockpit on either side of the boat, depending on which way the boat was sailing. What is a fun look-back is that our group had been sailing the seas of health care for a long time together, and our trip was a metaphor for enduring what nature brought us. That is what it is like in business too. Endurance for what smacks you in the face from time to time.

While we were on the boat for a week, the crew was planning its transatlantic trip back across the ocean to prepare for summer sailing in the Mediterranean. It was going to take them three weeks to make it there, sailing twenty-four hours a day and taking turns on watch at the helm in shifts averaging about four hours. In my younger years, I would have taken the opportunity to experience that but decided that wishing I had not gone, somewhere between South America and Western Europe, would be a bad idea. But we kept trying to talk Doug into it.

When we were on the boat Doug and Brad leased, the captain and crew were going to sail back through the Panama Canal to its new destination after our trip. Doug almost went on that one. We all had great times on those trips, and we look forward to more in the years ahead.

HEALTH CARE STAFFING AND GROWTH CHALLENGES DURING COVID

Although we enjoyed the voyages and adventures during COVID, the business of health care had to continue despite the obstacles and barriers of caring for patients. We lost staff; we had payrolls based on larger revenues that were no longer there. We began to lose money, and it took all of us contributing in various ways to find solutions we needed so that when the pandemic ended, we would still be standing and able to grow back out of it. That is what happened.

From 2019 to 2021, life was all about the pandemic. There were government mandates on who could be open and who had to shut down. There was hypocrisy at every turn by government officials who told us how to live but did not comply themselves. There was virtue signaling with wearing or not wearing masks, arguments in shopping lines about the distance to keep between customers, and Joe-Main-Street business owner being arrested for staying open. To make things worse, particularly for us in the health care business, was a government mandate for vaccinations of all health care workers. People quit over it. Many people did not go back to work, and we had disagreements among our boards as to what we should do to protect our businesses.

The government started sending signals that businesses receiving funds from Medicare would be in jeopardy of losing funding if they did not comply with laws that we had no negotiation or debate in. Nobody doubted the severity of the virus, and everyone took it seriously, but pragmatism was out the window. The draconian government approach was simply unreasonable and out of touch with mainstream America. Hindsight is the final word on these things, and hindsight says that masks did not work, and we shut down the economy to great economic peril when it did not need to be. Schools were shut down, and our kids were taken advantage of, some say for political purposes, but other legitimate questions remained.

It was hard, at first, to tell the difference between honest and helpful policy assessment and political bending of the pandemic. Who do you believe? All of us in our family ultimately got sick with COVID and fully recovered, and we are thankful to God that we did.

Now, at the beginning of 2023, with the world emerging out of the pandemic crisis and returning to normal, we need a sea change in the political composition of our government. Herd immunity has been a factor to our recovery, just like the flu. Congress has lost touch with real Americans out here, trying to do the right thing for their businesses, families, and society at large. Inflation is at a forty-year high; we keep passing new laws with new taxes and increased inflation as a result. Interest rates are approaching 10 percent; our southern border is letting two million illegal aliens into our country; supply chains are still limited; crime is out of control; and biologically born men compete with biologically born women in women's sports. Nuts, just plain nuts. It must change.

The social and economic experiment under radical liberals and radical conservatives, both sides of the aisle, is out of hand, and we need to return to the fundamentals of freedom and liberty that America was founded on. As with most things, the answer is somewhere in the middle. We are a constitutional republic, where the power rests with the people, and it is how we keep our democracy balanced and resilient, with no fascism and protection for all. But the scorecard of how our country managed the pandemic has a few F's and 0's on it, which is what we should expect when anyone takes on the challenge of a lifetime for the first time.

As previously stated, the first version of anything is usually not very good, including solving for a pandemic. We endured it and got through it, and now we must all come together and drop our divisiveness. But our work in post-acute care must go on, and we must find solutions to the myriad challenges facing patients, payers, and providers. There will be new ways to receive health care, and we want to be active in those leading changes as we develop new companies brought together by Grapetown Healthcare Partners.

Due to the demanding work of our boards and management teams, we are beginning to see organic growth that is showing good signs of progress. We have also started another new company sponsored and founded by Grapetown Healthcare Partners. We purchased a post-acute care physician practice company called Trumen Physicians + Associates in Houston in October 2021. Woody and I partnered with Petra again and Capital Alignment Partners, also in Nashville. We have built out the management team and put our own money into the new company. Our intent is to build it with organic physician growth and acquisitions of similar practices in other new markets, beginning with Texas. We are now considering our next Grapetown Healthcare Partners company and plan on founding at least one new company per calendar year.

21

From pandemic to jet captain, turning trouble into opportunities, horsing around, the kids growing careers and families, keep accelerating

HOW TO TURN TROUBLE INTO A MEMORABLE EXPERIENCE

In June 2020, I decided to sell the turboprop airplane, the TBM 930, and buy our first jet, a Cessna Citation M2. It was obvious I was never going to be an airline pilot like my college roommates Randy Smith and Gene Massad, and quite frankly, I wanted to see if I could do it. I had valuable flying experience, but jets are a different workload and complexity from piston and turboprop airplanes.

We bought the M2, had it painted, put on a new tail number, and I flew N681GG around the US with my mentor pilots, Parker Madill and Aaron Hawkins. After stacking up fifty hours flying all over the place, when the rest of the aviation world, including the airlines, was grounded, it was a perfect time to train in a new airplane because the skies were empty, and we could concentrate on my training.

When I was not flying the airplane, I was studying in my office with charts, checklists, and online courses. By the time I went to training in August 2020, I was ready. After seventeen days of classroom ground school and full-motion level D simulator sessions, I took my FAA check ride on a Friday night. I finished at 10:30 p.m. and went out for a steak and a beer by myself, but also with the spirit of my dad next to me. In fact, before I started my check ride in the dark cockpit, I said a little prayer for success and asked Dad to ride in the right seat to make sure I passed.

I did pass, and when the sim bridge lowered to connect us to the land bridge in the simulator bay, I stood there and screamed in joy. I had done it, and it was one of the most difficult intellectual accomplishments I can remember . Thank you, Lord.

The next morning, I flew home in the jet as a newly type-rated jet pilot with captain's bars on my shoulders and my ProCard. Awesome feeling that is hard to describe. It is never too late to challenge yourself with big dreams. Accomplishment at any age is extremely gratifying and is a wonderful learning experience. From riding your first bicycle by yourself to flying an airplane solo to getting FAA approval acknowledging you are a ProPilot flying a jet, it's all very much the same. If you can dream it and if you want to accomplish it, complete it and claim it, it can be done, and you are the one to do it! It's never too late to show yourself what you got! Yeah, mule! Bury me in those stripes, please.

PROUD PARENTS AND GRANDPARENTS

While Sandee and I, along with our dogs and horses, who have been with us for years (two dogs, Lucy and Dolly, three horses, Casey, Nic, and Yello Cat), have been at the ranch, chipping away at survival in the country from the feral hogs and other predators that need shooting every week, our adult children, Natalie and Charlie, and Charlie's wife Corey and their two beautiful children, Caleb, born in May 2021, and his sister Collins, born in June 2022, keep building their lives in wonderful ways.

After two college degrees, including her master's degree from Baylor University, Natalie has built an incredible career of arduous work in education, beginning as a classroom teacher in a couple of different schools. Then, after six years in the classroom, followed by two years as an instructional coach, she was promoted to assistant principal (AP) and continued to build her experience. She can tell you better than I can that the AP is the enforcer of the school and is like a COO of a company that requires minute-to-minute attention and exceptionally long hours dealing with exceedingly difficult issues with students, parents, and teachers.

After four years as an AP, Natalie was recruited to lead a fine elementary school in Prosper, TX. She simply loves leading a school and building teams in education. It fits her work ethic, leadership style, and ambition. And most importantly, she loves the kids in her school like they are her own. I have always told Natalie that one day there will be a school with her name on it. I genuinely believe it. Those kids come first to Natalie, and she is building quite a legacy—and she is early in her career. I am so proud of her and love her like no other! I just reach out to her with an abundance of blessings. She is an incredible daughter, and I love her with my life without exception.

ON OUR WAY TO GRANDCHILDREN

In 2017, Charlie met the love of his life in Corey Lynn Page. They were married in late November that year, and we were so excited for them both and for Corey to become our daughter-in-law. The whole experience was amazing and surreal. It seemed like for me and Sandee, life was speeding up and we were falling behind with the events that were taking place in Dallas. Their wedding was stunning, and Sandee, Natalie, and I were all included in very meaningful ways. I was Charlie's best man and was so honored that he would ask me. He has so many solid friends that he had a lot of choices, but I made the cut.

I threw a bachelor's party for Charlie and his twelve groomsmen. I rented a large house near Lake Texoma, and we all stayed up virtually all night. It was great fun. On their wedding day, as the best man, I was responsible for delivering a gift to Corey while she and her bridesmaids were getting dressed. The wedding was outside at the Four Seasons Hotel in Las Colinas, adjacent to the eighteenth green of the TPC course where they play the Byron Nelson Classic golf tournament each spring. The weather was glorious, and everyone looked so nice, and I had a bird's-eye view of the proceedings, standing there with Charlie and Corey as they took their vows. It was impossible not to be emotional.

Such a wonderful event, and the reception was of great proportions, with a great band, wonderful specialty culinary delights, and an open bar. What a night. They drove away from the party in our 2016 Bentley Continental GT. It was a classy affair, and we are so happy they are married. Charlie, Corey, Caleb, Collins, and Natalie all live within a mile of each other and see each other often.

ENTREPRENEURS AMONG US

After and during some time in the corporate world of mergers and acquisitions for two large health care companies, Charlie's sense of business adventure began to change. As a youth and in college, he created a couple of different businesses, sort of his Petri dish of entrepreneurship. He built a banking transaction application at Baylor and also took a run at learning retail by starting his own barbecue sauce company, Big Bear Barbeque Sauce. He made a recipe with a friend of mine, Chris Nichols, who still makes it today.

With that early experience, he and a business partner built a small start-up education company called Boss Club. His sense of entrepreneurship drove him to build a company teaching young students how to start their own businesses. He and his business partner created a curriculum that has been purchased by school districts from coast to coast, introducing the concept of capitalism, but also, and maybe more importantly, combining this new knowledge with the students' personal interests and ambitions.

It is quite an impressive opportunity for students and parents alike to unlock and encourage a life skill that can be life changing in many regards. If that wasn't enough, Charlie also took some of his own medicine and built a solid business around his personal passion for flying. His aviation company is called Airplane Academy, and it includes a website, blogs, articles, and a growing YouTube channel by the same name. With nearly one hundred thousand subscribers interested in his platform, he is reaching a population of people interested in learning how to fly, how to afford to fly, and all things new-pilot/new-airplane-owner-related. Not only is he a great pilot and purchased his own airplane to pursue his dreams, but he now shares that passion and insight with others to give them the encouragement to dream big and to follow those dreams. Both of his businesses have a consistent theme to the participants who are interested in pursuing their personal interests. It takes a lot of ambition to see yourself where others don't even try, but with encouragement, persistence, and intellectual might, it can be done!

NEW TRANSITIONS

For us living in Fredericksburg, and after twenty years at the ranch, we are feeling the tug of our heartstrings toward our kids and grandkids in Dallas and have every intention of being there more often as the kids grow older. To that end, we have purchased land in Dallas and have plans to build a home there soon. It will give us more of an existence with our family so that we can be involved in their lives as they all grow, and we grow older. We have accomplished the life building/survival of raising a family and seeing them pursue their education, friends, dreams, and family traditions. We have done our heavy lifting of life, and now we want to participate in the building of their dreams and do some spectating along the way, caring for our grandkids.

We will slow down sooner or later, but when we do, we want to be around our kids more often, which is another good reason to keep flying as long as I am safe and qualified to do so. The day will come when I pass the family flying baton to the kids.

In Fredericksburg, Sandee's two terms serving on the Gillespie County Historical Society Board ended at the end of 2022. Now, for both of us, our new other priorities are our adult children and grandchildren living in Frisco, Texas. Shortly before my dad died, he bared his soul to me about things tugging at his heart. One thing he told me was that he wished he had moved closer to us kids and been part of our lives and our children's lives. He said it was one of his few regrets as he knew his life was ending.

I will always remember his words to me and will take them as a strong suggestion, a piece of advice from Dad, in the here and now. Sandee and I have fun trips planned with each other and with our entire family, to whom our heart and souls are devoted. I plan to continue to build Grapetown Healthcare Partners along with Woody Grossman, Bill Ward, Andrea Bohannon, and Bob Sarna, as we try to make our mark on health care services. We are even talking about raising a fund of our own. We will see. We enjoy what we do, as long as it revolves around our private family lives. Family, faith, and friends. Those are the priorities. Now and forever.

As Augustus McCrae said to his sidekick Woodrow Call in the television miniseries *Lonesome Dove*, "It's been a hell of a party, hasn't it, Woodrow?" I'll say it has, and I hope there is a lot more to come. After all, it can be done!

22

Flights of joy with Sandee, Natalie, and Charlie, with looks back

As part of my look-back research I also took other memorable trips with Sandee, and trips alone with each of our children, kind of a quick-trip-with-Dad kind of thing.

In June 2022, Sandee and I took a trip to visit St. Louis. I wanted to show her where I spent nine years of my life before meeting her in Dallas in 1969. I guess when people think back to the very early days of their lives, where they lived, what they did, and who they knew, there must be a curious nostalgic craving to dig deep into those memories. But not everyone cares to do so. I am very nostalgic, probably due to such good memories of family and friends that I had in those early years.

Another notable mention that I think is in play here for me is that we moved six hundred and forty-eight miles from St. Louis to a vastly different land with a Big Sky. Texas! If you never leave the town that you grew up in, there certainly will not be any curiosity about where you grew up. You will not really say you are *from* somewhere unless you are on vacation. But leave a place in the rearview mirror that meant so much to you, and it is likely you will want to return one day, for context of your past against the backdrop of all that has happened in your life.

I can honestly say it is those memories that created the desire to write my book. There has been a lot of research for my writings on these pages. Research of history, but also of family events, locations, and the inside stories that make the memories very real. In the more than fifty years since we lived in Glendale, the city of St. Louis has changed quite a bit, but so has most of America. When you return to your childhood neighborhood and the surrounding city that occupies it, you have a hope that things will return to black and white, as they were on the television when you lived there. You want to reminisce about the innocent times that shaped your view of the world then.

While on our trip, we had a wonderful anniversary dinner at Tony's Restaurant in St. Louis. Our waiter had left St. Louis years ago to explore San Francisco and then Denver, and finally returned to St. Louis. He summed it up for us when he said, "St. Louis is a wonderful place to live. It has art and history that neither San Francisco nor Denver has. Now that I am older, I realize that I should never have left my home here."

We went to Grants Farm during our trip to St. Louis. I remember going there on field trips during elementary school to learn about Ulysses S. Grant and the Busch family, made famous by inventing Anheuser-Busch beer in the mid -800s. It was a throwback for me to simpler times, with all the same history and family fun that Grant's Farm provides.

We also toured our old neighborhood with plans to grab a sandwich and maybe a Pomac soda pop at the old Tom Boy's neighborhood store, which is now named Westwood Catering. While there, we enjoyed a great sandwich, chips, and a fountain drink, just like the old days. Four fifth-grade boys rode up on their bikes and came into Tom Boy to get candy and a soda pop, just like we did all those many years ago. Instead of a pencil-written account card system for the neighborhood residents to track their purchases, which was then billed each month, these boys had a card with store credit on it and they were going deep on those cards in the candy inventory.

We were checking out behind them when one of the little fellas put his card in the reader, saying, "I think I have $13 on this card."

The lady running the register said, "Nope, you don't have enough."

The four boys looked at each other, trying to decide which candy to put back to get under the mandated $13 mark. The one boy decided to set aside the peanut M&M's, when I intervened and said, "We'll pay for the difference. Give the boys their candy and put it on us."

The boys were in silenced awe. It was so cute. I could picture that being me and a good Samaritan recognizing our plight, stepping in to save the day without being begged to do so. One kid let out a gasp. "Oh wow!" I think he said.

I told the boys to enjoy their summer and be careful on their bikes. When I got out to the car, I realized I had left my sunglasses at the sandwich counter and went back in to find them. I walked by the boys, who were devouring their spoils, and they started to help me find my glasses. I told them to just enjoy their lunch, have a safe summer, and be good to their family and friends. Then I returned to the car. Such an example of today's glimmer of hope that small neighborhoods and the kids that grow up there can also find their legacy of great memories, of people and friends who will shape their lives, not recognizing it until it matters and means the most.

Another memorable treat was when Sandee and I visited Nipher Middle School, which used to be a junior high school when I attended there from 1966 through 1969 for seventh and eighth grade. It was a hoot to stand in the cafeteria in the basement, with the low-hanging 1960s ceilings and support posts every fifteen feet in every direction. That cafeteria had a lot of lunch memories, but also the junior high dance I proudly attended wearing a polka dot tie, staring at the girls all staring at the boys. We made our way to the office to let them know we were in the building, which they were fine with since school was out for the summer. The office lady there asked if I knew her mother, who might have been in classes with me in grade school at Henry Hough Elementary School. She asked, "Do you remember Jan Whitson?"

I said, "Yes! Of course, I do!"

She said, “I will text her to see if she remembers you.” A moment later, she said, “Were you a stinker in school?”

And Sandee said, “Yep! That would be him!”

So fun to reconnect, and now we are planning on going to the next reunion there in October 2023. Some people care to do those things, and some do not. I do because it can be done, and I will be grateful to see very old friends. Sandee and I had a memorable time together on our trip back to where I left tracks as a lad.

Of particular joy for me was when I flew the jet to Oklahoma City with Natalie and spent a weekend there. And another was with Charlie when he and I (he did most of the flying, including the takeoffs and landings) ventured back to Toledo, Ohio.

With Natalie, we flew from Addison Airport in Dallas to her birthplace of Oklahoma City. We stayed downtown at the Omni Hotel, and after landing at Wiley Post Airport (named after the aviator and writer Wiley Post, who died in the same airplane crash that also killed American legend Will Rogers during a trip together in Alaska) we drove to the rejuvenated area of downtown called Bricktown. We found a fun Cajun seafood restaurant, ate oysters, and drank beer, and just talked.

I enjoy these one-on-one trips with both Natalie and Charlie as it gives us a chance to really catch up as parent and adult child. Natalie is beginning her second year as principal at Cockrell Elementary in Prosper, so we always have a lot to talk about. We always seem to talk about challenges to overcome in work and relationships. I often ask her for advice on things that I need help thinking through. I do the same with Charlie.

After lunch, we went to the Oklahoma City Memorial, where the Alfred P. Murrah building was bombed by a madman in the 1990s. We took the entire tour and were deeply moved by the exhibit, and it was a good time to reflect on our days in Oklahoma City and Edmond in the mid-eighties.

That night we enjoyed a very swank dinner downtown, where we had wonderful steaks and Natalie gave me the full lowdown on her leadership initiatives and dreams for her new school. She is very bright, has a leadership style all her own, and is constantly looking for ways she can up her game even more. She may not have a lot to say in the mornings at home, but over a good steak dinner out or at home, she likes to talk and reflect, and I am immensely proud of her.

The next morning, before we flew home, we went for a walk down the Riverwalk in OKC. It is an impressive rebirth for the city. We did a little bit of running, too, if you can call it that. We grabbed a brief time by the pool at the Omni before checking out and flying home. On the flight home, we flew right over Lake Texoma and saw Cedar Mills, Cedar Bayou, and Duck Cove, favorite family places we enjoyed for many years. We laughed as we looked down from fifteen thousand feet, traveling four hundred miles per hour. A few minutes later, we were having lunch with Sandee at Mi Cocina. A great father-and-daughter trip, and it only took thirty-six hours. Quality family time, I tell you!

On the trip with Charlie, he and I flew around weather nonstop to Toledo from Dallas. We departed Addison airport in the morning, and by noon we were enjoying a nice lunch in Toledo. I had not been in Toledo since I was a kid. More dramatic is the fact that I had not been to my birth home since I was a baby. I do not remember much about Toledo because I was so young, but after lunch, Charlie and I drove to 1349 Leith Dr. This twelve-hundred square foot house was tucked on the south side of a small narrow street, off a main artery boulevard. It was an older part of town, to say the least, and the lawn and vegetation around it spoke of years of light maintenance and attention.

As we pulled up to the house on the right, I was holding two pictures so that I could verify it was the correct house. The pictures were of the house with the address on the front elevation to the right of the front door. One with me, Mom, and Dad sitting on the concrete front step, and I could not have been more than six months old. The other was a picture of Mom, Minnie or Grandma Gasmire, also sitting on that same porch, and I looked even younger. Jay was not born yet, so this is one of the earliest photos I have of me as a baby in a social setting, not just a sleeping-baby-in-a-bed photo.

I turned off the rental car at the driveway and the angular walkway to the front door. We just sat there and took it all in. I imagined my mom and dad bringing me home from the hospital in November 1955, parking the car and walking into the house from the west-side entrance, which looked like it had not been opened since. This was where I was given my start in life. A humble little clapboard house with one small tree in the front, built in 1953, so it was new when Mom and Dad bought it when they were married that same year.

Charlie asked, "Dad, are you going to knock on the door?"

I said, "Yes, we've come a long way to get here, and my curiosity is unmatched, so cover me—I'm going in!"

I slowly walked up that angled strip of seventy-year-old concrete and turned sideways to get through the overgrown flowers, grass, and shrubbery that nearly blocked the pathway to the porch. Over the concrete steps seen in the photographs, a small wooden deck had been built, and it needed structural repair and paint. I thought it might collapse as I stepped onto it. There was a glass outer door that had been closed, but the main door to the house was halfway open, and there were three little yappy dogs trying to meet me through the glass door. I took a deep breath and knocked with my knuckles on the frame of the door, which also needed paint and attention.

I took a slow step backward just in case I was not a welcome visitor. A middle-aged man with a dirty ball cap came to the door, pushing the dogs out of the way so he could crack open the door to greet me. When he pushed the door open about six inches and looked at me, I said, "Good afternoon, sir. I hope this is not an inconvenience for you, but this was my first boyhood home when I was born in 1955, and I haven't been back since. My son Charlie and I happened to be in Toledo and wanted to stop by and remember the place where my life started. I hope you do not mind if we take some pictures from the front of your house." Then I said, "My name is Dave."

He said, "Oh, okay. I'm Bob; everyone calls me Boomer." Bob from Toledo.

We shook hands through the small opening in the door. Then he just stared at me. I asked him how long they had lived there, and he turned his head toward the inside of the house and asked his wife or friend, then said, "We moved in here in 2013." He told us to meet him around the back of the house and that he had something he wanted to show us.

As Charlie and I walked deeper down the driveway, we stopped and stood at that side door where I was brought home as a baby. It was a very moving moment for me. I imagined the complete trust and dependence that I had as a tiny baby in my mother's arms, where she cared for me every day in this little house. A home. The home where I first slept nearly sixty-seven years ago. I thought about all the houses and apartments and cars I have slept in since. All the stories, each connected to the other, that would never have been told if my first breaths had not started here.

Home is where family is. The size of the home never matters; where it is located does not matter; what is in it does not matter. I was not curious about those things, standing there looking at the picture of my time then and standing in the same place now. I was just happy to still be alive. And oh, how I would have loved to have my dad with us standing there, talking to Boomer. What would that conversation have been like? I can imagine, and it puts a smile on my face.

The backyard was a jungle of vegetation, some intentionally planted and most of it growing out of control. A bit creepy, but I was in another world in my mind, trying to recall any of it. The big backyard in which I have pictures of Dad teaching me to play golf was gone. And in my mind, I may be confusing this backyard with the backyard in St. Charles near Chicago, which is where we moved after living in this home in Toledo. Behind this home were other homes, and beyond them, office buildings. But standing there now, I was snapped back when we saw a small aluminum pool about eight feet in diameter and filled with six inches of water. The wall of the pool was about eighteen inches tall, so it was a little fold-up pool.

Boomer told us that sometimes he and his wife got in it and had a couple of beers. Next to the pool, a small aluminum trash can was full of empty beer cans. I could only imagine. He told us he had owned burger joints around town and made the shape of a burger with his hands, which Charlie thought was noticeable, as if we did not know what a burger was shaped like. We never met his wife, and he never invited us into the house, and I was not going to ask but would have ventured inside if we had been given the chance.

Before we left, Charlie went back to the car and brought back the picture of me learning to play golf in Boomer's backyard. I showed it to him, and I do not think he quite got the enormity of it for us. He told us to stop by, and for some reason, also said that if we brought friends with us, he would be okay with that. Charlie took some photos of me at the front of the house, holding the old pictures that we had. We drove down the street, turned around and drove back by the house, stopped and took one more picture, then drove off, never to see the house again.

It was worth the time and the expense to stand where I once crawled. Where my mom and dad and my grandparents first enjoyed my presence as their baby and grandbaby. It was good for Charlie also, and I appreciated his interest and the respect he showed toward me and this little twenty-four-hour journey. So many good memories of trips back to Toledo, even when we lived in St. Louis, as we would come visit Uncle Al, Aunt Lilian, and all our cousins. Great memories of snowy winters and stormy summers and the long drives in the family car to get there. Thanks to Dad and to Mom for making this all happen.

Then Charlie and I went to play golf at Maumee Bay on Lake Erie. We had a lakeside dinner, and he flew us home the next morning in two hours and fifteen minutes. Wow. What fun trips. Whatever is next, I know It Can Be Done.

EPILOGUE AND EXPECTATIONS

An interesting aspect of writing that I have learned is that you are never finished with the story. For my story, it would take sixty-seven years to tell it, so by nature of storytelling and setting priorities for what an author wants to tell, things are left out. This effort has taken more than two years, with all the fits and starts that go with attempting something a person has never done before. I hope you reflect on your own life, the vicissitudes, the victories and the defeats, the beautiful and the macabre, the fun and the tears, the love, and the search for more love. God has a plan for all of us. It is my prayer that as you think about your life's story, you will find or recognize His hand in your life.

We only get one opportunity to walk on this earth, where Jesus came to save us. The next life will be a story unimaginable, so let us do our best with the one we have here now. Get on with it—you've got things to do and people to touch. Blessings to you! It can be done!

David Charles Gasmire, January 2023

No memoir would be complete without mentioning, in high praise, our wonderful pets who have experienced, or at least been with me and our family, through all of life's laughter, tears and jeers. I can't remember not having a dog at anytime in the last 40-50 years. Except for college, when my parents were the dog owners and keepers, but since then, trusty companions by my side. As I write this, three days earlier I was with our beloved King Charles Cavalier, Lucy, when we humanely "put her down" after 14 years and 8 months to the day she was born. We wept a bucket of tears. That's what we do when our most devoted mans-best-friend reach the limit of their life's span. We are thankful in our mourning, but we still mourn, and although there are few mentions of them in this book, I want to give each of them thanks and recognition here, these wonderful furry friends who have paved the way with me.

Gone before us are: Mickey, Ginger, Belle, Bandit, Honey, Lily and Lucy. And still with us are Clara, Scarlett, Dolly. And a tip of my cowboy hat to Sandee's beloved first horse, "Pork Chop," who is buried and honored at our ranch in Fredericksburg, Texas.

Lily and Lucy on my truck at the Flying G Ranch...sisters forever!

ABOUT THE AUTHOR

In a career spanning four decades, David Charles Gasmire has achieved his life's dream of leading remarkable healthcare companies. He has won the coveted Three Oaks Hospice Lifetime Achievement Award, and his companies have won the North Texas Top 100 Fastest Growing Companies four years in a row. He began his career in a large corporate healthcare entity which led to pure play startup companies, including an initial public offering just a few weeks after the 9/11 attacks in New York City. David has competed in seven marathons. He's passionate about flying, playing guitar, golfing, hunting, and horses. He has been married to his wife, Sandee, for over forty-two years; they live on an 1800s ranch near Fredericksburg, Texas. The couple has two adult children, a daughter-in-law, and two grandchildren, along with a cat, two dogs, and three horses.

Printed in the USA
CPSIA information can be obtained
at www.ICGtesting.com
LVHW042025200923
758628LV00009B/261/J